The Economics of
Urban Amenities

STUDIES IN URBAN ECONOMICS

Under the Editorship of

Edwin S. Mills
Princeton University

The Economics of Urban Amenities

EDITED BY

DOUGLAS B. DIAMOND, JR.

Department of Economics and Business
North Carolina State University
Raleigh, North Carolina

GEORGE S. TOLLEY

Department of Economics
University of Chicago
Chicago, Illinois

ACADEMIC PRESS
A Subsidiary of Harcourt Brace Jovanovich, Publishers
New York   London
Paris San Diego San Francisco São Paulo Sydney Tokyo Toronto

ACADEMIC PRESS, INC.
111 Fifth Avenue, New York, New York 10003

United Kingdom Edition published by
ACADEMIC PRESS, INC. (LONDON) LTD.
24/28 Oval Road, London NW1 7DX

Library of Congress Cataloging in Publication Data
Main entry under title:

The Economics of urban amenities.

(Studies in urban economics)
Includes bibliographies and index.
1. Urban economics. 2. Space in economics.
3. Homesites. 4. Real property--Valuation. 5. Land
use, Urban. I. Diamond, Douglas B. (Douglas Byrnne),
Date. II. Tolley, George S., Date.
III. Series.
HT321.E33   330.9173'2   81-22794
ISBN 0-12-214840-1   AACR2

PRINTED IN THE UNITED STATES OF AMERICA

82 83 84 85   9 8 7 6 5 4 3 2 1

Contents

I

THE AMENITY CONCEPT

II

METHODS OF AMENITY MARKET ANALYSIS

III

URBAN AMENITY MARKETS

IV

REGIONAL AMENITY MARKETS

Contributors

Numbers in parentheses indicate the pages on which the authors' contributions begin.

GLENN BLOMQUIST (89), Department of Economics, University of Kentucky, Lexington, Kentucky 40506

DOUGLAS B. DIAMOND, JR.[1] (3), Department of Economics and Business, North Carolina State University, Raleigh, North Carolina 27650

PHILIP E. GRAVES (211), Department of Economics, University of Colorado, Boulder, Colorado 80309

ORVILLE F. GRIMES, JR. (143), Eastern Africa Projects Department, The World Bank, Washington, D.C. 20433

C. HARRELL (55), Department of Economics and Business, North Carolina State University, Raleigh, North Carolina 27650

R.N.S. HARRIS (55), Food and Agriculture Organization, Via Delle Terme di Caracalla, 00100 Rome, Italy

DONALD R. HAURIN (195), Department of Economics, Ohio State University, Columbus, Ohio 43210

LARRY E. HUCKINS (125), Center for the Study of Business and Government and Department of Economics and Finance, Baruch College, New York, New York 10010

PETER LINNEMAN (69), Finance Department, Wharton School, University of Pennsylvania, Philadelphia, Pennsylvania 19104

[1] *Present address:* Department of Housing and Urban Development, Washington, D.C. 20410.

ROBERT POLLARD (105), Department of Economics, University of Texas, Austin, Texas 78712

JOANNA REGULSKA (211), Department of Geography, University of Colorado, Boulder, Colorado 80309

BARTON A. SMITH (165), Department of Economics, University of Houston, Houston, Texas 77004

GEORGE S. TOLLEY (3,55), Department of Economics, University of Chicago, Chicago, Illinois 60637

ROGER J. VAUGHAN (125), Office of Development Planning, State of New York, Albany, New York 12224

LAWRENCE WORLEY (89), Department of Economics, Texas A & M University, College Station, Texas 77843

Preface

Amenities are increasingly recognized as a major determinant of people's well-being. However, the analysis of amenities has remained outside the mainstream of economics. Only in the past two decades have concerted attempts been made to bring the tools of economics to bear on them. These efforts, while useful, have been somewhat fragmented. Though amenities are important to behavior generally, most analyses have focused on a particular regional, urban, or neighborhood phenomenon, such as air pollution, crime, education, housing, taxes, or commutation. General principles for the analysis of amenities have not been formulated.

Amenities have proven to be difficult to analyze using traditional tools. The dimensions of amenities are not those in which most other commodities are measured, nor do amenities have observable prices in the usual sense. Despite the fact that a great deal of effort is devoted to their production and distribution, amenities are not directly bought and sold. Some amenities, like clean air and open space, have been ubiquitous over wide areas in the past and did not have a positive price. In the increasingly prevalent cases in which amenities are scarce, amenities are priced indirectly through the prices of other things—notably land and human resources as well as buildings and other capital—with which they become inextricably related. The demand and supply of amenities must be analyzed through these indirect effects on other markets.

Another reason that amenities are challenging to analyze is that they are spatially differentiated. As in the case of amenities, the analysis of the spatial dimensions of activities has remained underdeveloped. One of the best hopes for progress in understanding spatial phenomena is through their joint analysis with amenities.

The importance of amenity analysis to policy and planning can hardly be overestimated. Governments from federal down to local units use such analysis, either implicity or explicitly, to determine service and tax levies and to regulate and zone. Policies to influence the location of people and jobs must be grounded in an understanding of amenity markets. Private firms and individuals must also make periodic location decisions, which will determine their access to amenities. Beyond those decisions based on the given pattern of amenity supplies, there are public policies which seek directly to change amenities such as pollution, crime, and neighborhood public services of various kinds, to name only a few.

This book advances the analysis of amenities by providing conceptual, methodological, and empirical foundations for such analysis. It also applies amenity concepts to a wide variety of specific phenomena. These phenomena are associated with access to places for buying and selling outputs and inputs, as well as with environmental and topographic features, collectively provided goods, and people themselves in their roles as neighbors. The topics range from benefit–cost analysis to gentrification, from the effect of climate on regional migration to the effect of racial prejudice on urban housing markets.

Part I deals with amenities most generally. Diamond and Tolley (Chapter 1) develop a framework within which to place the heretofore disparate parts of amenity analysis. Extensions within the framework are also developed. Based on a rigorous definition of amenities, the chapter examines approaches to modeling effects of amenities on urban form and other phenomena under static and dynamic conditions, giving attention also to the effects of amenities in a regional context. Harris, Tolley, and Harrell (Chapter 2) provide a model of the effects of amenities on the residence site choice. It demonstrates the great influence on land values of amenities other than distance to the central business district, indicating that models of urban form must move beyond those in which the latter variable is the single or dominant explanatory variable.

In Part II on methods of amenity market analysis, Linneman (Chapter 3) reviews a wide range of issues in the hedonic demand estimation literature as it bears on estimating the determinants of residential location. Blomquist and Worley (Chapter 4) examine a specific controversy in the hedonic literature, the degree of endogeneity in the levels of dwelling characteristics and amenities. They specify and illustrate a hedonic demand and supply framework in which econometric tests for simultaneity can be made.

Part III is concerned with the empirical analysis of urban amenity markets. Pollard (Chapter 5) provides a unique analysis of the joint effects on building heights of access to downtown and view amenities. Vaughan and Huckins (Chapter 6) develop the benefit–cost analysis for evaluating measures to control the disamenity, urban expressway noise. Grimes (Chapter 7) estimates rent gradients connected with recreational amenities near a large urban center. In doing so, he models and estimates the effects of competition for recreational land by people from towns and cities outside the dominant urban center. Smith (Chapter 8) investigates racial composition as a neighborhood amenity, estimating how racial preferences effect house prices and testing whether it is preferences or discrimination that causes segregation.

Part IV turns to regional amenity markets. Haurin (Chapter 9) develops a rigorous model of how regional amenities jointly affect regional wage rate differentials and city size. Graves and Regulska (Chapter 10) estimate the effects on migration of climate, access to recreational opportunities, and other amenities, showing how the effects depend on life-cycle variables and race.

Much of the work in this book began as thesis or other research by the contributors while they were associated with the Department of Economics and Center for Urban Studies at the University of Chicago. The contributions in this volume go well beyond that research, however.

We wish to thank Dennis Carlton, Gideon Fishelson, Arnold Harberger, J. Vernon Henderson, D. Gale Johnson, Ronald Krumm, Robert Lucas, Margaret Reid, Sherwin Rosen, Larry Sjastadd, and other colleagues who contributed to the thinking underlying this book. Special recognition is due to Charles Upton whose contributions were immeasurable in dissertation advising and in the Urban Economics Workshop. The patience and help of the members of the editors' families—Alice and Catherine Tolley and Alice Diamond—should also be acknowledged, as should the painstaking and good-spirited help by Betty Raff and June Nelson.

GEORGE S. TOLLEY
DOUGLAS B. DIAMOND, JR.

I

THE AMENITY CONCEPT

1

The Economic Roles of Urban Amenities

DOUGLAS B. DIAMOND, JR.   GEORGE S. TOLLEY

I. INTRODUCTION

Urban and regional economics address a large set of market and social phenomena that intrinsically possess a spatial dimension. That is, the location of the activity matters to the economic agents. There are, undoubtedly, hundreds of reasons why location matters. However, all of these reasons can be captured in one general concept, that of locational amenities. Amenities, like other goods, affect the level of either firm profits or household satisfactions. But, unlike for other goods, increments to amenities can be gained solely through a change in location. This unique characteristic of amenities means that location matters to people. It also means that amenities are the essence of urban and regional economics.

This chapter will demonstrate that amenities provide a unifying concept central to the explanation of

1. Urban land values
2. Patterns of urban density
3. The locations of households and businesses within and among cities

These subjects encompass topics as diverse as hedonic estimation, the timing of residential land use, neighborhood filtering or gentrification, industrial location, and household migration. All of these involve locational decisions and therefore amenities.

Traditionally, this central role in spatial analysis has been held by a subset of all amenities, the transportation or access amenities. The analy-

3

THE ECONOMICS OF
URBAN AMENITIES

sis of firm location has emphasized the transportation costs of inputs and outputs. Intraurban patterns of land prices and residential location were said to be driven by the desire for access to workplaces. However, much work (e.g., Bradford and Kelejian, 1973; Diamond, 1980; Graves and Linneman, 1979; Harris, Tolley, and Harrell, 1968 and in this volume; Wheaton, 1977) on these and other urban phenomena has concluded that nontransportation amenities can be as important or even more important than transportation costs. Thus it is appropriate to delineate in detail just what all amenities have in common and how they influence so many facets of economic life.

The pursuit of amenities is clearly an important household undertaking. Locational amenities affect such major determinants of household well-being as personal security and health, leisure time, housing quality, child quality, and the opportunity set facing the household for maket consumption activities. The effects of amenities on firm location can be just as profound. The choice of both a region and the location within the region will reflect the pursuit of factors affecting profits (such as transportation facilities and work force characteristics) over which the firm has no other influence.

In addition to providing an understanding of how amenities shape economic activity, another major reason for examining amenities is that governmental units can directly influence the spatial pattern of amenities and the course of urban economic events. The presence and growth of this power has raised a number of policy concerns that can be addressed only through the analysis of amenity markets. What is the value of decreased noise and pollution? What is the spatial impact of heavily subsidized mass transit? Is the decay of some cities and the sprawling growth of others an efficient use of resources? How can racial and economic integration be achieved? These questions and many others being pondered by the public and its public servants can be at least partially answered through the careful empirical and theoretical analysis of urban amenity markets.

In this chapter we provide a conceptual structure for synthesizing a wide variety of urban and regional economic analyses. We also attempt to summarize the most important insights of amenity market analysis. References to earlier and more recent works in these areas are given. However, the amenity phenomenon is too pervasive to permit a complete review of the amenity-related literature since that would be equivalent to a review of nearly all the literature in urban and regional economics.

The approach is first to *describe and classify amenities* (Section II) and to explore the implications of their peculiar properties for the way they are *allocated through an implicit price system* (Section III). We find that, since they are part and parcel of the residence and firm site choice, amenities are sold through a tie-in with either vacant land or existing structures. The analysis suggests how *the demands for amenities* might be *estimated from property prices* (Section IV).

Since all locational distinctions are captured in the amenity bundle, we then analyze *residential location patterns* of various socioeconomic groups by examining how the residence market allocates amenities over such competing groups in a given city (Section V). In the allocation process, the pattern of lot sizes, and thus *urban density,* is determined (Section VI). More generally, the whole gamut of the structural characteristics of development is influenced by amenities. The *dynamic nature of this development* is also recognized in Section VI. The fact that structures are durable implies that both past and future expected conditions in the amenity market will influence present location and density patterns. Moreover, the attractiveness of *maintaining* or *renewing* structural characteristics of dwellings is very much a function of amenity market conditions (Section VII) since the amenity market determines the payoff to such investments at a given location.

A quite different allocation process operates to determine the residential location choice across urban areas or *regions*. Since movement across areas implies a change of labor market and perhaps relative prices and the price level, the regional amenity market intrinsically involves wages as well as property prices. These links among amenities, household migration, and compensating differentials in wages and prices are developed in Section VIII.

II. THE AMENITY CONCEPT

An amenity may be defined as a location-specific good. As we shall see, this simple definition covers a broad range of things.[1] In doing so, it encompasses all aspects of the consumption or production decision that influence the location of the household or firm. However, such a concise definition also hides important nuances of the amenity concept that must be clearly understood before applying the concept to the full scope of urban and regional analysis.

First of all, an amenity is a good. Thus, things such as food and utensils

---

[1] The vernacular meaning of the word "amenity" is similar but somewhat narrower. Developers and realtors use it to describe features which are specific to their development or to particular houses (e.g., tennis courts, walk-in closets). To the extent that such features are easily replicable elsewhere, they are not truly location-specific. However, the more general advantages and disadvantages of a location are also amenities and are really the focus of our discussion.

could be amenities, as could steel and labor. However, in modeling the markets for these goods, the usual assumption is that they are available in homogeneous units at a price which is independent of location. In other words, the markets on both the demand side and the supply side are not location-specific. As described, these items are not amenities.

For other goods, the market is totally location-specific. Consumption of goods such as air quality, views, or local public services can be varied only by movement into another "market" or location. These are all examples of one major type of amenity. They are components of the social, physical, or legal environment. As with most other environmental goods, they are ambient elements available for consumption (or production) at zero cost. In this sense, consumption is nonexcludable, at least once access to the particular location is obtained. This implies that there is a public good aspect to these goods, an aspect which will be examined further below.

However, even ordinary goods can easily have an element of location-specificity about them. For example, when food and utensils are combined to produce fine restaurant meals they become a location-specific good. Fine restaurant meals cannot be purchased in every town, much less on every block in a given town. Similarly, a ton of steel in Pittsburgh is not the same as a ton of steel in Montana. The services of a cigar roller in Miami are not the same as similar services in Topeka, Kansas.

There is a question, though, as to how to model these location-specific but nonenvironmental goods. Physically speaking, steel is steel, wherever it is located. What makes some of such goods location-specific is the presence of significant transportation costs, either for transporting the good from producer to user or to transport the user to the producer. In these cases, the amenity aspect of the good is really one of access. The greater the distance or costliness of transportation, the higher the price gross of transportation costs. The amenity in this case, access to a location-specific market, has value because it serves as a substitute for an ordinary good, transportation services. It is the access to a good which is location-specific and thus an amenity.

We shall model access amenities and all other amenities as goods entering the utility function. However, in the case of access amenities, there could be effects on the price of nonamenity goods in the budget constraint (e.g., the price—including transportation costs—of fine restaurant meals). In other words, they shift the budget constraint or the cost function, with an attendant income or profit effect. In this sense, these amenities are different from the other, purely environmental goods.

An obvious case of this spatial variation in the budget constraint arises in modeling household location decisions with respect to access to the workplace. Alonso (1964) placed access to the Central Business District (CBD) both in the utility function as an ordinary good and in the budget constraint as a monetary cost. This reflects the fact that access to the workplace affects utility not only directly through the pleasure or displeasure of the time spent commuting, but also indirectly through the reduction in the price of work trips and thus in the income available for expenditure on other goods.

A more general amenity model would recognize explicitly that the prices of goods gross of transportation costs may vary over space. However, this is an important distinction only when the demand for a particular good is responsive to price variation. For example, if one makes the assumption that households will make as many trips to the CBD independent of the price, then no predictive power is lost by modeling access to the CBD solely as a direct determinant of utility. Access has value as a substitute for other household consumption goods, such as gasoline and automobile services. Similarly, we will generally model other access amenities as entering the utility function directly.[2]

Another generalization of the amenity notion could be toward viewing them as either inputs into the household production function or shifters of that function. This is attractive, considering the characteristic of many amenities as elements of the environment in which other consumption takes place. However, the analysis of most urban phenomena has not made use of the distinction between household commodities and market goods.

As noted, consumption of an amenity is usually nonexcludable once access to its location is gained. To see this, assume for the moment that exclusion at a location is possible. If so, consumption of the good would not be purely location-specific, that is, consumption could vary at a given location. This distinction can be unclear in some cases. For example, a good may be excludable and thus rationed by price at a given location, but the price may vary across locations. In this case, it is the option to buy the good at a given price, and not the good itself, which is location-specific and thus an amenity. In turn, this nonexcludability means that most amenities are not private goods, that is, consumption by an additional individual does not reduce the consumption of all others by an equal amount. If in fact consumption by one person reduced the consumption of others by

---

[2] The price shift effects of access amenities may be important in other contexts. For example, firms will substitute across inputs based on relative prices gross of transportation costs. If input ratios are the focus of an analysis, then access amenities should be explicitly entered into the cost function.

the full amount, the good usually would be subject to price rationing at a given location and thus not be an amenity itself.[3]

If an amenity is not a pure private good, it must have an element of "public good" in it. However, the amenity need not be a pure public good. Consumption could involve some congestion effects, such that consumption by another person reduces the levels available to others. This is not surprising, since many amenities are environmental goods subject to technological external effects. There may also be external effects on the social or legal environment and on access.

Another way of thinking about amenities is that they are goods that are not fungible (i.e., subject to transfer or exchange) across space. That is why they are location-specific. Traditionally such goods had not been the focus of much analytical interest. However, nonfungible environmental goods have become widely recognized as important to consumption and production and provide much of the impetus to the amenity literature. But nonfungibility across space also applies to legal access to local public goods and transportation access to work.

The location-specificity of amenities also implies that the level of any amenity available at a site to the individual household or firm is independent of the choice of the individual household or firm. This does not mean that the level of the amenity cannot be a function of the number or type of individuals at a location. There can be congestion or other external effects. It does mean that the functional relationship between, say, density and an amenity such as air quality is given exogenously and that the number or type of other individuals is determined exogenously to the wishes of each individual. For example, a high-income household may be considered an asset to any community. Moreover, the magnitudes of its external effects may vary across potential residence locations. We assume, though, that the fiscal and social environment of each potential neighborhood, after accounting for its presence, is what matters to the household. Yet that is what is beyond their direct control. In this specific sense, amenity levels at a location are exogenous to the control of any individual and are only variable to the individual by movement in space.

Having noted that amenity levels are exogenous to individual choice, it should be recognized that usually there is a human agent behind the supplies of amenities at a given location. Those few amenities that are bestowed by nature are the only true exceptions. These would be things

---

[3] An important class of amenities for which consumption is perfectly congestible at a location is the indivisible and durable characteristics of an existing dwelling. Consumption can be perfectly congestible for practical reasons of privacy and security. Yet the good is not subject to price rationing because it can not be unbundied.

such as natural weather, natural water routes, natural topography, and natural views.

Even these can be directly or indirectly altered by people other than the consuming household. The federal government builds highways and recreational areas. State and local governments build transportation systems and other facilities, provide a wide range of services, and also impose taxes. Firms and households produce a variety of externalities on the physical environment. Households collectively create a social environment. The characteristics of neighboring households may be important to each household. All of these factors beyond the direct control of the household determine the amenities available to the household at a particular location. Yet the only way that the individual household can determine its consumption of amenities is through movement in geographic space. Such is the distinctive nature of amenities.

Since amenities are not fungible, there is no simple way of aggregating demands for an amenity. However, the modeling of an amenity in the utility function of the individual household is quite conventional. An amenity has a marginal utility, and a marginal rate of substitution can be formulated between an amenity and another good or between an amenity and money. The latter is also the marginal willingness-to-pay for an increment of the amenity.

A large number of factors can affect the marginal willingness-to-pay (or marginal value) of an amenity, either through the marginal utility of the amenity or through the marginal utility of money. For example, increased consumption of market substitutes for the amenity will reduce the marginal value of the amenity. Increases in income will very likely raise the marginal value, if it is a normal good. Most importantly, anything that systematically shifts the utility function itself over households may change marginal valuations. Family size or structure and labor force participation in the household are only two of these kinds of "taste" shifters that may be important determinants of the individual household's marginal valuations of an amenity. Since the locus of these marginal valuations are the household's "demand" for the amenity, these shifters can be called *demand shifters*.

The nature of the household demand for an amenity can be illustrated by the demand for clean air. The amenity in this case must be defined more precisely. Let us say that it is the absence of particulate matter in the air. Even more precisely it is a decreasing function of the annual mean level of particulate matter at 6 ft above the ground at each location. In terms of the production of household commodities, particulate-free air reduces the cost of commodities such as health, a clean interior environment, and a high quality exterior residential shell. Alternatively, one can view it as a direct input into the utility function without specifically considering the reasons for its value.

The value placed by a household on a marginal unit of this amenity will depend at least on the household's income and probably also on the number of members in the household. On an individual household basis, those households for which health is more closely related to particulates (e.g., with elderly members) or which occupy the dwelling environment more of the time (e.g., retired or homemaker households) may value clean air more.

The marginal value of cleaner air will also be a function of the level of clean air. In fact, it is very possible that, above a certain level of cleanliness, no value is placed on further increments, whereas below a certain level, life itself is threatened. Since the levels of some amenities (at a given location) are beyond control by anyone and in all cases the amenities available to the individual are beyond the control of that individual, locations with extreme amenity levels may exist (e.g., Death Valley). Existence of the locations does not mean, though, that someone must reside there (e.g., in the case of mortally low amenity levels) or that the market can charge for unvalued increments (e.g., in the case of very high amenity levels).

A household's demand for an amenity may vary also with the level of other amenities or the price of ordinary market goods. For example, clear air is more desirable when there is a view from a location, but it may be less (or more) important if other noxious but less visible pollutants are at low levels. On the other hand, the clarity of the ambient air is less important when the services of an air filtration device are cheaper (i.e., a substitute) and more important the higher the number of sunny days (i.e., perhaps a complement).

Thus the theoretical determinants of the household demand for an amenity are similar to those for any conventional market good. It is the assumption of a perfectly elastic supply of the good to the household at an exogenous price that does not apply to amenities. By the location-specific nature of an amenity, increments to the consumption by the household are unobtainable at any (relevant) price without changing its location. Nor is there a perfectly elastic supply of bundles of amenities, since the area conveying a given bundle of amenities is fixed. Therefore, both the dimensions of any given bundle and the number of such bundles are fixed. This implies that amenities are allocated through a bidding process. We turn next to a closer examination of how households behave in amenity markets.

III. MARKETS IN AMENITIES

Since amenities are location-specific goods, there exists no market in the usual sense for amenities. Variation in consumption is feasible only through relocation. However, the right to reside or to produce in an area with more amenities must be purchased in order to increase consumption. In other words, there is a tie-in sale between the property market and amenity consumption. More generally, the choice of a location to live or produce at also involves the choice of labor and consumption (or input and output) markets, inasmuch as prices in those markets vary over urban areas. The amenity market is implicit in the markets for land and labor.

The usual model in urban economics assumes the existence of a single market in labor, goods, inputs, and outputs. Regional analysis, on the other hand, emphasizes the variation in wages and prices across urban areas. In this section, we shall focus on intraurban amenity markets and return in Section VIII to examine regional amenity markets. Moreover, we will develop only the residential amenity market, although the analysis can be extended to the production or firm amenity market.

The most important behavioral element of the intraurban residential amenity market is the demands of individual households. Supplies of amenities in the form of the geographic area providing eligibility to given levels are strictly fixed, at least in the simpler amenity models.[4] Aggregate demand, in the sense of the number of households in the city and the general level of their demands, is an important determinant of the general level of property prices (or wages) but not usually of their intraurban variation, which is the force behind most interesting urban spatial phenomena. So we begin by examining the amenity consumption decision of an individual household with a given level of income in a given city of given population.

A. Individual Household Demand

There have been several different approaches to the analysis of an intraurban amenity market. Most analyses include only one amenity, access to the CBD, and assume that it declines uniformly with distance from the center. Within this approach, though, there have been those studies that have assumed that the purchase of vacant land provides access to the amenity (e.g., Alonso, 1964), those that have hypothesized instead that

---

[4] We shall discuss the endogeneity of certain neighbor-related amenities, including effects of congestion, in Section V. Ellickson (1979) provides a more rigorous discussion of how supplies of areas with a given level of amenities may interact with household demand.

firms offer housing services produced from land at a given location and malleable capital (e.g., Mills, 1967; Muth, 1969), and those that have emphasized how the durability and nonmalleability of housing capital adds further constraints on the choice set of residents (e.g., Kain and Quigley, 1975; Straszheim, 1975).

Each approach has its advantages for particular purposes. Muth was able to provide a systematic analysis of spatial patterns of residential location and housing quality from both the theoretical and empirical viewpoints by assuming that housing services and access to the CBD were what households were seeking. Straszheim was able to give more weight to the constrained characteristics of dwellings in addition to the influence of the desire for access. However, Alonso's approach was the simplest and most vivid as far as implications for urban form and residential location. Thus we use that approach here, as modified for the presence of multiple amenities in Diamond (1980).

We assume that the household takes a one-period perspective and resides at only one location. It allocates its money resources over land, amenities, and other goods in such a way as to maximize its utility, or

$$\text{Max } U(L, A, Z) \qquad \text{subject to} \quad Y = Z + P_L(A)L, \tag{1.1}$$

where

L = land services consumed at a residential site with given levels of amenities,

A = a vector of the services of all amenities at the residential site,

Z = a composite of all other goods, and

P_L = the marginal price (or rent) for land services at a point in amenity space.

The first order conditions required for an optimum for each household are obtained by partially differentiating Eq. (1.1) with respect to land, amenities, and other goods:

$$U_Z = \lambda, \tag{1.2}$$

$$U_L = \lambda P_L, \tag{1.3}$$

$$U_{A_i} = \lambda(\partial P_L/\partial A_i)L, \tag{1.4}$$

where λ is the Lagrange multiplier. Dividing Eqs. (1.2)–(1.4) by (1.2), we obtain the usual conditions that the marginal rate of substitution between any two goods is equal to the ratio of their prices. In particular the marginal rate of substitution between each good and the composite good is equal to the price of that good, or

$$U_Z/U_Z = 1, \tag{1.5}$$

$$U_L/U_Z = P_L, \qquad (1.6)$$

$$U_{A_i}/U_Z = (\partial P_L/\partial A_i)L. \qquad (1.7)$$

Equation (1.7) is particularly interesting. It implies that households will move along the land price function, $P_L(A)$, in every direction (i.e., increase consumption of each amenity) until the marginal value of each amenity, U_{A_i}/U_Z, equals the increment to land costs, holding constant the quantity of land. *The increment to the price of land times the amount of land purchased is the price of an amenity.* It is not a fixed price. It varies with both the partial of the equilibrium land price function and with the quantity of land consumed.

Equations (1.6) and (1.7) are central to urban analysis. In Eq. (1.6), both U_L and U_Z are functions of land, amenities and Z. Solving the budget constraint for Z, substituting it in for Z in (1.6) and solving for L yields

$$L = L[P_L(A), A, Y]. \qquad (1.8)$$

The level of amenities enters both directly (but probably modestly) through interaction with land in the utility function and indirectly (but more strongly) through the price of land. Since per household consumption of land determines residential density, Eq. (1.8) may be viewed as the basic relationship in density analysis.

The same kind of manipulation can be performed on Eq. (1.7) to derive the demand for amenities. The consumption of a particular amenity will be a function of income, the partials of the land price function $[P'_L(A)]$, and the level of the other amenities (A_j) and lot size, that is,

$$A_i = A_i[P'_L(A), A_j, L, Y]. \qquad (1.9)$$

Since household consumption of amenities determines residential location, Eq. (1.9) may be viewed as the basic relationship in residential location analysis.

An additional insight can be drawn from Eq. (1.7). By dividing both sides of Eq. (1.7) by L, we have

$$V_{A_i}/L = \partial P_L/\partial A_i, \qquad (1.10)$$

where

$$V_{A_i} \equiv U_{A_i}/U_Z$$

(i.e., V_{A_i} is the marginal value of A_i in terms of money). Equation (1.10) implies that for a household to be in equilibrium, the marginal value of each amenity, divided by lot size, must be equated to the increment to land price. For example, if the household's marginal value of A_i were \$100 per year and land consumption (at the given P_L) is 10,000 ft², then the household will be in equilibrium only if, for another unit of A_i, the rental value of the land increases by one cent per year.

Equation (1.10) is of interest for at least two reasons. Since the supply of land with any particular bundle of amenities is fixed, the price is purely demand determined. Thus the gradients of the market price or rent function are being determined by the marginal bids for additional amenities by households. Those bids are the left-hand side of (1.10), and they are determining the partials of the land price function in the process of generating equilibrium in the land market. We shall consider that process further later in this section.

At the same time, the individual household takes the partials of the land price function as exogenous to its own location decision. It maximizes its welfare by moving along the land price function until the incremental amount per square foot equals the marginal value of the amenity per square foot of land consumed. The implications of this condition for (a) estimating the demands for amenities; and for (b) analyzing the residential location decisions of different socioeconomic groups are developed in Sections IV and V, respectively.

B. Land Market Equilibrium

We have described the determination of the equilibrium consumption of amenities by the individual household. We now move on to the equilibrium in the total land and amenity market. These demands must be somehow aggregated, matched with supply constraints, and an equilibrium land price (and amenity price) schedule arrived at. This process of clearing the amenity markets is developed in Alonso (1964), Mills (1972), and Wheaton (1974). Some of the details and conditions are complex and problematic. However, the rough outlines can be drawn directly from Alonso's work.

Alonso focused on each household's equilibrium conditions. He proposed that there are a set of land prices and partials implied by those prices that would put each household or group of similar households in equilibrium everywhere in the city. That set of prices was called the *bid-price function* of that household or group. In fact, each household had a continuum of such bid functions, the higher ones associated with lower levels of utility. In the case where the presence of the household in the urban area is a given, the household's utility as well as location is determined by which bid function it ends up on. In any case, equilibrium for all households in a group of similar households requires that enough of the total geographic area of the city have land prices along one of the group's households' bid functions to provide space for all the households in the group. Otherwise there will be excess demand (or supply) for space and members of the group will raise (or lower) their bids to the next highest (or lowest) bid function.

The supply of land to each household or group of households depends on the geographic area associated with the portion of amenity space in which the land price function follows the bid function of the group. The total supply of land for urban use is determined by the geographic area for which equilibrium bid prices by urban residents are greater than the price of the land in other uses. The general level of the bid-price functions must be such that the total land drawn into use for that urban area exactly equals the sum of the demands of the individual households, based on the bid function each household ends up on.

When the number and type of households in the city are fixed (i.e., a closed city), excess demand for land leads to a rise in the general level of land prices, bringing more land out of the nonurban use and reducing land consumption per household. However, the analysis of regional amenity markets must allow for migration and the general endogeneity of city size. One assumption is that of an open city where utility levels of each household are given by the option of achieving that utility in another city.[5] In this city, it is the number of each type of household that adjusts until the equilibrium bid function of each household yields the exogenously given utility level.

An equilibrium outcome in either case is illustrated in Figure 1.1. On the horizontal axis is distance from the center of the city. On the vertical axis is the one-period price (i.e., the rent) per unit of land. Let us assume that amenity levels and thus land prices are uniform at any given distance from the center. However, there are several amenities in the city, not just access to the center. In particular, the areas closer to the center suffer from higher levels of a number of disamenities, such as crime, pollution, or poor schools.

There are three socioeconomic groups in the city. In Section V we will examine how the relative amenity consumption of these three groups is determined. For the moment, we are only concerned with how the bid-rent function of each group contributes to the formation of the market-clearing land price function.

In Figure 1.1, all bids at the edge of the city are less than the exogenous price of land outside the urban area, except for that of Group 2. Their bid-price function of B_2 is set at the exogenous price P_0 at the amenity levels attainable at distance k_5. This in turn determines their utility level.

---

[5] See Polinsky and Shavell (1976) for a discussion of land market adjustment to an amenity change under the closed and open city assumptions.

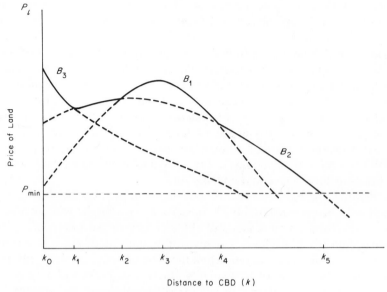

FIGURE 1.1. Equilibrium bid functions.

Since one of those amenities is access to the CBD, a bigger city is associated with lower utility since the CBD is less accessible from the edge.

If the city is an "open city," additional members of Group 2 will enter only as long as utility remains above that achievable elsewhere. If it is a "closed" city, utility levels will simply depend on how many people of each group live in the city and on the amenity levels on the fringe of the city. In either case, the equilibrium radius of the city depends on the density of development in the city, which is a function of the level of land prices and of the demands for land by the inhabitants. In other words, the level of land prices depend on the radius, and the the radius depends on the level of land prices. These relationships are generally so complex that an analytical solution for the land price function is unattainable except under extremely simplifying assumptions.

However, the linkages between bid functions are clear. Land market equilibrium requires (*a*) that no resident can increase utility by changing location or land consumption; and (*b*) that all residents who wish to live in the city at those land prices be accommodated. If Figure 1.1 portrays such an equilibrium land price function, the aggregate demand for land by each group is satisfied at those prices over those areas in which each group is the high bidder. Thus, Group 2 just fills the area from k_1 to k_2 and k_4 to k_5 Group 1 occupies the area from k_2 to k_4, and Group 3 lives in the relatively small area from k_0 to k_1.

The distance to the edge of the city is determined by the number of residents of each type and their demands for land and amenities. Once the location of the edge is known, the level of the other land prices can be determined. Land prices within the city move along the portions of each group's bid function in the area in which that group is high bidder. The slope of the price function with respect to k is the slope of the bid function for that group, which is given by Eq. (1.10) (where A_i is now the bundle of amenities associated with distance).

Land price levels and partials must adjust until each household and household type is in equilibrium relative to other locations in the city and relative to other cities. The latter adjustment process is just as important as intraurban amenity market adjustment. In this process the labor market also serves as an allocator of amenities, particularly regional amenities. We have been assuming that work location and incomes were exogenously determined. Going back a step further, amenity consumption may also depend on workplace. Income may vary because the marginal product function of labor may vary over space. Moreover, households do not simply locate to maximize money income. Although we are assuming that the prices of most goods are the same within a city, this need not be the case across regions. Thus the more general choice of a residential location over regions takes account of variation in wages, prices, and amenity levels. For the marginal resident of any given city, variation in wages must compensate for differentials in the other two if he is to be indifferent between areas.

The implications for the allocation of people across cities of this three-way relationship between wages, prices, and amenities are discussed in Section VIII of this chapter. Before that, we examine the implications of the amenity market-clearing process for estimating the demands for amenities and for the allocation of people to residential locations within a given urban area. Then we turn to the profound effects of the variation in land prices on urban form. Finally, we consider how amenity markets influence the filtering and renewal process.

IV. ESTIMATING HOUSEHOLD DEMANDS FOR AMENITIES

Since firms do not explicitly produce amenities for household consumption, it might seem that the estimation of the demands for amenities would be of little importance. However, private-sector housing producers have an interest in what types of households are most attracted to particular amenities because they must package dwelling characteristics and land with those amenities in the bundle of goods called a new house. Similarly, analysts of urban phenomena are interested in the demands for amenities since they are important determinants of residential density, location patterns and urban growth or decline.

Perhaps the most important reason for estimating the demands for amenities is the fact that many governmental bodies can and do influence the supplies of those amenities. In the absence of competitive markets in the supply of "neighborhoods" or jurisdictions (e.g., as envisioned in a pure Tiebout, 1956, world), whether optimal levels of amenities are provided depends on how well public decision makers can assess and respond to the values that households place on them.[6] This need has been the motivation behind many of the studies of specific amenities (e.g., Brown and Pollakowski, 1977; Ridker and Henning, 1967; Vaughan and Huckins, this volume) and of efforts at refining the methodology of such measurements.

If amenities were publically provided goods, the electoral process would provide the only possibility of directly estimating the demands for them. However, amenities are site-specific. That is, variation in consumption can be achieved through choice of residential location. This implies that amenities are involved in a tie-in sale with something that is traded in ordinary markets—residential land and housing. The joint bundle is traded in an *explicit* market with each amenity having an *implicit* price depending on relative bundle prices. Demand can be inferred from these implicit markets.

As Rosen (1974) points out in his pathbreaking analysis of implicit markets, there is an aspect of all implicit markets that makes their analysis different from that of ordinary markets. The difference is that the market marginal price of any implicit good may vary with the quantity of the good. In other words, the price of another unit of an amenity may be a function of the quantity consumed of the amenity and of the other amenities in the bundle. This nonlinear form of the budget constraint arises because amenity bundles cannot be divided or repackaged by any relevant market participants. Thus, the arbitrage that would guarantee equalization of marginal prices across locations cannot occur.[7] Arbitrage is possible only in the markets for bundles of amenities. This guarantees equalization of *bundle* prices across equivalent *bundles* but does not lead to equalization of the implicit marginal prices for individual increments of the amenities.

---

[6] The political system provides some signals of consumer demands but only in a fairly gross way, particularly at the Federal level.

[7] This same argument applies to a market in a good such as "housing services". The indivisibility of such a good implies that the marginal cost of production need not be constant. The implications for the analysis of the demand for housing are drawn in Diamond and Smith (1981).

This quantity-dependence of price is both a blessing and a curse. It permits variation in the prices facing participants in a single market at a single time. Thus price elasticities can be estimated from a single cross-section. On the other hand, income elasticities are more difficult to estimate from such a cross-section because price is varying also.[8]

This nonconstant price term can be measured in two different ways, depending on the market being observed. If lot size and dwelling characteristics are freely variable, that is, not part of the tie-in sale, then the price of an amenity increment is the partial of the land price function times the amount of land consumed. This result comes out in Eqs. (1.7) and (1.8). In the case of amenity markets in areas where lot size has been fixed by previous development, the price of a marginal unit of an amenity is more simply the increment to the price of a house with given other characteristics and amenities.

In either case, the marginal price of an amenity at any point in amenity space must first be inferred from an estimate of the land price or house price function defined over all residence sites in the city. The partials of such estimated price functions with respect to each amenity contain the information needed by the household to choose its consumption of amenities.[9]

We shall first examine the case of freely variable lot sizes. Once a data set including land prices and amenity information has been gathered, land price should be regressed on amenity levels to recreate the information assumed to be available to households. In other words,

$$P_L = P_L(A_1 \cdot \cdot \cdot A_n). \tag{1.11}$$

This is essentially what most studies of amenities and land prices have done, including Brigham (1965), Brodsky (1970), Harris, Tolley, and Harrell (1968 and this volume), and Mills (1969). However, Eq. (1.11) does not directly yield estimates of the prices paid by households for amenities. To find that, the partial of the estimated land price function at the point in residence space that the household settles must be multiplied by the land consumption of the household, that is

$$P_{A_i} = (\partial P_L / \partial A_i) L \tag{1.12}$$

---

[8] Unfortunately, the presence of the quantity-dependence of the price term also implies a form of simultaneity bias. This and various other issues arising in the estimation of amenity demands are discussed in articles by Linneman and by Blomquist and Worley in this volume.

[9] It is an open question whether households, even with the help of a full-time real estate broker, have very accurate knowledge of the price function they are facing. However, inasmuch as they focus only on the small relevant part of the market, they actually may have excellent information.

The quantity consumed of each amenity can then be regressed on the "prices" of each amenity, on the "prices" of other amenities, and on demand shifters such as income, or[10]

$$A_i = A_i(P_{A_i}, P_{A_j}, P_L, Y),$$ (1.13)

where P_{A_j} is a vector of the implicit prices of other amenties and P_L is included as the price of a substitute or complement.[11]

The analysis is only slightly different for a market in which lot sizes are fixed by previous development. In that case, there is no longer a tie between the choice of amenities and land price. Instead there may be correlation in an incomplete choice set between amenities and lot size or other dwelling characteristics due to the impact of amenities on lot size at time of development. However, we can examine the choice of any particular amenity with all other aspects being held constant, at least conceptually. In that case, as Rosen shows, the relevant price of an increment to the amenity is the partial with respect to the amenity of the function describing house prices in the city, that is, the hedonic. In other words,

$$P_{A_i} = \partial P(A, L, H)/\partial A_i,$$ (1.14)

where H is a vector of dwelling attributes.

The demand equation, Eq. (1.13), can be rewritten to use the hedonic definition of the marginal prices of the amenities, Eq. (1.14), and to include the implicit prices of the dwelling attributes. This yields a demand function to be estimated of

$$A_i = A_i(P_{A_i}, P_{A_j}, P_L, P_{H_k}, Y),$$ (1.15)

where P_{H_k} is a vector of implicit prices for dwelling attributes other than land.

Equations similar to Eq. (1.15) have been estimated recently by a number of researchers. Among the earliest studies were Straszheim (1975) and King (1976). Since these studies preceded the recognition that the implicit marginal prices were inherently nonconstant, they relied on the empirical findings that the implicit prices varied over "submarkets" within a city. More recent studies have explicitly taken advantage of the nonconstancy of prices in implicit markets. Most studies, such as Harrison and Rubinfeld (1978), Nelson (1978), and Witte, Sumka, and

[10] This two-step procedure was first proposed by Rosen (1974) for use with property prices. This chapter is the first place it has been applied to land prices. There is no identification problem of the type noted by Rosen in the second step here because we assume that the market is in long-run equilibrium with respect to its price structure (see Rosen, p. 48).

[11] Land prices were used by Diamond (1980) to estimate an inverse demand function of a form related to Eq. (1.13). This seems to be the only study explicitly estimating amenity demand functions using land prices.

Erekson (1979), have estimated inverse demand functions, (i.e., implicit prices paid are a function of the levels of the amenities and other residence characteristics). Others, such as Linneman (1981), have used the more traditional demand formulation, as expressed in Eq. (1.15).

Despite the major progress made towards a methodology for estimating the demands for amenities, there remain a number of conceptual and econometric problems. Some are examined in Freeman (1979) and others are discussed by Linneman in this volume. Here we shall only treat one that seems not to have been clearly recognized so far.

That problem arises in the choice of the functional forms for the estimation of the hedonic function and of the demand functions. Much has been written recently on the choice of functional form for the hedonic (see Bender, Groenberg, and Huang, 1980; Halvorsen and Pollakowski, 1981; or Linneman, 1980). The consensus seems to be that the best fit should be sought. Less attention has been paid to the specification of the demand functions, although some authors such as Wheaton (1977) and Quigley (1980) have based that specification on the choice of a form for the utility function. However, the inherent linkage between the form of the hedonic and of the demand function has not been properly treated.

Since the implicit prices of the amenities are not directly observable, they must be estimated as the partials of the market hedonic price function [see Eq. (1.14)]. This implies that

$$P_{A_i} = P_{A_i}(A, L, H). \tag{1.16}$$

The exact relationship depends on the functional form chosen for the estimation of the hedonic price function. This market-level relationship between the levels of amenities and the implicit prices of amenities can lead to a spurious relationship between the two in the demand estimation. At the extreme, the adoption of a functional form for the demand function that is the same as the form of the first partials of the hedonic can lead to a perfect relationship being estimated between amenity consumption and implicit prices alone, leaving nothing to be explained by income and other demand shifters.

Such an outcome would be correct if in fact all demand shifters had no effects. In that case, the price function would exactly correspond to the single bid function of all households. Assuming instead that some demand shifters do indeed shift demand, then the functional form of the demand equation must differ from that of the implicit price function. It is clear that some external notion of the true functional relationships in demand functions must be imposed to separate out the effects on consumption of the prices and the demand shifters.

Of course, this is the case in any demand estimation. However, ordinarily there is some independent variation of prices and quantities, and thus some criterion as to the best fit can guide the choice of functional form. In the case of quantity-dependent prices, a more arbitrary element must be introduced since prices are an *exact* function of quantities alone. One option would be to work from a utility function with desirable properties to a form for the demand function. This method has the advantage of making clearer what behavioral assumptions underlie the estimation. Its disadvantage of arbitrariness seems unavoidable in working with a single cross-section of property prices.[12]

In any case, there is much need for estimates of the demands for amenities. As we shall see, amenity demand parameters are central to the analysis of many urban phenomena as well as to informed policymaking. We turn now to the discussion of those analyses with the expectation that ongoing methodological and empirical advances over time will provide more and better parameter estimates.

V. AMENITIES AND RESIDENTIAL LOCATION PATTERNS

The choice of a residence location by the individual household is the outcome of its pursuit of urban amenities.[13] This is because the consumption of a bundle of amenities simultaneously involves residence on land at some geographic location. It is true that there may be more than one geographic location conveying a given bundle of amenities. However, the total area available with precisely a particular bundle of amenities is generally small since some of the most important amenities are access to other points. Such access, by definition, varies with any movement in geographic space. Thus, although the choice of an amenity bundle does not imply residence at an exact site, the range of locations with the same amenities is usually small enough to closely link amenity consumption with geographic location.

[12] One interesting alternative would be the estimation of demand over unrelated housing markets, that is, across cities. In that case, there is not an exact correspondence between implicit prices and amenity levels. In other words, price varies (over cities) while holding quantity constant, permitting independent estimation of the functional forms.

[13] The effects of amenities on firm location can be just as profound. The choice of both a region and the location with the region will reflect the pursuit of factors affecting profits (such as transportation facilities and work force characteristics) over which the firm has no other influence. Moreover, analysis of firm location also permits consideration of how work location is determined simultaneously with residential location (e.g., Steinnes, 1977). However, space limitations and the relatively undeveloped state of the firm location literature preclude an extended discussion here. The interested reader might consult Struyk and James (1975) or Schmenner (1978).

A. Land versus Amenities

We considered the household's choice of an amenity bundle in Section III. From the point of view of the individual household, the first-order condition for an equilibrium with respect to any particular amenity was given by Eq. (1.7), which was rewritten to become Eq. (1.10)

$$V_{A_i}/L = \partial P_L/\partial A_i,$$

where V_{A_i} is the marginal value of A_i in terms of other goods. What does this tell us about the consumption of A_i by one household relative to another? If we know nothing about how land prices vary with amenity levels, we cannot say. However, household equilibrium and optimization in the amenity market also require that the second partial of the Lagrangian be negative, which implies that[14]

$$V_{A_iA_i}/L < \partial^2 P_L/\partial A_i^2 \tag{1.17}$$

under the simplifying assumption that the demand for land is independent of the amenities. This assumption eliminates the second-order effects of A_i on the denominator of the left-hand side, land consumption. $V_{A_iA_i}$ is the partial with respect to A_i of the marginal value of A_i. The left-hand side essentially is the second-partial of the household's bid function.

Equation (1.17) states that the second partial of the market land price function with respect to A_i must be *greater than* the second partial of the equilibrium resident's bid function at the point of equilibrium amenity consumption. But Eq. (1.10) implies that the first partial of the land price function be *equal to* the first partial of the bid function at the point of residency. *Thus equilibrium residency at the higher of two levels of an amenity, holding other amenities constant, will be allocated to the household with the more steeply sloped bid function.* In other words, anyone living at a location with incrementally higher A_i must *ceteris paribus*, have a higher marginal value for A_i per unit of land than the household consuming the lower level of A_i. This also implies that households can be ranked in their consumption of A_i, holding the other amenities constant, according to the ranking of their marginal values per unit of land, if the latter ranking is independent of the level of A_i.

This notion is the basis of the Alonso–Muth–Mills model of location by income. The model assumes that there is only one amenity, access to the CBD (ACSCBD). The marginal value of the amenity was further as-

---

[14] This is required for utility to reach an absolute maximum. If, as is likely, there are a number of points from the household's bid function on the market land price function, then along that portion the household achieves a constant maximum utility. Over that portion Eq. (1.17) holds as an equality.

sumed to be determined by the value of the savings in time and money associated with greater access. If the value of time is proportional to the wage rate and the marginal money cost of commuting does not rise significantly with income, the sum of the two savings will rise less than proportionally with income. Assuming that the demand for land rises at least proportionally with income, the value per square foot of land of greater access will fall as income rises and thus so will the consumption of access. The implication is that neighborhood income should decline as distance to the CBD declines (i.e., as ACSCBD rises).

The model can easily be generalized to a world with additional amenities (see Diamond, 1980) and demand shifters other than income. The sign of the partial relationship between any demand shifter and an amenity, holding constant other amenities and demand shifters, is given by the sign of the partial of the marginal value of the amenity per unit of land consumed with respect to that demand shifter. The partial can be further expressed as a function of the elasticities of the demands for the amenities and land, or

$$\partial(V_{A_i}/L)/\partial D_j = (V_{A_i}/LD_j)(\eta_{V_{A_i} D_j} - \eta_{LD_j}), \qquad (1.18)$$

where D_j is the jth demand shifter and the η_{km} is the elasticity of the kth variable with respect to the mth variable.[15]

Equation (1.18) highlights the economics underlying the Alonso–Mills–Muth model. Households are facing a choice between cheaper land or more amenities. Any given increase in land price per square foot will be more costly, the greater the number of square feet consumed. Thus a household will be less likely to consume more of a amenity, the greater its demand for land and the less its demand for the amenity. Any shifter of household demands for either land or amenities will influence the willingness to pay an increment to land prices in return for an increment to amenities. Specifically, the impact of the demand shifters on the consumption of an amenity depends on whether the shift in the *marginal value* of the amenity (i.e., the height of the demand curve for A_i) is greater or less than the shift in the *quantity* of land demanded.

B. Location in a Multi-Amenity City

The power of this insight and its limitations can be illustrated for the relatively realistic case of two amenities and two demand shifters. We

---

[15] The derivation proceeds as follows:

$$\frac{\partial(V_{A_i}/L)}{\partial D_j} = [(\partial V_{A_i}/\partial D_j)L - (\partial L/\partial D_j)V_{A_i}]/L^2$$

$$= (V_{A_i}/L^2 D_j)[(\partial V_{A_i}/\partial D_j(LD_j/V_{A_i}) - (\partial L/\partial D_j)(LD_j/L)]$$

$$= (V_{A_i}/LD_j(\eta_{V A_i} - \eta_{LD}).$$

shall examine location patterns with respect to distance from the CBD. Distance from the CBD does not matter for its own sake. However, the amenities will be assumed to be correlated with it.

The amenities are

A_1 = access to the CBD
A_2 = quality of schools

A_1 is negatively correlated with distance to the CBD (k), whereas school quality A_2 is positively correlated. The demand shifters are household income Y and size of family N.

The value (cost) of living another mile from the CBD is the sum of the marginal value of the decline in access to the CBD and of the rise in the quality of schools. Specifically,

$$V_k = V_1(\partial A_1/\partial k) + V_2(\partial A_2/\partial k) \tag{1.19}$$

under the assumption that the demands for the amenities are not interdependent.[16] Location patterns with respect to income or family size can be evaluated with an expression similar to Eq. (1.18). Such an expression indicates the impact of the demand shifter on the marginal bid for greater amounts of k and thus whether the bid function is becoming steeper or flatter. For income we can derive that

$$\partial(V_k/L)/\partial Y = (1/LY)[V_1\eta_{V_1Y}(\partial A_1/\partial k) + V_2\eta_{V_2Y}(\partial A_2/\partial k) \\ - (V_1\,\partial A_1/\partial k + V_2\,\partial A_2/\partial k)\eta_{LY}]. \tag{1.20}$$

Equation (1.20) says that the effect of income on the marginal bid for the composite amenity (or disamenity) distance to the CBD (k) depends on the income elasticities of the marginal values of the amenities, weighted by the partials between each amenity and k and by the marginal values.

We can easily quantify Eq. (1.20) and the parallel expression for the size of family if we know the parameters of the demand functions for land, for A_1, and for A_2 and the correlation between the amenities and k. By arbitrarily choosing the units of the amenities, and under the assumption that the amenities are perfectly correlated with k, we can assert that

$$\partial A_1/\partial k = -1 \tag{1.21}$$

$$\partial A_2/\partial k = 1. \tag{1.22}$$

We will further assume that we know that the true parameters of the demand functions, which are given by

$$L = (558)Y^{.7}P_L^{-.7}N^{.4} \tag{1.23}$$

[16] It would be an enlightening exercise to include interaction terms, such that the level of other amenities affects the demand for a given amenity. Such interaction effects, though, are not our primary interest here.

$$V_1 = (6.7)Y^{1.5}N^{-.5} \tag{1.24}$$

$$V_2 = (9.4)Y^{2.0}A_2^{-2.0}N^{2.0}. \tag{1.25}$$

The constants have been chosen to yield reasonable values. Equations (1.24) and (1.25) are actually inverse demand functions where marginal value is a function of quantities. The exponents on Y and N are thus the values of $\eta_{V_{A_i},Y}$ and $\eta_{V_{A_i},N}$ required to evaluate Eq. (1.20) and the comparable expression for family size.

It is important to recognize the substantive assumptions underlying these demand functions. The demand for land is assumed to take approximately the values reported in Diamond (1980) and other studies, except that family size has been introduced as a positive shifter. The marginal value of access to the CBD is assumed to be independent of the level of access but is quite elastic with respect to income, again in line with Diamond (1980). Smaller family size increases the value of access to the CBD, presumably because of more nonwork trips there. Finally, the marginal value of school quality rises with income and family size but declines as a function of the level of school quality.

In the calculations reported below, income (Y) has been measured in thousands of dollars, school quality (A_j) is measured as hundreds of dollars of expenditure per student, and access to the CBD (A_i) is measured as miles *from the edge of the city*. From a more general perspective, access and school quality are proxies for all the good and bad things, respectively, associated with living closer to the city center.

We can now solve for the sign of the partial relationships between income or family size and distance from the CBD. First, we need to know the sign of the marginal bid for living further from the CBD. Using Eqs. (1.21), (1.22), (1.24), and (1.25) to solve Eq. (1.19) for a typical household at the midrange levels of the amenities, we have

$$V_k|_{X=X_1} = 300(-1) + 150(1) = -150, \tag{1.26}$$

where X is a vector of locational and household characteristics. In this case, X_1 takes the value $N = 4$, $Y = 20$, $A_1 = 10$, $A_2 = 20$.

Equation (1.26) implies that distance from the CBD is on net a disamenity for this household in this situation. This need not be the case, though, for every household or even this household at every distance. The slope of the bid function for this household at the center of the city is

$$V_k|_{X=X_2} = 300(-1) + 602(1) = 302, \tag{1.27}$$

where X_2 is $N = 4$, $Y = 20$, $A_2 = 10$ and $A_1 = 20$ (i.e., the radius of the city is 20 mi). The sharply lower level of school quality has raised the marginal value of another unit of school quality above the marginal value of greater access, so that locations further away from the center are preferred at that point.

This tells us that this household's bid function first rises and then declines with k, as did the bids of Groups 1 and 2 in Figure 1.1. However, it tells us nothing about location by income in the city (holding family size constant at 4). We could evaluate that pattern most quickly by calculating the marginal bid per square foot of land for a high- and a low-income household. The more general procedure is to evaluate an expression such as Eq. (1.20) to see the general influence of income on marginal bids. Doing so at our first location yields

$$\partial(V_k/L)/\partial Y|_{X=X_3}$$
$$= [-300(1.5) + 150(2.0) - (-150).7]/(7910)(20) = -.00028, \quad (1.28)$$

where X_3 is $N = 4$, $Y = 20$, $P_L = 1.00$, $A_1 = 10$ and $A_2 = 20$. This result indicates that increases in income make the bid function more steeply negative and thus higher income will be associated with living closer in (i.e., avoiding the net disamenity of living further out).

The same calculation at the center of the city, however, indicates that, at the low levels of school quality found there, the slope of the bid function, which is positive according to Eq. (1.27), becomes more steeply positive as income increases. Specifically,

$$\partial(V_k/L)/\partial Y|_{X=X_4}$$
$$= [-300(1.5) + 602(2.0) - (302).7]/(4869)(20) = .0056, \quad (1.29)$$

where X_4 contains $N = 4$, $Y = 20$, $P_L = 2.00$, $A_1 = 20$ and $A_2 = 10$.

Equations (1.26)–(1.29) imply that the bid price function of this household defined with respect to distance to CBD will look somewhat like B_1 in Figure 1.1, whereas the bid function of households with less income but the same family size will be somewhat flatter, like B_2. Thus up to some distance, higher income households of size $N = 4$ will live further out, but after that point (e.g., k_3 in Figure 1.1) incomes will tend to decline with distance. The overall correlation between income and distance will be weak, even holding constant family size, because distance from the CBD is initially desired on net, and only after school quality reaches some minimum does distance become a bad. As a good, higher income leads to greater consumption. In the range that distance to the CBD is a bad, income will fall as distance increases.

The point of switching for the relationship between income and distance is a function of family size. Households of size greater than four will place greater weight on school quality and land consumption and thus have a tendency to live out further, holding income constant. Alternatively, smaller families will place greater weight on access to the CBD and less on schools and land. In fact, for a family size of one, the marginal bid at the center of the city is strongly negative [compare with Eq. (1.27)]

$$V_k|_{X=X_5} = 599(-1) + 38(1) = -561, \tag{1.30}$$

where X_5 is the same as X_2, except that $N = 1$.

Similarly, increases in income at small family sizes will strengthen the tendency to live closer to the center. Recalculating Eq. (1.29) for a family size of one yields

$$\begin{aligned}
&\partial(V_k/L)/\partial Y|_{X=X_6} \\
&= [(-599)(1.5) + (38)(2.0) - (-561).7]/(2797)(20) = -.00769, \tag{1.31}
\end{aligned}$$

where X_6 is $N = 1$, $Y = 20$, $P_L = 2.00$, $A_1 = 20$ and $A_2 = 10$. This implies that among singles, and perhaps childless couples, increases in income uniformly lead to living nearer the CBD, with the further implication that high-income, small households will live nearest the center. They could constitute Group 3 in Figure 1.1.

This example illustrates how amenity demands and the land–amenity trade-off lead to differential bid patterns and from that to residential location patterns. In the process, it utilized some common notions of what motivates current patterns of residential location. Presumably, the lack of family-oriented amenties, such as school quality in the inner-city, and their relatively higher demand for land propagates suburban locations among larger middle-class households, whereas smaller middle-class households are free to ignore the low levels of family-oriented amenities and the higher land prices to live nearest the center. Lower income households fill the remaining space in the inner-city and also appear nearer the fringes of the city.

In this example, lot size and all other characteristics of the dwelling are treated as freely variable. This is clearly not the case over the many portions of an urban area where redevelopment does not pay. In these areas there is no explicit trade-off between land consumption and amenity consumption. Instead, lot size and other characteristics of the dwelling unit at a given location take on the characteristics of amenities themselves. In this case, the partial relationship between income or other demand shifters and consumption of any particular amenity or dwelling characteristic simply depends on the shift effect on the demand for that characteristic alone. For example, if income raises the marginal value of air quality, the *partial* relationship between income and air quality will be positive.

The parallel expression for Eq. (1.18) is[17]

$$\partial V_{A_i}/\partial D_j = V_{A_i}/D_j \eta V_{A_i} D_j. \tag{1.32}$$

The impact of D_j on the demand for land is now irrelevant.

It should be emphasized that the fruits of this type of analysis of residential location pattern are limited to an indication of the *partial* relationship between a given household characteristic and an amenity. Much further analysis and more detailed information is needed to predict the magnitude or even the sign of the *general* relationship. For example, the correlation between income and family size would be needed in the case illustrated above in order to tie income or family size with amenity consumption. Linkage with distance to the CBD required knowledge of the relationship of the amenities with distance. Even the simple relationship assumed yielded nonmonotonic bid functions and location by income. In the most general case, the general correlation between income and any amenity depends on the correlations between all the amenities, the relative strengths of the demands for the amenities, the relative strengths of the impact of income on each of those demands, and the correlation between income and other demand shifters.

C. Location Patterns and Endogenous Amenities

Although the analytical and empirical requirements are challenging, the richness and realism of the general amenity model makes it attractive for the analysis of location patterns. It is already useable for developing hypotheses on current and evolving patterns of location. Verification of hypotheses primarily awaits accumulation of further estimates of the parameters of amenity demand functions. However, there remains a conceptual hurdle to clear. The complication is the macroendogeneity of many amenities.

In the preceding illustration, school quality is an important amenity assumed to increase with distance from the CBD. The relative importance of school quality to higher income families with children caused them to foresake the short commutes of closer locations for middle distance locations with a balance of access and schools. Thus, it could be concluded that school quality is an important determinant of location by income and family size. However, from another perspective, the school quality at any given location may be entirely dependent on the characteristics of the households that live there. If there were only one truly exogenous

---

[17] See Diamond and Smith (1980a) for an extended discussion of this model.

amenity (e.g., access to the CBD), it would determine both the pattern of household location and of school quality.[18]

Most amenities are somewhat influenced by the composition of the area population. At one extreme are amenities, such as the characteristics of one's neighbors, that are totally determined by the levels of other amenities.[19] But even such amenities as access to the CBD, air quality, and recreational options are partially functions of residential location patterns through their impacts on the provision of transportation facilities and parks and on auto usage.

In these cases, the more exogenous amenities may be exerting a more powerful influence on overall locational patterns than the relatively endogenous amenities. Thus, the explanation of locational patterns would give special emphasis to the exogenous components of amenities. The question of why an individual household lives where it does becomes different from the question of why particular patterns form. The search for ultimate causation is an important topic, both for the determination of individual location decisions and for aggregate urban form. Meanwhile, much analysis can proceed taking the location patterns of amenities as given.

The durability of dwellings introduces an element of historical endogeneity to the determination of current amenity levels. Amenity levels in the past determined the lot sizes and other characteristics of dwellings through their effects on land prices and location by income. Some of the characteristics of those dwellings became amenities once they were "set in concrete," and they affect residential location today just as other amenities do. These very durable elements of dwellings will affect the socioeconomic composition of the area's residents, which in turn may influence the levels of other amenities (e.g., school quality or public safety) in the area.

Similarly, in the evolution of residential location patterns as a city grows, the dominant amenities determining development at the fringe may be those associated with the socioeconomic characteristics of nearby residents. In the absence of major variation in natural advantages at the edge of a growing city, the only important variation in amenity levels may be in the "neighbor amenities." Thus location patterns may be more oriented along sectors of a city (e.g., as proposed by Hoyt, 1939) than be uniform functions of distance from the CBD, as in Figure 1.1.

The endogeneity of amenities can also raise issues of the stability of

---

[18] School quality would continue to influence land prices since it is still a true amenity, that is, location–specific from the point of view of the household.

[19] This point is central to Smith's (in this volume) analysis of how prejudiced households seek to assure the racial composition of their neighborhoods.

equilibrium in the amenity market. This issue has been particularly troublesome in the literature on racial prejudice (e.g., Courant and Yinger, 1977) and the literature on locally provided public goods (e.g., Hamilton, 1975). In any case, the subject of how endogenous amenities are determined is one that is attracting the attention of urban and public choice economists alike (see Segal, 1979 for a more detailed discussion).

VI. AMENITIES AND URBAN FORM

The density of development is a highly visible and important manifestation of urban form. Higher densities are denoted by a rising roofline, sometimes culminating in lofty spires offering millions of square feet of space within the confines of a single block. Even suburban areas are dotted with apartments and attached units of all kinds. Detached homes may be squeezed onto a tenth of an acre or repose on a two acre "estate." The density of development in turn greatly influences the pace and density of traffic, the density of shopping and other services, and the general aesthetic of an area. Thus density itself may become an amenity or affect other amenities (e.g., Richardson, 1977).

Density is also the most commonly analyzed aspect of urban form. Thus it will be the focus of the discussion here. Other aspects, such as type of land use or other characteristics of development, also deserve attention but will be less emphasized here.

A. The Static Model

In the one-period model above, households choose an amount of land services to consume depending on their incomes, the rental price of land, and the level of amenities at the location. The current rental price for the land is essentially determined by the amenity market in that city in a manner described in Section III. The residential density of an area is primarily determined by the price of land and the incomes and other characteristics of the residents. Moreover, as we saw in Section V, the incomes and other characteristics of the residents in an area also depend heavily on the amenity levels. In these ways the spatial distribution of amenities strongly influences the face of a city.

There are a number of different ways to model the determination of residential density patterns. Traditionally, land has been treated as an input into the production of a homogeneous good—housing services. A simple but illustrative example of such an analysis can be found in Mills (1980, pp. 222–232). In that model, an equilibrium schedule of prices for housing services is calculated, based on the need for price differentials to compensate for differences in commuting costs. Higher prices lead to lower consumption per household and thus to the expectation of a negative relationship between density and distance from the CBD. This relationship will take on a negative exponential shape under some reasonable assumptions. This approach can be generalized to include amenities other than access to the CBD, but the close link between distance to the CBD and density would be severed.

An alternative and more general approach is to view housing as a bundle of implicit goods, as described by Rosen (1974). In this case, each dimension of the bundle is valued for its own sake and has an implicit price in the market for houses. In the long-run equilibrium, ignoring the durability of housing, the price of any particular component will be equal to the marginal costs of production.[20] However, the marginal cost of producing land is assumed to be zero. Instead its value is a residual out of revenues after costs which is to be maximized.

Total revenues from developing a given tract of land at a given location are assumed to be a function of the amenities at the location and of the characteristics of the individual dwellings and of the number of dwellings, or

$$\text{Total Revenues} = R(A, L, H)N, \qquad (1.33)$$

where

R = rent per period per unit,
A = the vector of amenities,
L = lot size,
H = a vector of dwelling characteristics, and
N = the number of units in the tract.

The total costs of development are a function of the cost per unit and the total number of units. Cost per unit depends directly on the characteristics of the dwelling (H) and indirectly on the density of development (L). The latter effect is most pronounced in the case of multifamily development, where the cost per unit is clearly an increasing function of the height of the building. Thus in general we have

$$\text{Total costs} = C(H;L)N, \qquad (1.34)$$

where $C_L < 0$. This implicitly assumes that there are no economies or diseconomies of scale with respect to the number of units in the relevant ranges of development.

---

[20] As noted in Section IV, in the case of an indivisible good, the cost function need not be linear homogeneous because arbitrage is not feasible. Thus the marginal cost need not be independent of the quantity.

The producer's profit maximization can be expressed as

$$\max \pi = R(A, L, H)N - C(H;L)N \qquad (1.35)$$

with respect to the choice variables, L and H. Just as households took the land price function as exogenous in Section III, so do developers take the house price or rent function as exogenous for their purposes. It reflects not only the willingness of individuals to pay for amenity differentials but also the market returns to increases in lot size (L) and dwelling characteristics (H).

The first-order conditions for a profit maximum are

$$\left(\frac{\partial R}{\partial L} - \frac{\partial C}{\partial L}\right) N + (R - C)\frac{\partial N}{\partial L} = 0 \qquad (1.36)$$

$$\frac{\partial R}{\partial H} - \frac{\partial C}{\partial H} = 0. \qquad (1.37)$$

Note that amenities are not a choice of the developer since they are assumed to be outside his control. To the extent that an amenity from the point of view of the household (e.g., the presence of sidewalks) is subject to the choice of the developer, for this analysis it would be treated as an element in H. Also note that the number of units on the tract (N) is not an independent choice of the developer since it depends solely on L.[21]

Equation (1.37) is more or less a standard result. Marginal revenue equals marginal cost in the provision of dwelling characteristics (although marginal cost may be a function of the quantity of the characteristic).

The implications of Eq. (1.36) for density are less straightforward. They may be clearer if it is rewritten as

$$(R - C)\frac{\partial N}{\partial L} = \left(\frac{\partial C}{\partial L} - \frac{\partial R}{\partial L}\right) N. \qquad (1.38)$$

The left-hand side is the negative impact of larger lot sizes on profits due to the decline in the number of units as lot size increases. The right-hand side is the impact on profit due to the change in the profit per unit times the number of units.

The level of amenities may affect both sides of this condition. Higher amenities directly affect the *level* of rents per unit, holding constant the other characteristics of the unit. Thus profit per unit increases, raising the left-hand side. Higher amenities may also indirectly affect the *partial* of profit per unit with respect to lot size. This effect operates through the

---

[21] Muth (1969) popularized the notion of housing services and of an alternative density notion, housing services per unit of land. This formulation incorporates the choice of H as well as L. However, housing services cannot be measured if the cost function is not linear homogeneous (see Murray, 1978). Thus we avoid this formulation.

influence of amenities on residential location. If higher amenity areas are more likely to be occupied by higher income households, a higher marginal rent for land will exist in those areas.[22] In addition, a higher level of dwelling characteristics will be demanded, thus adding to the value of lot size as a cost reducer.

It is highly probable that amenities most strongly affect density through their direct influence on the level of rents per unit. Higher amenity levels imply higher profits per unit and thus a higher implicit cost to lower density. Only a big increase in household income (or in another demand shifter) will stave off a decline in lot size. However the indirect effects on household characteristics need not always be neglible. Sometimes the amenity differentials between two areas are not dramatic enough to have significant impacts on land prices, yet the incomes of the equilibrium residents are very different because the amenity is particularly special to higher (or lower) income households. In any case, wealthy households will tend to have relatively large lots (or large units in high-rises) even if the land price is high. Similarly, lower income or single households will live in smaller apartments or on small lots even if the area is not "high-rent." This can be seen particularly in suburban areas, where the impact of amenity levels on location by income is often more dramatic than the impact directly on land prices.

These interacting influences can be seen in Figure 1.2. Figure 1.2 portrays the residential density gradient that might arise from the land price function in Figure 1.1 and the residential location pattern developed in Section V. Density is at its peak in the center, where single, higher income households live. It declines as land prices decline away from the center and at a rate influenced by both the decline in incomes of households and the increase in their size. At some point, land prices begin to rise as distance from the center becomes an amenity on net due to the increasing school quality. However, density does not rise as much as land prices do because both incomes and family size are now increasing and thereby raising the demand for land. Finally, beyond k_3, land prices are falling once again. Density will decline, although the rate of decline may be reduced by the accompanying decline in household incomes.

B. A Dynamic Model

Most models of urban form have the one-period perspective discussed earlier. However, the density of current development actually depends on

---

[22] The conditions for a positive link between the level of an amenity and income, that is, $\eta_{V_{A_i}Y} > \eta_{LY}$ can be seen operating in Eq. (1.38). The partial of R with respect to A_i is V_{A_i}. The impact of income on this partial is measured by $\eta_{V_{A_i}Y}$ and the impact on demand for land and thus $\partial R/\partial L$ is reflected in η_{LY}.

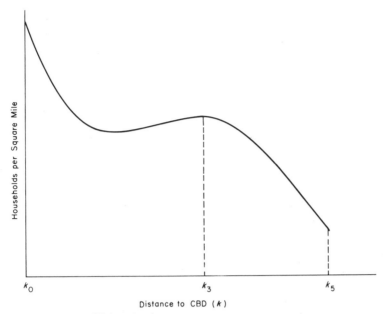

FIGURE 1.2. Equilibrium density pattern.

expected future, as well as current, rental prices and demands for the land. That is because it is quite costly to modify residential densities over time. Major modifications require the destruction of the existing structure. Even relatively minor changes may entail major remodeling. The result is that individuals or firms, in seeking to reap the maximum locational rents over the life of the structure, take into account the future value of land services and land uses in the area as well as the current values.[23]

The fact that density is not variable without cost also implies that current residential densities in areas of older development are primarily determined by *past* levels of current and expected value and use for the land, that is, by the density of previous development. If those expectations came to pass, the density may be fairly compatible with *present-day* current and future expected demands. However, this need not be the case. Expectations of radically different demands for land in a distance future, though accurately formed, will carry little weight in the current density decision. In general, it is very likely that densities in areas developed over 30 years ago will not be similar to the densities appropriate to today's land market.

The importance of these considerations is especially apparent in cities

---

[23] This proposition has been addressed in several papers on the dynamics of urban growth (e.g., Arnott, 1980; Fujita, 1976).

that were heavily developed before the automobile era. Residential densities in what is now called the "inner-city" are very high, reflecting the relatively low incomes and high land prices at the time of last development. Transportation was relatively expensive in time and money, so differentials in access to workplaces were worth relatively more then.

However, the high value of access at the time will not adequately explain the high densities if only current use value of the land had mattered. The capital prices of residential land at the developing edge of the city would have, in that case, only depended on agricultural rents. Instead, people at the time usually expected the city to grow very rapidly. The actual value of the access provided by areas currently at the fringe was expected to climb. Thus, if a site were to be developed only once over a 50-year period, the development would reflect the use value of space at that location in the future as well as the present. For similar reasons, there may be no development of a site until expected high rents come closer in time or actually occur.

The results can be more formally modeled. The developer's problem now is to choose the time of development as well as the quantity of land per dwelling unit and the characteristics of the unit that maximize net profits from developing a site. To simplify the analysis of the development issue, we shall assume that dwellings, once constructed, are perfectly durable and, in addition, that the option of redevelopment is not considered. This is probably close to the mark, given the kind of discount rate applied to potential returns in the risky development business.[24]

To solve such a problem, the developer must have some expectations of the future market rents at a given location for different combinations of land (L) and dwelling characteristics (H) for the current and future periods. He faces an intertemporal dilemma if those rents will be changing over time or if the demand for the amenity bundle or the bundle itself changes. As the rents rise, the shadow price of the land rises and the single-period optimal amount of land per unit falls. Similarly, the single-period optimal amounts of H may change, either because of variation in the rent on land or in the demands for H by the highest bidder for the location. The moment the developer proceeds, though, the levels of L and H are fixed forever. Thus the three decisions—land, structure, and timing—will depend on the expected future characteristics of the amenity market.

Assume that land earns no rent and bears no expenses before development. The builder attempts to maximize the present value of rents for a

[24] See Brueckner (1981) for a discussion of the effect of perfect foresight in a model of decaying housing capital.

tract of land, less the costs of development, or

$$\text{Max } \pi = \int_T^\infty R(A, L, H, t)Ne^{-rt} \, dt - C(H;L)Ne^{-rT}, \qquad (1.39)$$

where T is the time of development and the other variables are defined as before. The rent function and the cost function are assumed to be independent of the developer's choices (in contrast to Markusen and Scheffman, 1978, where future market rents are a function of individual developer's decisions). Rents are expected to change over time in a way known for certain. Costs of development per unit are once again a function of the dwelling characteristics per unit, with lot size acting as a negative shifter. Total development costs are proportional to the number of units.

First-order conditions are

$$\int_T^\infty \left(\frac{\partial R}{\partial L} \cdot N + R \frac{\partial N}{\partial L} \right) e^{-rt} \, dt$$

$$- \left(\frac{\partial C(H;L)}{\partial L} \cdot N + C(H;L) \frac{\partial N}{\partial L} \right) e^{-rT} = 0 \qquad (1.40)$$

$$\int_T^\infty \frac{\partial R}{\partial H} \cdot Ne^{-rt} \, dt - \frac{\partial C(H;L)}{\partial H} Ne^{-rT} = 0 \qquad (1.41)$$

$$R(A, L, H, T)Ne^{-rT} - rC(H;L)Ne^{-rT} = 0. \qquad (1.42)$$

Rewriting Eq. (1.40) to parallel Eq. (1.38), we have

$$\left(\int_T^\infty Re^{-rt} \, dt - Ce^{-rT} \right) \frac{\partial N}{\partial L} = \left(\frac{\partial C}{\partial L} e^{-rT} - \int_T^\infty \frac{\partial R}{\partial L} e^{-rt} \, dt \right) N. \quad (1.43)$$

Now revenue per unit and marginal revenue are seen to be functions of the present discounted value of a whole stream of rents. Costs are all in the period of development. Equilibrium lot size reflects the same revenue and cost calculations as in the one-period model. However, revenue gained per unit and revenue lost by the change in the number of units are functions of the expected future levels of amenities, the value of those amenities, and the demands for lot size. The closer in time a change in any one of these things is expected to occur, the greater the impact on equilibrium lot size at the time of development.

Development itself will be deferred until current rent equals the interest on the cost of total dwelling capital. If rents are expected to rise rapidly in the future, optimal development will be at a higher density and thus involve more capital costs. The higher rents are expected to be in the future, holding constant current rents, the more likely that development will not be optimal today. At the extreme, flat expectations for total rents implies that development will occur immediately or not at all. The actual time of development in general, though, will depend on precisely the path rents are expected to follow.

The expected future amenity market conditions affect the initial development decision. On the other hand, once that decision is made, current and future amenity market conditions may have little influence on some characteristics of the dwelling stock.[25] For example, profit maximizing decisions by developers in 1880 continue to profoundly influence the densities of older cities, despite drastic changes in amenity market conditions. The value of access has declined, the demand for land by the typical household has grown, and other amenities have declined in the inner-city. Redevelopment of many such areas would be at lower densities today.[26] Yet the large, multifamily structures still stand. In fact, the high densities and other "obsolete" characteristics of the existing structures may be making those areas relatively more attractive to the poorest segments of the city's inhabitants.

Meanwhile, the same process is occurring today in growing urban areas. Development in the suburbs will determine the densities of those areas for many years to come. Yet those densities will be too high if the city unexpectedly stops growing since the value of the amenities available there would be lower than had been expected. Alternatively, if the value of access to employment centers were to rise sharply (e.g., due to a sharp rise in explicit or implicit gasoline prices), large lots might become things of the past in all new development. However, the densities of previously developed areas would tend to remain too low for an indefinite period.

Thus it is that amenities—past, present, and future—shape urban form. Changes in amenities over time may modify that form to some extent. Drastic changes, such as the construction of a major highway or employment subcenter, can make it profitable to replace existing dwellings with much higher density development. Declines in amenities or in the value placed on them can lead to declines in expenditures to maintain decaying capital elements. But it is generally not profitable simply to replace sound buildings with lower or only moderately higher density development. Meanwhile, densities in areas of new development and redevelopment are governed by current expectations of future amenity flows, the

---

[25] See Section VII for a discussion of how the amenity market affects the levels of the relatively more "flexible" aspects of dwellings.

[26] This is not always true. Some areas have maintained high amenity premiums over the years and others have regained them. In fact, premiums for some areas have grown so much that they have been redeveloped at a higher density.

value placed on them, and the demand for land by those who are or are expected to be the equilibrium residents at each location.

VII. AMENITIES, FILTERING, AND RENEWAL

This section develops the roles that amenities might play in the determination over time of the attributes of existing dwellings. Section VI examined how the initial attributes of a dwelling are very much a function of amenity levels. For that analysis, the simplifying assumption was made that dwellings were expected to retain those attributes "forever." However, the fact is that wear and obsolescence can noticeably reduce the service flow from capital components of a dwelling in as short a period as 4 or 5 years (e.g., for paint or carpeting) or as long a period as 50 years (e.g., wiring, plumbing). Neglect of all maintenance and repair can reduce a dwelling to a ruin in even less time. Alternatively, market conditions can lead to major upgrading of already high-quality dwellings or total renovation of deteriorated structures.

In all of these maintenance or renovation decisions, amenities play a role similar to their role in the initial development process. In other words, amenities influence the maintenance and renewal processes through their influence on the residence site choice. Most of the maintenance and renewal literature focuses on the production specification, taking demand as exogenously determined and spatially undifferentiated. We shall emphasize the influence of amenities on the spatial pattern of the demand for housing "quality." That is because the extent to which it is optimal to maintain or renew depends on the willingness-to-pay of potential residents for the extra services provided.

There are two crucial differences between dwelling attribute determination in new development and in existing dwellings. The first is that effectively some of the most important attributes of the dwelling, such as lot size and interior space, are fixed.[27] These are no longer determined by the rents and the socioeconomic characteristics of the highest bidder for that location. Instead these fixed attributes act as amenities themselves, influencing the type of resident in the dwelling and also the resident's demands for maintenance and renewal. Secondly, most maintenance and renewal requires the destruction and replacement of durable attributes that are still capable of providing future services. This fixed opportunity

[27] The assumption that some of the attributes are effectively fixed can more precisely be stated as an assumption that the opportunity cost of demolishing them is nearly always greater than the *excess* of the market value of the replacement structure over the cost of construction.

cost makes the provision of higher attribute levels in existing dwellings more expensive (or less rewarding on net) than in new construction.

A. A Model of Maintenance and Filtering

Before analyzing the role of amenities through the demand side, we must more fully model these peculiar supply constraints. We take as the central features of the supply side that (a) many characteristics of dwellings decay over time; and (b) replacement of decayed capital requires foregoing the services of the remaining capital. The former seems self-evident. The latter reflects the presence of technological constraints on the maintenance or renewal process and the absence of a low transactions-cost market in used dwelling components. These imply that the economic value of the remaining services of deteriorated or obsolete capital components is lost upon replacement. For example, replacing flooring or wiring usually involves destruction of the current flooring or wiring. Replaced kitchen cabinets or bathroom vanities have little market value. Even repainting results in the loss of the remaining services of the current paint.

We shall further assume that there are important interactions in the demands for the various durable components. This assertion makes it essential that distinctions be made between the lives of different capital attributes of dwellings. Those attributes that are more durable or infinitely durable may strongly influence the value placed by consumers on replacements of the stock of shorter-lived capital. For example, the quality of the interior appointments may be a substitute for interior space. We would expect, though, that many interior appointments are complements with each other and with interior space.

We can now proceed to a more formal statement of these propositions. We shall define the dwelling as a multidimensional bundle,

$$Q = (L, S, F, A), \qquad (1.44)$$

where

L = land associated with the dwelling,
S = a vector of very durable structural components of the dwelling,
F = a vector of infrastructure or less durable components, and
A = a vector of locational amenities.

This is essentially the same bundle analyzed in Section VI, except that the vector of dwelling characteristics (H) has been divided into two groupings, S and F.

These four categories reflect the important supply-side distinctions among dwelling attributes.[28] First, land (L) must be distinguished both because it is presumably very durable and because it is the only attribute remaining after complete demolition. Secondly, there are elements of the capital stock (S) that are durable enough to be treated as fixed over the planning horizon and also can be altered only at great expense or only with the destruction of existing levels of other attributes. The interior floor space of the dwelling can be considered one of these elements in most contexts. Thirdly, there are components of the capital stock that we call infrastructure (F) that depreciate relatively rapidly but also must be destroyed before replacement. These are the focus of our analysis of renewal. Finally, there are neighborhood and access amenities (A), which do not depreciate but are subject to change by exogenous events.

We shall also assume that there is a Rosen-type (1974) market for these bundles of housing attributes. For the moment, the demand side of the market consists of a large number of households with identical utility functions but varying income levels. These households shop over the bundles by examining the prices of alternative bundles. We further assume that the choice space over all the attributes is complete and continuous. The supplies of bundles with different attributes are generally fixed except under conditions discussed later. For simplicity, we shall assume that both sides of the market have only a one-period perspective.

Having conceptualized housing in such a manner, we can now approach the questions of filtering, maintenance, and renewal. These phenomena are all closely related. In our model, dwellings will tend to filter in quality as infrastructure levels decline. Whereas the rate of decline in the level of infrastructure components is exogenous, the level of infrastructure can be raised at any time. When increases in relatively minor components of infrastructure occur, they are commonly called *maintenance* or *repair*. A window breaks, carpets or floors get worn, paint becomes dingy or unfashionable. Upgrading of more major components of infrastructure, such as walls, ceilings, or kitchen and bathroom equipment, are more commonly labeled *renovation* or *renewal*. However, these activities differ economically only in magnitude, not in their conceptualization. All maintenance, repair, and renovation we shall call *rehabilitation*.

All infrastructure components of a dwelling are subject to decay or rehabilitation. The current level of any particular infrastructure compo-

---

[28] Ingram and Oron (1977) make similar distinctions between structure type, quality capital, and neighborhood location. Muth (1976) assumes instead that all structural inputs decay at a constant rate.

nent in a dwelling is assumed to be equal to the intial level (at construction or last rehabilitation) depreciated at some constant rate d_i. Thus F_i^t is given by

$$F_i^t = F_i^T \exp - d_i(t - T), \tag{1.45}$$

where F_i^t is the level of component i at time t, T is the time of the last rehabilitation, and F_i^T is the level of the component after rehabilitation or construction. Note that, aside from the rehabilitation option, the level of infrastructure components in a given dwelling is exogneous to the pattern of house prices and to construction costs. But the level after rehabilitation is independent of the level before since the previous level is destroyed.

Rehabilitation will occur when there is a net profit to it. The basic condition for this being the case is similar to that for demolishing and replacing the entire structure. The difference between the market value of the new building and the current structure must be greater than the cost of constructing the new one. Similarly, rehabilitation (including maintenance) will occur when

$$P(L_0, S_0, F^*, A_0) - P(L_0, S_0, F^t, A_0) > C(F^*), \tag{1.46}$$

where F^* is the optimal level of F after rehabilitation and C is the cost function for replacement of infrastructure. In other words, rehabilitation will occur when the net increase in market value from raising the infrastructure level from F^t to F^* is greater than the cost of doing so. There must be a net gain despite the fact that all of an infrastructure component must be replaced in order to increase it from its current level by even one unit.

The existence of heterogeneous infrastructure permits us to describe a realistic scenario of progressive filtering (by quality), partial rehabilitations, and eventual major rehabilitation. In the absence of changes in amenities and macroshifters of the demand side of the housing market over time, the individual components of the infrastructure of a dwelling may decay only to be restored. Some components, such as painting and carpeting, have relatively rapid depreciation rates. It is likely that they will be rehabilitated at frequent intervals. However, at that time the levels of other components may not be such that full replacement is optimal. This is for two reasons. Given that such longer-lived components as walls, floors, plumbing, and wiring are somewhat decayed, the level of income (and thus the demand for infrastructure) of the postrehabilitation resident will be lower than that of the initial residents. Moreover, the demands at each income level for infrastructure will be reduced if there are complementarities among the types of infrastructure. Thus, until the basic components of the infrastructure are replaced, replacement of the more superficial components will tend to be at ever decreasing levels.

B. The Spatial Pattern of Decay and Renewal

We now need to complement this theory of filtering and renewal with our theory of residential location. As developed in Section V, our analysis was an extension of the Alonso bid-rent framework to a world of multiple locational amenities and demand shifters. To extend it further to a world of fixed lot sizes and other dwelling characteristics involves changing the trade-off between land prices and amenities to one involving house prices (not the price of housing) and both amenities and dwelling characteristics. The same bid-price analysis applies, with individual households bidding for the different bundles with incremental bids depending on income and "tastes." Taste shifters include location of workplace, size of family, and number of workers in the households as well as more idiosyncratic shifters of the utility function. The characteristics of the highest bidder for an existing dwelling will depend on the complex conditions in the market for amenities and the fixed components of the dwellings. However, in the presence of decaying but replaceable dwelling attributes, bids based on the option of rehabilitation will also arise.

It is through the influence of amenity levels on the differential between prerehabilitation and postrehabilitation values that the amenity market most directly affects filtering and renewal. For example, let us first examine the effect of an increase in amenity levels on the likelihood and extent of maintenance and repair. We assume that maintenance and repair are relatively minor changes in infrastructure that do not themselves influence the incomes of the equilibrium residents. Assuming that amenities are normal goods (and holding constant dwelling characteristics), an increase in their level, however, will raise the level of income associated with the highest bidder for the dwelling. If the incomes of the equilibrium residents are now higher, the premium placed on higher levels of infrastructure will also be higher. This will both raise the minimum level of F_i at which enhancement will become optimal and also raise the level to which F_i is increased.

Increases in amenity levels also raise the probability and extent of major renovation. Such renovation itself may lead to an increase in the income of the resident household. An increase in amenities raises the incomes both of the household that would be high bidder for the unrehabilitated structure and of the household that would be high bidder for an optimally rehabilitated structure. Higher income tends to imply a greater demand for infrastructure and thus a greater differential between the un-rehabilitated and postrehabilitation prices, that is, the left-hand side of Eq. (1.46).[29] The rise in the income of the postrehabilitation resident will also raise the level of F^* in the right-hand side cost function, but the increase in the premium for a rehabilitated dwelling will ordinarily be enough to cover the increase in the cost.[30]

Thus increases in amenity levels tend to promote both maintenance and renewal. On the other hand, declines in amenity levels will promote progressive filtering by quality and income. Similarly, shifts in the demands for the existing amenities or for the fixed characteristics of the dwellings may also influence the socioeconomic characteristics of the prerehabilitation and postrehabilitation high bidders for the dwelling and thus the probability of rehabilitation.

The extent of the shift in prerehabilitation and postrehabilitation income levels also depends on the correlation of income with other determinants of the demands for infrastructure and for the amenity that has changed. If the demand for that amenity is highly related to a particularly powerful demand shifter for infrastructure, the likelihood of rehabilitation after a change in that amenity is greater. For example, if a hospital moves into an area, there will be increased demand to live there by health professionals. In this example, being a health professional is a shifter of the demand for the amenity, access to the hospital (or access to work). Since this demand shifter is highly correlated with income, an increase in the level of access to a hospital will lead to an increase in the value placed on infrastructure and thus in the value of the unit as a potential rehabilitation.[31]

Similarly, the existence of multiple demand shifters provides a basis for a commonly observed type of gentrification. An inner-city area may have levels of amenities and dwelling characteristics (e.g., large, run-down units in poor school districts) such that lower-income households with large families and one worker are the equilibrium high bidders. On the other hand, middle-income, two-worker, childless households may

---

[29] This need not hold if the rise in the amenities causes an increase in the incomes of the high-bidder for the unrehabilitated dwelling that is much greater than the increase in the income of the potential postrehabilitation resident. This would not ordinarily be the case, though.

[30] This depends on the shape of the cost function, among other things. These issues are examined in more detail in Diamond and Smith (1980b).

[31] The impact of a special access amenity on maintenance and renovation is frequently seen in university towns and neighborhoods. Housing in areas with special amenities for students is maintained at one level while similar housing with other features or amenities attractive to faculty is maintained at another level. In most cases, both faculty and student housing is in better condition than housing of similar age and original characteristics elsewhere in the city.

bid nearly as much for the existing structures based on the possibilities of rehabilitating the structures. A slight shift in amenity levels, say toward greater access to the CBD due to the opening of a subway, or a shift in household demands, say toward greater value placed on access to the CBD, could lead to a major shift in the income of the high bidder for the area and the rapid infusion of large amounts of additional infrastructure.

VIII. AMENITIES AND REGIONAL LOCATION

The last major role played by amenities is in the distribution of households and firms across regions within a nation and ultimately across nations. The cost functions of firms depend on amenities such as access to raw materials or other inputs. Households seek certain weather conditions or consumption opportunities. Regional variation in these amenities implies that the demand for labor by firms and the supply price of labor by individuals will also vary across regions. Thus the size of any given urban area and its wage rates will reflect the firm and household amenities available there. The long-run spatial distribution of population across the country will reflect the pattern of attraction to both firms and households.

A. Wages, Prices, and Regional Amenity Differentials

As noted in Section III, the choice of an urban area to locate in involves more than the choice of an amenity bundle and land price. It also ties in with the choice of the markets in which the firm or household will buy and sell. Differences in prices in markets across urban areas arise from the high transportation cost of many goods and services. Input costs may differ up to the cost of transporting the input from one area to the other. Output and consumer prices may also differ up to the costs of arbitrage.

This variation in market conditions across areas arises from the presence of region-specific goods. Some of these goods, such as natural resources or natural transportation advantages, are exogenous to the presence of firms or households. Others, such as a low average cost for rail shipment or gourmet restaurant meals, are the result of scale effects achievable due to the presence of a large local market. In either case, these regional advantages to production or consumption can be treated as amenities.

The first step in understanding the regional market in amenities is to specify what level of an amenity is associated with migrating to a region.

In some cases, the answer is simple. If the amenity is uniform regionwide, then that uniform level is what is relevant. However, if there is significant variation within the region in the level of an amenity, the relevant level is the one at the location most attractive to the migrating firm or household.

In the simplest case of homogeneous households, the level of consumption amenities that matters is that at the marginal residential location in the urban area (e.g., at the edge of the city). Someone will have to move there to make room for the in-migrant. Since all households are the same, it does not matter whether it is the in-migrant or another household who locates at the marginal location. In the case of firms, the analysis may be even simpler. If all firms are assumed to produce at a point in the center, then the amenity levels at the center point are the levels that matter for the marginal firm.

Note that, in the case of households, the amenity levels at the marginal location are likely to depend on the size of the city. This is because the most desirable locations will be utilized first, with worse locations (e.g., with lower access to the CBD) being used only as the city grows. This decline in the amenity level at the marginal location acts to eventually stop the growth of the urban area.

It is important to recognize that intraurban variation in amenities, or even the average levels of the amenities, need not directly influence the regional amenity market.[32] In the case of homogeneous households, such variation affects only the intraurban equilibrium pattern of land prices, and not wage rates. However, in the more realistic case of heterogeneous households and heterogeneous labor, the relevant level of amenities depends on what type of household and labor is marginal. If the marginal job is relatively high-paying, then the relevant level is the level of amenities and the land price at the location in amenity space at the margin of being occupied by higher income households. In Figure 1.1, such locations would be k_2 and k_4 if Group 1 is higher income. Similarly, it is the general price level for the bundle of goods consumed by higher income households that matters, rather than the price level for the "average" household.

Prominent examples of amenities that vary for marginal residents across different urban areas are weather conditions, air quality, specific aspects of the available consumption set, and access to the CBD from the edge of the area. These and similar amenities are used in Graves and Regulska in Chapter 10 and in other papers on regional amenity markets.

The issue of particular interest here is how wages and prices for ordi-

---

[32] In models of city size with flexible lot sizes, the level of amenities anywhere in the city has indirect effects on the regional level of amenities through the impact of land price on density and thus on the geographical extent of the city.

nary goods serve as a "price" for amenity consumption at the regional level. The argument follows those of Izraeli (1979) and Kenny and Denslow (1980). Wage and price differentials arise and will persist because of the willingness of firms and households to accept higher or lower real money incomes in return for lower or higher amenities. In other words, both the supply and the demand for labor (and thus population in a region) in terms of nominal wages are functions of the amenities, both the exogenous amenities and the scale amenities. Equilibrium differentials in the real wage (from the point of view of the household, that is, deflated by the consumer price level) will compensate for differentials in household amenity levels. Equilibrium differentials in the real wage (from the point of view of the firm, that is, deflated by the output price) compensate for differentials in the marginal physical product of labor due to the differentials in firm amenities.

Figure 1.3 illustrates the forces behind the wage differentials. Assume that households are homogeneous, labor is homogeneous, and labor supplied per household is fixed. In the absence of city scale effects, there is some differential in nominal wage rates between this region and the base or reference region that changes real income by an amount equal to the total premium placed on the amenity differential. The region being illus-

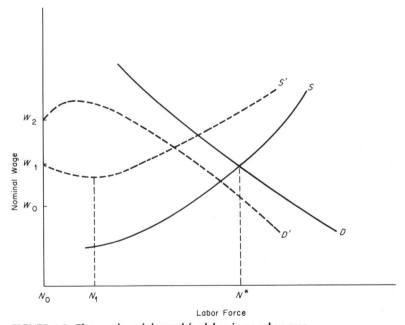

FIGURE 1.3. The supply and demand for labor in an urban area.

trated is assumed to have an inferior bundle of amenities and so a pre-mium is required by households. However, that premium is expanded fur-ther by the feedback effects of local wages on the prices of locally pro-duced goods. The nominal wage differential $(W_1 - W_0)$ thus reflects both the real value of the amenity differentials and the differentials in price levels.

However, as city size expands, amenities become subject to scale ef-fects. Over a certain range (e.g., N_0–N_1), the positive effects of city size on amenities may predominate. For example, tax rates may decline as the average cost of providing municipal services declines (e.g., Hirsch, 1968). In this range, the required nominal wage differential will shrink. As city size continues to increase, though, some of the important amenities, such as access to the CBD, decline at the marginal location.[33] Eventually these negative scale effects prevail, and the wage differential required to attract the homogeneous labor expands with city size. Once again, the expansion in the nominal wage also reflects the feedback effects on the regional price level. The effective supply curve of homogeneous labor from homoge-neous households for the region is S'.

The existence of heterogeneous tastes for amenities among households simply steepens the supply curve of labor relative to the homogeneous household case. Each household has a reservation wage differential that will compensate them for the given amenity differential. Those house-holds which place the greatest value on living in the area and have the lowest reservation wage differential (probably negative) will move there first, with the needed differential rising at larger city sizes to attract less inclined households. The supply schedule of labor for an area (S) will be more steeply sloped than S' since each incremental resident has a higher reservation wage differential than the current residents.

If firms produce only one good and the good is costlessly traded throughout the economy, if non-labor input prices are independent of regional location and if there are not firm external effects on other firms, firms would all wish to locate where they could pay the lowest wage. If households are homogeneous and there are no diseconomies to scale for consumption amenities (including commuting), all production would occur in the most desirable part of the country. The presence of disecon-omies in consumption (e.g., declining access to the CBD) or heteroge-neity in tastes for amenities would spread production over several rela-tively desirable areas. However, nominal wages would still be uniform. Areas with higher amenity levels initially would grow larger until the scale

[33] The decline in the level of access and other amenities at the marginal location leads to an increase in the price of land for all other households at presumably more desirable loca-tions. It is sometimes this increase in land costs that is seen as the brake on city size.

effects reduced some of the amenities to the point that no nominal (or real) wage differentials would be required. Essentially, the demand for labor facing each region is perfectly elastic at the uniform wage.

The presence of locational advantages for firms would change this outcome somewhat. In the absence of firm external scale effects, the demand for labor at each location would still be perfectly elastic but at different nominal wage rates. In Figure 1.3, W_2 might be the value of the marginal product of labor in this particular region, relative to W_0 in the reference region.

In reality, the presence of other firms has important external effects on production amenities, which act to raise or lower the marginal product of labor as the number of firms and employment expands. For some firms, such as those in financing or advertising, these effects may be always positive in the relevant range. For industrial firms today, a major concern is the concentration of air pollution arising from the spatial concentration of production. These firms may find that the positive economies of industry scale run out fairly quickly. The net effect may be an initially rising demand curve from labor that eventually declines as scale diseconomies set in (e.g., D').

This analysis of the regional demand for labor has assumed so far that all goods are traded costlessly across areas and that each area produces only a small part of the total output. Thus, prices were taken as exogenous to the area. However, there are a large number of goods, and particularly services, that are not traded and for which local firms as a group face downward sloping demand curves. Moreover, the demand for them is a function of the population of the area. Therefore, demand is downward sloping for these firms as a function of price, but it is rising as a function of region population. Total regional demand for labor is composed of the demands for use in the production of local and traded goods and probably has the conventional shape of D in Figure 1.3.[34]

Equilibrium employment, and thus population, is determined by the point of intersection between supply and demand for labor in the region. However, as Tolley (1974) and Tolley, Graves, and Gardner (1979) emphasize, this need not be an optimum since marginal technological externalities are not accounted for by either firms or households.

The determinants of city size and wage differentials are clearer now. High levels of exogenous amenities that raise the marginal product of labor or household utility levels will increase city size and lower the wage rate at any given size. Exceptionally large cities (e.g., New York) proba-

[34] More complex models of city size, and particularly of the firm role, can be found in Henderson (1977). A more sophisticated analysis of regions is developed in Tolley and Krumm (1981).

bly have relatively high levels of production amenities and positive industry scale effects that dominate negative scale effects on household consumption. Exceptionally small cities presumably have few amenity advantages for either firms or households.

In summary, there are both wage and size effects of regional amenity differentials that matter to both firms and households. At the equilibrium city size, nominal wage differentials exactly compensate or penalize firms producing the traded good for the production amenity differentials associated with that city size. Households are compensated or penalized for consumption amenity differentials and price level differentials.[35] If firms and households are not homogeneous, though, the relevant amenity differentials and the relevant wage and price differentials will depend on the type of firm or household that is the marginal in-migrant.

B. Amenities and Migration

Within the static model of wage rates and city size sketched out previously, migration arises as a response to disequilibrium. That is, it occurs solely when the existing structure of city sizes and wage rates no longer puts all firms and households into an equilibrium. A wide variety of disturbances can lead to this. Population growth must be redistributed over areas. Income growth shifts demands for amenities unevenly. Even the aging of individual households may be related to shifts in the demands for specific amenities, leading to migration of individual households (but not necessarily net migration).

Similarly, firms are subject to shifts in relative factor prices or in technology. These will lead to shifts in the derived demands for production amenities and labor. If there are heterogeneous traded goods in the economy, shifts in the relative prices or in the relative demands for those goods will be a major force toward relocation of economic activity as industries using certain locational advantages are supplanted by industries needing others.

Although amenities have been long used in the analysis of intra-urban phenomena, they have only recently been emphasized in inter-urban analysis and even more recently in household migration research (see Chapter 10 for references). Even less is known about what determines the location of new firms or the migration of existing ones. However, the conceptual and empirical potential of the amenity approach seems significant. Its use would also promote greater integration of regional and urban analyses.

---

[35] Izraeli (1979) and Rosen (1979) report the results of efforts to estimate the demands for regional amenities from observed interurban wage differentials.

IX. CONCLUSION

Urban and regional economics incorporate into economics the spatial dimensions of economic activity. The recent growth of urban and regional economics as a specialty reflects the importance of location for many ordinary economic phenomena and for many public policy questions. Pollution control, bussing, fiscal distress, blight, mass transportation, regional redistribution, housing inflation, redlining, urban redevelopment, jurisdictional fragmentation, land use controls, urban enterprise zones: all of these pose policy issues that demand new analytical insights and empirical techniques. Meanwhile, our understanding of basic urban phenomena, such as density and residential location, is evolving to provide a stronger foundation for such policy analysis.

In this chapter we have suggested that the evolution of the basic analyses in urban and regional economics will gain from the recognition that all the relevant attributes of locations share a common identity as amenities. Each central topic in these fields was redeveloped with the amenity concept at its core. We have shown that the same things that influence house prices also determine location patterns, the maintenance and renewal of the housing stock, and city size and migration. For this reason, it should be clear that analyses of urban phenomena that focus on only access amenities may be poor guides to reality. For example, since the levels of crime and school quality matter for house prices, they also probably affect residential location, density, filtering, and even city size.

The amenity concept is indispensable for spatial analysis because it facilitates modeling with more than one amenity. However, empirical analyses need not be overwhelmed by the size of the universe of potential amenities. Clearly, some amenities are more important than others and are more useful for some purposes than for others. The relative importance of an amenity depends on the degree of variation within or across urban areas, the value of (demand for) the amenity to firms or households, and the degree of variation across firms or households in that value. The determination of the relative importance of individual amenities is a pressing empirical question and is a key to further development of analytically tractable yet realistic models of urban and regional economic phenomena.

REFERENCES

Alonso, W. *Location and Land Use,* Cambridge, Mass.: Harvard University Press, (1964).
Arnott, R. J. "A Simple Urban Growth Model with Durable Housing." *Reg. Sci. and Urban Econ.* 10 (January 1980): 53–76.

Bender, B., Groenberg, T. J., and Huang, H. S. "Choice of Functional Form and the Demand for Air Quality." *Rev. Econ. Stat.* 62 (March 1980): 638–643.

Bradford, D. F., and Kelejian, H. H. "An Econometric Model of the Flight to the Suburbs." *J. Polit. Econ.* 81 (May 1973): 566–589.

Brigham, E. F. "The Determinants of Residential Land Values." *Land Econ.* 41 (August 1965): 325–334.

Brodsky, H. "Residential Land and Improvement Values in a Central City." *Land Econ.* 46 (August 1970): 227–247.

Brown, G., and Pollakowski, H. "Economic Valuation of Shoreline." *Review Econ. Stat.* (August 1977): 272–277.

Brueckner, J. K. "A Dynamic Model of Housing Production." *Journal of Urban Economics,* 10 (July 1981): 1–14.

Courant, P. N., and Yinger, J. "On Models of Racial Prejudice and Urban Residential Structure." *J. Urban Econ.* 4 (October 1977): 272–291.

Diamond, D. B., Jr. "Income and Residential Location: Muth Revisited." *Urban Stud.* 17 (March 1980): 1–12.

Diamond, D. B., Jr., and Smith, B. A. "The Role of Spatial Goods in a Model of Residential Location." Unpublished paper, North Carolina State University, June 1980(a).

Diamond, D. B., Jr., and Smith, B. A. "A Theory of Rehabilitation and Gentrification." Paper presented at the AEA meetings, September 1980(b).

Diamond, D. B., Jr., and Smith, B. A. "Housing as an Implicit Good." Unpublished paper, North Carolina State University, June 1981.

Ellickson, B. "Local Public Goods and the Market for Neighborhoods." In *The Economics of Neighborhood,* edited by D. Segal. New York: Academic Press, 1979.

Freeman, A. M. *The Benefits of Environmental Improvement: Theory and Practice,* Baltimore, Md.: Johns Hopkins Press for Resources for the Future, 1979.

Fujita, M. "Spatial Patterns of Urban Growth: Optimum and Market." *J. Urban Econ.* 3 (July 1976): 209–241.

Graves, P. E., and Linneman, P. D. "Household Migration: Theoretical and Empirical Results." *J. Urban Econ.* 6 (July 1979): 383–404.

Halvorsen, R., and Pollakowski, H. O. "Choice of Functional Form for Hedonic Price Equations." *J. of Urban Econ.* 10 (July 1981): 37–49.

Hamilton, B. "Zoning and Property Taxation in a System of Local Government." *Urban Stud.* 12 (1975): 205–211.

Harris, R. N. S., Tolley, G. S., and Harrell, C. "The Residence Site Choice." *Rev. Econ. Stat.* 50 (May 1968): 241–247.

Harrison, D., Jr., and Rubinfeld, D. L. "Housing Prices and the Willingness to Pay for Clean Air." *J. Environ. Econ. Manag.* 5 (1978): 81–102.

Henderson, J. V. *Economic Theory and the Cities.* New York: Academic Press, 1977.

Hirsch, W. Z. "The Supply of Urban Public Services." In *Issues in Urban Economics,* edited by H. Perloff and L. Wingo, Jr. Baltimore, Md.: Johns Hopkins, 1968.

Hoyt, H. *The Structure and Growth of Residential Neighborhoods in American Cities.* Washington: U.S. Government Printing Office, 1939.

Ingram, G. K., and Oron, Y. "The Production of Housing Services from Existing Dwelling Units." In *Residential Location and Urban Housing Markets,* edited by G. K. Ingram. New York: National Bureau of Economic Research, 1977.

Izraeli, O. "Externalities and Intercity Wage and Price Differentials." In *Urban Growth Policy in a Market Economy,* edited by G. S. Tolley, P. E. Graves, and J. L. Gardner, New York: Academic Press, 1979.

Kain, J. F., and Quigley, J. M. *Housing Markets and Racial Discrimination.* New York: National Bureau of Economic Research, 1975.

Kenny, L. W., and Denslow, D. A., Jr. "Compensating Differentials in Teachers' Salaries." *J. Urban Econ.* 7 (March 1980): 198–207.

King, A. T. "The Demand for Housing: A Lancastrian Approach." *So. Econ. J.* 43 (October 1976): 1077–1987.

Linneman, P. "Some Empirical Results on the Nature of the Hedonic Price Function for the Urban Housing Market." *J. Urban Econ.* 8 (July 1980): 47–68.

Linneman, P. "The Demand for Residence Site Characteristics." *J. Urban Econ.* 9 (March 1981): 129–148.

Markusen, J. R., and Scheffman, D. T. "The Timing of Residential Land Development: A General Equilibrium Approach." *Journal of Urban Economics,* 5 (October 1978): 411–424.

Mills, E. S. "An Aggregative Model of Resource Allocation in a Metropolitan Area." *Am. Econ. Rev.* 57 (May 1967): 197–210.

Mills, E. S. "The Value of Urban Land." In *The Quality of the Urban Environment.*, edited by H. S. Perloff. Washington, D.C.: Resources for the Future, 1969.

Mills, E. S. *Studies in the Structure of the Urban Economy.* Baltimore, Md.: Johns Hopkins, 1972.

Mills, E. S. *Urban Economics.* 2d ed. Glenview, Ill.: Scott, Foresman, 1980.

Murray, M. P. "Hedonic Prices and Composite Commodities." *J. Urban Econ.* 5 (April 1978): 188–197.

Muth, R. F. *Cities and Housing.* Chicago, Ill.: University of Chicago Press, 1969.

Muth, R. F. "A Vintage Model with Housing Production." *Mathematical Land Use Theory,* edited by G. J. Papageargiou. Lexington, Mass.: Lexington Books, 1976.

Nelson, J. P. "Residential Choice, Hedonic Prices, and the Demand for Urban Air Quality." *J. Urban Econ.* 5 (July 1978): 357–369.

Polinsky, A. M., and Shavell, S. "Amenities and Property Value in a Model of an Urban Area." *J. Pub. Econ.* 5 (1976): 199–229.

Quigley, J. M. "Non-Linear Budget Constraints and Consumer Demand: An Application to Public Programs for Residential Housing." Unpublished paper, University of California at Berkeley (1980).

Richardson, H. W. "On the Possibility of Positive Rent Gradients." *Journal of Urban Economics.* 4 (January 1977): 60–68.

Ridker, R. G., and Henning, J. A. "The Determinants of Residential Property Value with Special References to Air Pollution." *Rev. Econ. Stat.* 44 (1967): 246–255.

Rosen, S. "Hedonic Prices and Implicit Markets: Product Differentiation in Pure Competition." *J. Polit. Econ.* 82 (January 1974): 34–55.

Rosen, S. "Wage-based Indexes of Urban Quality of Life." In *Current Issues in Urban Economics,* edited by P. Mieskowzki and M. Strazheim. Baltimore, Md.: Johns Hopkins, 1979.

Schmenner, R. W. "The Manufacturing Location Decision: Evidence from Cincinnati and New England." Report to the Economic Development Administration, March 1978.

Segal, D. *The Economics of Neighborhoods.* New York: Academic Press, 1979.

Steinnes, D. N. "Causality and Intraurban Location." *J. Urban Econ.* 4 (January 1977): 69–79.

Straszheim, M. R. *An Econometric Analysis of the Urban Housing Market.* New York: National Bureau of Economic Research, 1975.

Struyk, R., and James, F. J. *Intrametropolitan Industrial Location: The Pattern and Process of Change.* Lexington, Mass.: Heath, 1975.

Tiebout, C. "A Pure Theory of Local Expenditures." *J. Polit. Econ.* 64 (1956): 416–424.

Tolley, G. S. "The Welfare Economics of City Bigness." *J. Urban Econ.* 1 (July 1974): 324–345.

Tolley, G. S., Graves, P. E., and Gardner, J. L. *Urban Growth Policy in a Market Economy.* New York: Academic Press, 1979.

Tolley, G. S., and Krumm, R. "The Economics of Regional Location." Unpublished paper, University of Chicago, March 1981.

Wheaton, W. C. "Linear Programming and Locational Equilibrium." *J. Urban Econ.* 1 (July 1974): 278–287.

Wheaton, W. C. "A Bid Rent Approach to Housing Demand." *J. Urban Econ.* 4 (April 1977): 200–217.

Witte, A. D., Sumka, H., and Erekson, H. "An Estimate of a Structural Hedonic Price Model of the Housing Market: An Application of Rosen's Theory of Implicit Markets." *Econometrica* 47 (September 1979): 1151–1174.

2

The Residence Site Choice*

R.N.S. HARRIS   GEORGE S. TOLLEY   C. HARRELL

Greater understanding of urban land use is needed for many planning purposes. Much theorizing has concentrated on travel savings motives as an influence on residential land use, ignoring amenity characteristics including beauty and neighbors that influence family choice of residential site. The present article develops a framework based on consumer demand theory for considering amenity in addition to travel cost considerations. A way of measuring the travel savings and amenity components of land value is suggested and consists of estimating the travel savings component as being the difference between actual travel costs and hypothetical travel costs if residence were at the low rent margin at the edge of the city.

Residential land values are analyzed for Raleigh, North Carolina. Making use of a travel habits survey, amenity and travel savings components of land values are estimated. Regression analyses are undertaken relating amenity values to supply attributes and relating amenity expenditures, lot size, and travel to demand attributes.[1]

* Reprinted from *The Review of Economics and Statistics* Published by Harvard University. Copyright, 1968, by the President and Fellows of Harvard College. Vol. L, No. 2, May 1968. This study was made possible by a grant from Resources for the Future, Inc. and was carried out while all of the authors were associated with North Carolina State University.

[1] The relation of this study to previous studies may be noted briefly. To explain residential land value, Alonso (1964) considered a model in which everyone works in a central factory and lives in a circular area around the factory. Lot size and location are determined on the basis of bids differing among households due to taste or income differences, where effects of travel time on leisure are substituted against living space and all other goods. Wingo

55

I. FRAMEWORK

The income constraint on the household specifies that total money expenditures add up to the amount available for spending. A second constraint specifies that total hours of the day are divided between work travel and nontravel leisure. Three further constraints pertain to residence location since travel by members of the household, expenditure on residence site, and amenity of the site vary with location. The household maximizes satisfaction from the consumption of amenity, lot size, leisure, and all other goods, subject to the foregoing five constraints. These remarks suggest how amenity can be included in a utility maximizing framework.[2]

(1961) considered a similar model. An aggregative model recently developed by Mills (1967) includes the same types of variables. These models do not permit explanations of value attaching to residential land other than for travel savings reasons. A primary purpose of the present article is to explain amenity, that is, nontravel savings, influences.

Muth (1964) recognizes amenity but does not try to measure it or explain its contribution to variation in land values. The same is true of Meyer, Kain, and Wohl (1965).

Richards (1963) among others has called attention to amenity as a consideration affecting residential land value and residence location decisions. Brigham (1965) and Crecine, Davis, and Jackson (1967) include variables to reflect amenity in regression analyses of land values for Los Angeles and Pittsburgh, but they do not attempt a separation of travel savings and amenity components of land value, nor is analysis of demand for land by individual families undertaken.

[2] The problem is to maximize:

(a)
$$U(A,Q,L,A) + \lambda_1[HW - P_Q Q - Z - P_M M]$$
$$+ \lambda_2[24 - L - vM - H]$$
$$+ \lambda_3[M - f(\mu)] + \lambda_4[P_Q - g(\mu)]$$
$$+ \lambda_5[A - Qh(\mu)],$$

where A = amount of amenity in dollars per day, Q = lot size in square feet, L = leisure in hours per day, Z = dollars worth of all other goods, P_Q = price of land expressed as rent per day, H = hours worked per day, W = hourly earnings in dollars, M = miles traveled per day, P_M = mechanical cost of travel per mile, v = average time per mile, μ = a variable identifying the coordinates of location chosen by the household, and $f(\mu)$, $g(\mu)$, and $h(\mu)$, are the functions relating miles traveled, price of land, and amenity per square foot to location.

The variables assumed to be beyond the control of the household are W, P_M, and v. Maximizing with respect to each of the remaining eight variables:

(b)
$$U_L/U_Z = W,$$

(c)
$$\frac{U_Q + U_A h(\mu)}{U_Z} = P_Q,$$

(d)
$$\frac{U_A Qh'(\mu) - [U_Z P_M + U_L v]f'(\mu)}{U_Z} = Qg'(\mu),$$

where U_L, U_Z, U_Q, and U_A are marginal utilities. These three equations refer to choice of H, Q, and μ. In light of these decisions, the five constraints determine the remaining variables A, P_Q, M, L, and Z.

The household has a choice of locating at point μ or out at the travel margin, which is the point beyond which demands for land motivated by travel savings have no effect on land values.[3] Let μ_0 be the point on the travel margin where travel cost would be smallest for the household among all points at the margin. The total amount of goods that would be given up, in order to live at μ, is the dollar cost saving plus the value of time saved:

$$t = [f(\mu_0) - f(\mu)]P_M + [f(\mu_0) - f(\mu)]\, v(U_L/U_Z), \qquad (2.1)$$

where $f(\mu)$ indicates travel by the members of a household if the residence is at site μ, P_M is mechanical cost per mile, v is the time required to travel one mile, and U_L/U_Z is the marginal rate of substitution of all other goods for leisure, that is, the value of time spent travelling. The amount that a household is willing to pay for travel savings reasons for one square foot of space located at μ is then $w' = t/rQ$, where r is the capitalization rate and Q is lot size.

To the travel savings bid is added the bid for the amenity of a piece of land. If amenity were completely divisible and producible at constant marginal cost, households could choose locations solely on the basis of travel savings and then obtain amenity desired at a price independent of location. Amenity can be varied to some extent by landscaping and related activities. It may not be reproducible at constant cost, first, because unique features such as existing buildings affect costs of endowing locations with esthetic characteristics. Second, some amenity is costly to reproduce because it is valued individualistically as reflected in the behavior of a person working in one town and living in another.

The value of a piece of land may be less than the travel savings value implying that its amenity is negative. The amenity is less than the amenity freely available at the margin. Some low income families choose negative amenity, living in deteriorated neighborhoods near the center of the city and saving on amenity and travel cost.

To illustrate the joint role of travel savings and amenity, Figure 2.1 depicts land value determination where developer decisions have already fixed size of lots demanded by people working in three places. At the bottom of the figure the separate demand schedules are added. The shaded area at the bottom of the figure shows the travel savings values corresponding to the household bids. Where households from different

---

[3] In Raleigh, North Carolina, the travel savings effect appears direct in that the upper limit on the bid for land of the marginal bidder is governed by his savings by not having to travel from the margin. The margin indirectly governs the travel savings effect in a megalopolis where there are many work centers, with workers in interior centers displacing workers from the near side of more exterior centers.

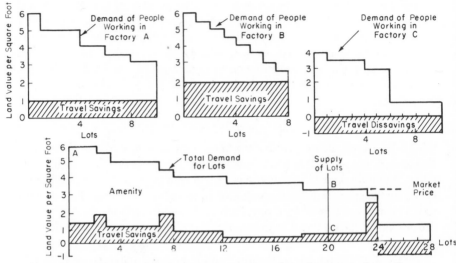

FIGURE 2.1. Determination of land value and separation of travel savings and amenity.

factory groups bid the same price for land, the average of their travel savings values was used. The figure suggests how it is possible for families to choose a pattern of residence location with cross-hauling in that people pass each other going in the opposite direction to work.

An hypothesis is that many amenity valuations are highly individualistic but that these ordinarily do not affect market prices because individualistic bids are likely to be among the highest (near the y-axis). Thus, there may be a presumption that the households who are just in the market and determine land value (near BC in Figure 2.1) reflect a broader similarity of tastes. As will be brought out in Footnote 6, this and related assumptions are important to the empirical analysis.

II. MEASUREMENT OF AMENITY AND TRAVEL SAVINGS COMPONENTS OF LAND VALUE

The method of separating land value into travel savings and amenity components was applied to Raleigh, North Carolina. A household survey was required, and funds available limited the study to one city. A third component of land value, not essential in the previous discussion, is agricultural value plus payment for utilities on residential land beyond the travel savings margin. For Raleigh, an identifiable margin is reached beyond which land values in outlying subdivisions are about $.13 per square foot. Essentially this reflects cost of utilities since the value of the land for farming is about $.005 per square foot.

In 1964, 20 blocks were randomly selected, and clusters of 3–5 blocks were obtained by combining each of the 20 blocks with contiguous blocks. Twelve households per cluster were interviewed. This was done at the rate of one household per day in each cluster for 12 days (Monday through Saturday, for 2 weeks). Each household reported on trips made the previous day by all family members over 16 years old.

For each trip, the distance was measured on maps. Out-of-pocket costs (excluding depreciation, license, and insurance) were computed from auto expense data,[4] on the assumption the family would own the same car regardless of location. Travel time reported in the interview was assigned a value in three alternative ways: (*a*) current wage rate estimated from household income; (*b*) zero wage rate; and (*c*) $1.55 per hour prevalent in road benefit studies.[5] The estimate of out-of-pocket costs plus time costs for the two weeks multiplied by 25 gives an estimate of yearly travel expenditures per cluster (50 weeks, allowing a 2-week holiday per year).

Total travel cost was then estimated for each household for the lowest travel cost location at the margin. In many cases this location was seen clearly to be the nearest subdivision on the city perimeter. Where there was doubt, trials of various locations were used to find the least expensive location at the margin. Travel distances were remeasured for each work, shopping, and school trip from residence. The place of work was considered to remain the same. Shopping and school destination points were changed to take in the nearest shopping center and school. It was assumed that social and recreation trip costs would be unaffected by moving to the margin.

Aggregation of the travel costs of the 12 households in each cluster again multiplied by 25 gives an estimate of hypothetical yearly travel expenditures if the household were located at the margin. Travel savings are the differences between hypothetical and actual travel costs. Lot sizes were used to put the travel savings on a square foot basis.[6]

---

[4] Reliance was placed on Crow (1964).

[5] American Association State Highway Officials (1960, p. 176).

[6] In terms of Figure 2.1, travel savings are estimated as the average height of the shaded area under the total demand for lots. Amenity value is then estimated as the height *B* minus the average travel savings. In Figure 2.1, the average travel savings is greater than the height *C*, which is the travel savings of the marginal bidder. For the method of this study to estimate the amenity and travel savings components of land value correctly, average travel savings per cluster should equal travel savings of the marginal bidder. Our survey does not permit identification of the marginal bidder if indeed he is in the survey. Average travel savings will tend to be higher than travel savings of the marginal bidder if the nonmarginal bidders would be willing to make higher bids primarily for travel savings reasons due, say, to having higher income; the average will be below travel savings of the marginal bidder if nonmarginal bidders value amenity highly for this reason, taking low travel savings to live in the neighborhood. There may be hope for lack of bias in view of these offsetting tendencies.

Total land value per square foot was estimated from the appraisal of land values for tax purposes. Since these values are from an external assessment made for the entire city in 1960 by one company, assessment errors are probably similar for all properties and may be small in relation to the neighborhood variation of interest in this study. The fact that there were numerous court cases protesting the appraisals suggests market values were not underestimated. Use of an average for a group of similar blocks tends to minimize effects of assessment errors due to qualitative differences of individual properties.

Amenity value per square foot was estimated for each cluster by subtracting the travel savings value per square foot and the $.13 markup found at the margin from average land value per cluster. The three time valuations and three alternative capitalization rates of 4, 7, and 10% gave 9 alternative estimates of amenity value for each cluster that were generally similar. Cluster land values and their estimated breakdown as between mark-up at the margin, travel savings, and amenity are shown in Table 2.1, assuming $1.55 leisure cost and 7% capitalization rate. The re-

TABLE 2.1
Components of Land Value per Square Foot (in Cents)

Cluster number	Land value mark-up at the margin	Travel savings value[a]	Amenity value	Total land value
1	13.3	1.0	11.2	25.4
2	13.3	2.9	2.8	19.1
3	13.3	34.8	−28.1	20.0
4	13.3	20.1	−10.0	23.5
5	13.3	11.0	−8.4	16.0
6	13.3	18.9	−4.8	21.6
7	13.3	30.0	−19.4	23.9
8	13.3	.3	18.3	31.9
9	13.3	.5	−1.3	12.6
10	13.3	−1.5	−1.3	10.5
11	13.3	2.5	12.6	26.3
12	13.3	4.2	9.3	26.7
13	13.3	3.0	5.1	21.4
14	13.3	8.6	−14.9	7.0
15	13.3	−.2	−5.2	7.8
16	13.3	4.6	21.9	39.9
17	13.3	.4	16.5	30.2
18	13.3	5.2	.9	19.4
19	13.3	.4	−.8	13.0
20	13.3	6.2	9.9	29.5

[a] Travel savings were computed at $1.55 per car-hour, divided by number of passengers and capitalized at 7% discount rate.

sults are reasonable in light of observed neighborhood characteristics. The highest positive amenity values occur for the most stylish residential areas, and the highest negative values are found for the seriously run-down areas. The two negative travel savings values are for subdivisions beyond the margin.

III. SUPPLY ATTRIBUTES AFFECTING AMENITY VALUES

The contention made earlier that amenity values may be largely determined by attributes that people value similarly will be supported if measurable characteristics affecting amenity can be found to explain observed variations in value.

Variables are average lot size, W_1; discrete variables referring to zoning (zoned at least partly to nonresidential use, $W_2 = 0$, $W_3 = 0$; zoned all residential but touching on a commercial or other nonresidential zone, $W_2 = 0$, $W_3 = 1$; zoned to residential use touching only other residential use, $W_2 = 1$, $W_3 = 0$); discrete variables indicating class predominance in cluster, with upper class indicated by professional and managerial occupations and lower class indicated by laborers and domestic service workers (predominance of lower class, $W_4 = 0$, $W_5 = 1$; upper class predominance, $W_4 = 1$, $W_5 = 1$); class homogeneity, W_6, measured as percentage that the largest class is of the total number of residents in the cluster; physical condition of buildings, W_7, measured as the percentage of houses in a neighborhood receiving enough maintenance to preserve their present condition according to the 1960 U.S. Census of Housing; average value of land and buildings, W_8; percentage that upper class residents are of total residents in the cluster, W_9; percentage of occupants who are tenants, W_{10}.

A shortcoming is lack of better measures of characteristics determining amenity, but it was not feasible to attempt to obtain more detailed and subjective measurements of the factors influencing amenity in each neighborhood. The problem of quantifying quality characteristics that affect land values is perennial. Although value of land and buildings W_8 is included to measure effect of worth of neighboring property, this may introduce some spurious correlation (dependent variable is a component of one of the independent variables) since amenity value is part of land value. The class variables W_4, W_5, and W_9 are included to measure effects on amenity of desirable neighbors. However, these variables may reflect partly effect instead of cause of amenity (e.g., upper class residents may live in a neighborhood because it has higher amenity that it would possess anyway). A similar difficulty confronts the inclusion of the tenancy variable W_{10}. Tenants may be careless in maintaining property and downgrade attractiveness of a locality, but the effect of tenancy in the correlation may also be partly to stand in for low income. To this extent, tenancy would reflect the effect of amenity in that low income people would be living in the neighborhood because of their choice of a low amount of amenity, rather than their presence having an effect on the amenity.

The dependent variable V'' was amenity value per square foot. Regressions were carried out for the different V'' series corresponding to the three different leisure cost assumptions mentioned earlier, all with 7% capitalization rate. The equation with the highest r^2, .88, was obtained using $1.55 per car-hour:

$$V'' = .197 - .000007 \ W_1 - .058 \ W_2 - .089 \ W_3 - .041 \ W_4 + .007 \ W_5$$
$$(.000004) \quad (.042) \quad (.057) \quad (.102) \quad (.047)$$

$$- .0007 \ W_6 - .000003 \ W_7 - .000003 \ W_8 + .003 \ W_9 - .002 \ W_{10},$$
$$(.002) \quad (.0002) \quad (.000006) \quad (.002) \quad (.0009) \quad (2.2)$$

with standard errors given in parentheses. Only two of the variables, W_9 and W_{10}, for which the possibility was raised of spuriousness of correlation or for which cause–effect direction was questioned have coefficients greater than standard error. In view of the number of nonsignificant variables, the regression was performed again including only the significant or near significant variables:

$$V'' = .165 - .000004 \ W_1 - .070 \ W_2 - .125 \ W_3 + .003 \ W_9 - .003 \ W_{10}.$$
$$(.000003) \quad (.036) \quad (.040) \quad (.0009) \quad (.0007) \quad (2.3)$$

The r^2 was .85. Three of the coefficients in (2.3) are highly significant and have signs as expected: W_{10} (per cent tenancy), W_9 (per cent upper class), and W_3 (residential location near nonresidential activity). The coefficients of the remaining two variables, W_2 (highly residential location) and W_1 (lot size) are of questionable significance and have signs opposite to that expected.[7]

Results from the stepwise regression program are helpful in interpreting Eq. (2.3). The percentage of tenancy W_{10} explained about 68% of total variation. The percentage of cluster residents who are upper class W_9 came in next and added another 8% to explained variation. The zoning variable W_3 designating an impinging nonresidential area then added an-

---

[7] As a test for curvilinearity, a quadratic form was estimated using squared terms. However, the only significant variables were W_3 and W_9, no squared terms were significant, and the addition for r^2 was small.

other 5%. Whether W_{10} and W_9 reflect cause or effect of amenity deserves further study.

IV. DEMAND

A. Amenity

Observations of price are not available due to the heterogenous nature of the amenity commodity. In view of data availability, demand variables that can be used to explain household expenditure on amenity include: Z_1, family income; Z_2, family size; and Z_3, structure type (1 if single detached, 2 if single attached, 3 if 2–4 apartments, 4 if 5–19 apartments, 5 if 20 or more apartments).

Average amenity value per square foot V'' was multiplied by lot size L to give average amenity expenditure per cluster, E''. A quadratic appeared fairly consistent with the observed scatters and gave the following results:

$$E'' = 3042 - 1.33\ Z_1 + .00016\ Z_1{}^2 - 117\ Z_2$$
$$(1.09)(.00009)\phantom{Z_1{}^2 -}(5449)$$
$$- 89.6\ Z_2{}^2 + 46.9\ Z_3 - .758\ Z_3{}^2, \qquad (2.4)$$
$$(751)\phantom{Z_2{}^2 +}(183)(3.41)$$

with $r^2 = .60$. A logarithmic function cannot be fitted without a transformation, because of the existence of negative amenity values. A constant was added to each E'' amenity value, the constant of best fit being chosen by iteration:

$$\text{Log}\ (E'' + 4300) = 1.85 + .471\ \text{log}\ Z_1 - .074\ \text{log}\ Z_2 + .094\ \text{log}\ Z_3, \quad (2.5)$$
$$\phantom{\text{Log}\ (E'' + 4300) = 1.85 +}(.165)\phantom{\text{log}\ Z_1 -}(.363)\phantom{\text{log}\ Z_2 +}(.171)$$

with $r^2 = .39$. As with the quadratic, income is the only significant variable. The r^2 was not very sensitive to alternative values of the constant, but the income coefficient changed markedly for different values. In view of the low r^2 and the sensitivity of the income coefficient, an alternative functional form was estimated hypothesizing a relation between income and amenity per square foot. Using this form, since E'' equals $V''L$, the income elasticity for total amenity is income elasticity for lot size plus income elasticity for amenity per square foot:

$$\frac{\partial E''}{\partial Z_1} \frac{Z_1}{E''} = \frac{\partial L}{\partial Z_1} \frac{Z_1}{L} + \frac{\partial V''}{\partial Z_1} \frac{Z_1}{V''}. \qquad (2.6)$$

In line with the approach of Eq. (2.6), iterating for the constant to be added to V'', the result is

$$\text{Log } (V'' + .29) = -2.19 + .888 \log Z_1 - .852 \log Z_2 - 1.12 \log Z_3, \tag{2.7}$$
$$(.317) \qquad\qquad (.700) \qquad\qquad (.329)$$

where $r^2 = .73$.

As an indication that the three alternative demand relations that have been estimated are reasonably consistent, consider the income elasticity of demand for amenity at $10,000 income for a family of three living in an unattached single dwelling. The quadratic implies an income elasticity of 4.08.[8] From (2.5), the logarithmic relationship for total amenity gives an income elasticity of 3.41. From (2.6), (2.7) and (2.10) the logarithmic relationship using amenity per square foot leads to an income elasticity of 2.49.

B. Lot Size and Travel Expenditure

Explanations of lot size consumption L and of travel expenditures C were attempted using linear and logarithmic forms. Income, family size, and structure type as before were used as explanatory variables.

$$C = 3.69 + .00051 Z_1 + 1.01 Z_2 - .013 Z_3,$$
$$(.00013) \qquad (.424) \qquad (.031)$$
$$r^2 = .60. \tag{2.8}$$

$$\text{Log } C = -3.55 + .918 \log Z_1 + .946 \log Z_2 - .141 \log Z_3,$$
$$(.184) \qquad\qquad (.405) \qquad\qquad (.191)$$
$$r^2 = .73. \tag{2.9}$$

$$L = -4287 + 2.41 Z_1 + 1598 Z_2 - 182 Z_3,$$
$$(.615) \qquad (1893) \qquad (138)$$
$$r^2 = .64. \tag{2.10}$$

$$\text{Log } L = .504 + .943 \log Z_1 + .212 \log Z_2 - .927 \log Z_3,$$
$$(.193) \qquad\qquad (.426) \qquad\qquad (.200)$$
$$r^2 = .86. \tag{2.11}$$

The significant variables in explaining travel expenditure are income and family size and in explaining lot size, are income and structure type.

---

[8] From Eq. (2.4), $\dfrac{\partial E''}{\partial Z_1} \dfrac{Z_1}{E''} = (-1.330 + .00032 Z_1) \dfrac{Z_1}{E''}$.

V. CONCLUSION

The measurement of amenity and travel savings components of land value, through estimation of household savings over living at the margin, revealed that both are major components of land value. Regression analyses in terms of supply and demand attributes led to reasonable results. The estimates for low income families of negative amenity consumption, and for high income families of income elasticity of demand for amenity in the range of 2.5–4, indicate that amenity is one of the main commodities people wish to acquire when their incomes rise.

REFERENCES

Alonso, W. *Location and Land Use*. Cambridge, Mass.: Harvard University Press, 1964.

American Association of State Highway Officials. *Road User Benefit Analysis for Highway Improvements*. Washington, D.C., 1960.

Brigham, E. F. "The Determinants of Residential Land Values." *Land Econ.* 41, 3 (August 1965): 325–334.

Crecine, J. P., Davis, O. A., and Jackson, J. E. "Urban Property Markets: Some Empirical Results and Their Implications for Municipal Zoning." *J. Law Econ.,* 10 (October 1967): 79–100.

Crow, J. T. "The Real Costs." *Road and Track* Magazine. (February 1964): 21–22.

Meyer, J. P., Kain, J. F., and Wohl, M. *The Urban Transportation Problem*. Cambridge, Mass.: Harvard University Press, 1965.

Mills, E. S. "An Aggregative Model of Resource Allocation in a Metropolitan Area." *Am. Econ. Rev.: Pap. Proc.* 57, 2 (May 1967): 197–210.

Muth, R. F. *The Spatial Pattern of Residential Land Use in Cities*. 1964 (prepublication version).

Richards, J. M. "The Significance of Residential Preferences in Urban Areas." In *Human Resources in the Urban Economy*. Baltimore, Md.: Johns Hopkins, 1963: 123–150.

Wingo, L. *Transportation and Urban Land*. Washington, D.C.: Resources for the Future, 1961.

II

METHODS OF AMENITY
MARKET ANALYSIS

3

Hedonic Prices and Residential Location

PETER LINNEMAN

I. INTRODUCTION

The bid-rent models of residential location that grew out of Alonso's (1964) pioneering work possess the virtue of simplicity. This simplicity interprets into a simple set of predictions about the residential location patterns that would exist in our urban areas if these models were accurate. However, the superb simplicity of these models has also proven to be their major handicap. This chapter attempts to provide a "roadmap" to some of the new models of residential location, with special emphasis placed on recent empirical efforts. This examination begins with a brief summary of the original bid-rent model and proceeds to evaluate this model as a particular implementation of a more general multitrait implicit market model. Section III evaluates a variety of specification errors that plague the accurate measurement of housing market transaction prices. The fourth section details some of the more important empirical issues involved in implementing the implicit market multitrait model of residential location. The chapter concludes with a brief evaluation of whether the newer models of residential location provide sufficiently superior predictions to warrant their use despite their greater complexity.

II. THE BID-RENT MODEL OF RESIDENTIAL CHOICE

The Alonso (1964) model of residence choice in its simplest form views consumers as only caring about residential accessibility to a single work

THE ECONOMICS OF
URBAN AMENITIES

site. If all consumers are identical, this model implies a monotonic decline in site payments as distance from the work site increases due to the compensating differential required to offset the increased transportation costs associated with more distant residences. When the model includes residents with different incomes, it predicts that higher income families will live relatively close to the work site if transportation costs are a positive function of income and access is the only residential site characteristic. In this case the model continues to yield the prediction that site payments decline monotonically with distance to the work site.

Introducing a measure of housing quality reduces the magnitude of the compensating differential necessary to compensate identical consumers for less accessibility because the lower housing prices at less accessible sites lead consumers to substitute toward greater quality. When more than one income group exists in the presence of an index of housing quality, these early bid-rent models predict that only if the income elasticity for this quality index is greater than one (the assumed income elasticity of transportation costs) will higher income families reside at relatively distant locations. The simple trade-off involved in this two trait (access and housing quality), heterogeneous population (with respect to income) variant of the model is that higher income families desire to purchase relatively large amounts of housing quality and hence have an incentive to live at relatively distant sites in order to take advantage of the low site prices induced by higher transportation costs. However, higher income families also have higher transportation costs that induce them to live relatively near the work site.

Many recent efforts have expanded the simple bid-rent model by explicitly modeling the impacts of heterogeneous consumers on residential location patterns. Madden (1980) emphasizes that the impact of income depends on the source of income, whereas Smith and Campbell (1978) evaluate the differential effects of permanent versus transitory components of income. Analysts have also considered the existence and prevalence of discrimination and its impact on residential choice. Bailey (1966), Kain and Quigley (1975), King and Mieszkowski (1973), and Schaffer (1979) all develop analyses of the role discrimination plays in determining the residential pattern that characterizes urban areas. The residential location impacts of other household characteristics—such as family size, the sex of the head, and age of the head—have been examined by this author (1981) and Straszheim (1973, 1974, 1975). Other analysts, such as Domencich and McFadden (1975), indicate that urban transportation costs are best viewed as endogenous and dependent on the characteristics of the population.

A major shortcoming of the simple bid-rent models is their exclusive concentration upon access (or more precisely, distance) and general housing quality. Harris, Tolley, and Harrell (1968) and Ridker and Henning (1967) were the first studies to explicitly recognize that housing is composed of a variety of residence site characteristics and that the composition and level of housing quality are both important dimensions of residential choice. Specifically, these works suggested that the demands for both neighborhood characteristics (such as air pollution) and structural characteristics (like the number of rooms) of a housing site are key determinants of residential location patterns. More recently, Blomquist and Worley (1980), Diamond (1980), Freeman (1979), Harrison and Rubinfeld (1978), Mieszkowski and Saper (1978), Nelson (1978), Pollard (1977), and Vaughn (1974) have all developed models that give primary importance to the impacts of a variety of amenities on property values and residential location patterns. In addition to amenities, researchers such as Edel and Sclar (1974), Linneman (1980a), Oates (1969) and Rosen and Fullerton (1977) have emphasized the role of publicly provided neighborhood location traits, such as school quality and public roadways. This literature has largely proceeded in terms of the Tiebout (1956) hypothesis. The importance of structural traits, such as rooms and bathrooms, for residential location analysis has been developed by Kain and Quigley (1975), King (1975), Linneman (1980b, 1981), Quigley (1976), and Straszheim (1973, 1974, 1975). These works also emphasize that people are interested in obtaining access to a variety of locations in the urban area.

These models are generally variants of the multiproduct model of competition developed by Griliches (1961, 1971) and Rosen (1974). Specifically, they model housing as a vector of traits that directly enter the consumer's utility function. The demand for housing, therefore, is nothing more than the vector of demand functions for the housing traits. However, these demands are not satisfied through transactions in explicit markets for these traits. Instead, the demands for location specific traits are carried out through implicit markets that comprise what is generally referred to as the *housing market*. The total payment observed in the housing market is viewed as reflecting the sum of transactions made in each of the implicit trait markets. Following Griliches (1961, 1971), the implicit housing market models specify the price of housing through a hedonic price function that expresses the total payment for housing V, as a function of the vector of location specific traits $\mathbf{Z}$,

$$V = f(\mathbf{Z}). \tag{3.1}$$

Expanding upon the single trait model of Working (1927), Rosen (1974) developed the interpretation of the hedonic price function that is employed in most of the implicit housing market models. Rosen demonstrates that in general the hedonic function only reflects the set of market clearing prices associated with bundles of housing services. He indicates that the hedonic function is, in general, neither the demand nor supply function of housing. Instead the hedonic function and its associated partial derivatives are the locus of supply-equals-demand points for each location specific trait. Only if consumers are identical while suppliers differ will the hedonic price function trace out the housing demand function. Similarly, if all suppliers are identical and demanders differ, the hedonic function identifies the housing supply curve.

A simple, nonhousing market example demonstrates Rosen's insight that the hedonic function measures only what the prices are and not supply or demand functions. Consider the experiment of going to a supermarket and observing grocery shoppers as they come through the checkout line with different bundles of grocery items due to differences in their family size, income, and other factors. Suppose a researcher is interested in knowing the price of a 7-oz can of beans but cannot look on top of the can to determine this price. The hedonic price literature notes that if the researcher knows the total amount spent by consumers on groceries and the items purchased by these consumers, he or she can determine the price of a 7-oz can of beans. This is because total expenditures on grocery items G is simply the sum over all possible grocery items of price P_i times the quantity of item i consumed X_i,

$$G = \sum_{i=1}^{N} P_i X_1.$$

(3.2)

If the researcher can observe all of the X_i's, then the price of a 7-oz can of beans is the change in total grocery payments brought about by adding one 7-oz can of beans into the grocery basket holding the rest of the bundle constant. Mathematically this is the partial derivative of G with respect to X_{7oz},

$$\partial G / \partial 7 \text{ oz} \equiv P_{7oz}.$$

(3.3)

Thus, knowledge of the total payments for and exact composition of the grocery baskets can be combined with knowledge of the functional relationship of the expenditures on each particle item [that is, knowing Eq. (3.2)] to discover the price of any item by differentiating the hedonic function with respect to that item. Notice that no knowledge of the personal characteristics of the consumers (for example, their income or family size) or about suppliers (for instance, their production technology) was required to identify the market price of the item (for example, 7-oz bean cans). In fact, Griliches (1971) notes that in order to accurately measure the prices, no agent-specific information (such as income or productivity) should be included in the hedonic function. Alternatively stated, the hedonic function is designed solely to measure the market clearing prices and not to describe the market forces that cause these prices. This is because any price represents only a single point on the market demand and market supply functions and the connection of these prices is merely the locus of these supply and demand intersections.

In terms of the implicit housing market models, the hedonic price function for the housing market can be used to measure the market clearing marginal prices for each of the location specific traits Z. Specifically, the partial derivative of Eq. (3.1) with respect to any element of Z is the marginal price of that trait. Rosen (1974) demonstrates that by controlling simultaneity issues, these prices can be used to identify supply and demand functions for the various housing traits just as prices of any product are used to identify supply and demand functions.

III. HOUSING MARKET HEDONIC FUNCTION SPECIFICATION ERRORS

In general, researchers interested in estimating the housing market hedonic function do not have all of the information necessary to perfectly measure the hedonic function. Instead they must estimate a version of Eq. (3.1), which includes an error term e,

$$V = f(Z) + e. \tag{3.4}$$

It is essential to understand the properties of this equation in estimating and interpreting the hedonic function for the housing market. In particular, there are a variety of serious specification errors that confront the consistent estimation of the market clearing prices. This section examines several sources of specification error that appear to be present in the literature.

One source of specification error arises when one decides which traits to include in the hedonic function. Many studies omit a large number of location-specific traits because of multicolinearity between traits. These studies invariably note that the standard errors for the hedonic coefficients obtained in the presence of multicolinearity are biased. Although this claim is true, it is not true that omitting some of the colinear traits will solve this problem. In fact, the omission of variables that should be in the model only confounds the problem because the least squares regressor yields consistent and efficient estimates only when the model is correctly specified. The omission of important traits on the basis of multicolinearity insures that both the standard errors and hedonic coefficients of the remaining traits are biased. Thus, the omission of location-specific traits in the presence of multicolinearity creates (not eliminates) bias problems.

Since most housing market data sets contain information on a limited number of housing traits, a useful exercise might be to use a data set containing information on a variety of housing site characteristics to search for the small set (say, 20) of traits that maximize explanatory power with minimum loss of consistency. This could be accomplished by searching for the set of traits whose hedonic coefficients are the most robust of the variables included and provide the best fit.

Another important specification issue is the choice of the hedonic equation's functional specification. Since the use of an incorrect functional form induces inconsistent estimates, this issue deserves more attention than has been given by the housing literature. The choice of functional form presents an empirical question of obtaining a workable approximation to the data. Simplicity suggests the use of simple linear and log-linear functional forms; however, there is no theoretical reason to believe that these forms accurately describe the market clearing locus. In the grocery store example once the units of measurements were decided (for example, cans), the market hedonic was assumed to be linear. If, however, the units of consumption had been specified as ounces of beans rather than cans of beans, it is quite possible that the market clearing function would have been significantly nonlinear in bean consumption due to decreasing marginal prices generally associated with larger quantities of consumption. Incorrectly specifying the hedonic as linear when the units of consumption are measured in ounces instead of cans might well lead to seriously biased estimates of the market clearing prices facing bean consumers. Similar specification issues exist in the housing market since a price that may be linear in terms of one unit measurement (for example, rooms) might be nonlinear in terms of another unit of measure of the same concept (for example, square footage). Blomquist and Worley (1980), Goodman (1978), Harrison and Rubinfeld (1978) and Nelson (1978) all display an awareness of the importance of appropriate specification of the housing market hedonic functional form. Linneman (1980b) provides the most extensive discussion of the biases inherent in inappropriate functional form choice. This work indicates that the functional form that best describes the data is neither linear nor logarithmic, and it demonstrates that the measurement errors induced by an inappropriate choice of hedonic functional form may be quite substantial. This point is independently substantiated by Harrison and Rubinfeld (1978) and Blomquist and Worley (1980).

Sample selection bias represents a third serious source of specification error present in the estimation of hedonic price functions for the housing market. Since the hedonic function represents the set of market clearing prices, it is important that the sample be representative of the full housing market because as Heckman (1976) and others have noted, inappropriate sample choice may lead to biased estimates. Specifically, the use of sample selection criteria that are correlated with total payments for housing yields estimates that fail to accurately measure the set of market clearing prices.

Unfortunately, it is difficult to give precise empirical meaning to the extent of the housing market. Three dimensions of the scope of the housing market are of particular interest: (a) the geographic boundaries of the market; (b) the presence of racially segmented markets; and (c) the nature of the market in terms of ownership status. Straszheim (1975) and Schaffer (1979) clearly present the arguments for using narrowly defined geographic market areas. They argue that consumers are primarily interested in the consumption choices in a relatively small geographic area and that people are insufficiently mobile to fully arbitrage price differences across these areas. For example, in his analysis of the San Francisco Bay area, Straszheim specifies 73 separate geographic submarkets on the basis of housing and personal characteristics. This position has been attacked by Butler (1978) and Linneman (1980b). These authors argue that residential migration and housing capital funds are sufficiently mobile that arbitrage across geographic areas creates an efficient housing market. They suggest that specifying narrow market areas induces selection bias due to the use of subjective sample selection criteria that áre correlated with total housing payments. They also indicate that markets defined as broadly as the entire United States are appropriate when estimating housing market hedonic functions. Unfortunately, no definitive test of the geographic extent of the market has been developed, but the mobility of people and housing capital strongly support the efficient market view of the geographic extent of the market.

The potential existence of racial and other types of discrimination also presents a problem in terms of defining the relevant sample for use in estimating price functions for the housing market. If discrimination exists, there are two (or more) distinct housing markets present—one for blacks and another for whites. Most studies, including Kain and Quigley (1975) and King and Mieszkowski (1973), have tested for the presence of two housing markets by estimating a single hedonic function on aggregated data (such as census tracts) and including as an independent variable a measure of racial integration. A typical version of this specification is contract rent R as a function of a vector of housing characteristics Z and the variable percentage of black residents in the neighborhood:

$$R = a_0 + a_1 Z + a_2(\%\text{black}). \tag{3.5}$$

This specification is inappropriate to test the existence of multiple housing markets because it fails to test the hypothesis that the marginal prices paid by whites and blacks for housing traits are different. Equation (3.5) is more readily interpreted in terms of the %black being a neighborhood characteristic. Since most studies have found that a_2 is significantly greater than zero, this fact suggests that %black is a desirable good (just as school quality will have a positive coefficient)! The problem is that these studies assume that segregation and discrimination are synonomous. It is easily demonstrated that this is not necessarily true since people facing the same price structure may choose for reasons other than discrimination to segregate themselves (for example, similarities in income and tastes). A further problem is that the %black coefficient is generally plagued by omitted variable bias. In particular, most studies find it difficult to include accurate measures of accessibility. Since predominantly black neighborhoods tend to be disproportionately neighborhoods that are near the city center industrial sites, the coefficient of %black may be reflecting that access is a desirable characteristic that is correlated with %black.

Schafer (1979) correctly argues that to measure the presence of discrimination, one must include the race of the consumer and not the race of the neighborhood in the hedonic function. This allows one to test whether the price functions are significantly different for white and black populations. A common variant of this specification is to include a dummy variable for the race of the family in the hedonic regression

$$R = b_0 + b_1 Z + b_2(\%\text{black}) + b_3(\text{race of family}). \qquad (3.6)$$

If $b_3 > 0$ it is argued that blacks are discriminated against in the housing market. This interpretation is only appropriate if one believes that discrimination in the housing market occurs in the form of a ''buy-in'' fee. Specifically, Eq. (3.6) implies that the marginal prices paid for traits do not differ between whites and blacks but rather that the intercept is higher for blacks by an amount equal to b_3. This is analogous in the supermarket example to a grocery store charging the same prices to both whites and blacks for all items in the store but charging blacks a fixed fee for the right to enter the store. An alternative model of discrimination specifies that there is no ''entrance fee'' for blacks but that once inside the store, they find prices that are significantly higher than those paid by whites. This is tested by estimating separate hedonic functions for the sample of black families and white families and comparing the coefficient vectors for blacks and whites. Schafer (1979) concludes that the coefficient vectors for white families and black families are significantly different. However, an examination of Schafer's results reveals that the coefficient vectors differ because some of the marginal prices paid by blacks are greater whereas others are less than those paid by whites. A final note in this context is that even if it were found that blacks pay significantly higher prices for a set of housing market characteristics, this need not be evidence of discrimination since search costs and risk differentials between whites and blacks may be able to fully explain the findings.

A final market-definition sample selection problem is the sample choice with respect to ownership status. Most studies have analyzed the present value of the flow of services from housing (property values) and contract rent, which measures the annual flow of services from housing, as if they were separate markets. This treatment is primarily due to the lack of knowledge concerning the appropriate capitalization rate that converts the stock measure into an annual flow equivalent. Linneman (1980b) demonstrates that the capitalization rate for combined owner and renter samples is an identifiable parameter in the hedonic price function and also that failure to treat owners and renters as part of the same market may lead to significantly biased hedonic coefficients since this selection criterion is correlated with total housing payments. In that work a single capitalization rate is assumed to hold for all owners; however, that assumption can be relaxed to make the capitalization rate a function of family-specific characteristics (such as income and family size, which might effect the marginal tax bracket of owners). This area of research seems a fertile one for further development in estimation and a workable methodology for avoiding this source of specification bias.

The accurate measurement of property value (for owners) presents another source of estimation error. The use of assessed values is weak because appraisals often reflect political and historic influences rather than current market forces. Alternatively, a sample composed of recently transacted or new dwelling units introduces a potentially serious selectivity bias since these units are not in general representative of the housing market. Although the use of self-assessed property values may introduce measurement error, there is little reason to believe that the values are biased. Thus, the use of this measure reduces the efficiency but not the consistency of the hedonic estimates.

IV. SPECIFICATION OF THE LOCATIONAL DEMAND FUNCTION

Depending upon their objective, early housing market analysts treated the hedonic price function as either the bid or offer curve for housing. For example, Ridker and Henning (1967) discuss their hedonic price function results as if they reflect the bid curves for the various locational traits. Since Rosen (1974), researchers have realized that the hedonic price function is only a market clearing function that provides information about what prices are but not why prices come about. Further analysis is necessary to understand the determinants of the equilibrium market prices. Specifically, bid and offer curves must be identified. Since bid curves are the inverse of compensated demand functions and offer curves are the inverse of supply functions, identification of the bid and offer curves is the same as that for identifying the trait demand and supply functions. Following traditional demand theory, the demand for any location-specific trait Z_i is expressed as a function of the own price of the trait P_i, the set of prices of substitutes and complements P, family income I, and a vector of taste variables $\mathbf{T}$

$$Z_i^D = f(P_i, P, I, \mathbf{T}). \tag{3.7}$$

This set of demand functions for locational traits possess all the properties normally associated with demand functions. Similarly, the supply of location-specific traits is a function of own price, the vector of input costs $\mathbf{C}$, and the state of technology (τ).

$$Z_i^S = g(P_i, \mathbf{C}, \tau). \tag{3.8}$$

Recent studies of the housing market have attempted to estimate these demand and supply functions or their inverses by using data generated by the hedonic function (the P_i and some of the elements of P). These data are used in conjunction with information on income and the other variables in Eqs. (3.7) and (3.8) to estimate the various trait demand and supply curves.

In the past five years important strides have been made in the estimation of bid and demand curves for locational traits. Blomquist and Worley (1980), Diamond (1980), Harrison and Rubinfeld (1978), Linneman (1981), Nelson (1978), and Straszheim (1975) all estimate variants of the demand curves for location-specific traits. Several important estimation issues are addressed in these studies. One of these issues is whether it is more appropriate to estimate the demand curve or the bid curve. Since the bid curve is simply the inverse of the appropriately specified demand curve, the choice of which variable to use as the dependent variable is largely a matter of convenience and functional form assumption. If the fit of this relationship is good, there is little difference between a bid function obtained through direct estimation and one derived from the estimated demand curve. However, if the fit of the relationship is not precise, these inverse specifications may differ substantially.

Another important aspect of estimating the demands for location-specific traits is the impact of substitutes and complements. Nelson (1978) fails to include any cross-price effects whereas Harrison and Rubinfeld (1978) employ an "other quantity held constant" bid curve specification. Since the housing market hedonic function is exogenous, it seems more appropriate to alter the Harrison and Rubinfeld specification to include "other prices" rather than "other quantities" when estimating the bid or demand curve. This specification is utilized by the author (Linneman, 1980b, 1981) and Blomquist and Worley (1980). The "other prices held constant" specification allows the identification of traditional cross-price elasticities of demand.

The most important methodological issue involved in the estimation of the demand and bid curves for locational traits is the presence of simultaneity bias. The first type of simultaneity arises because of the endogeneity of prices in the presence of a nonlinear price function. When P_i depends on the quantity of the trait consumed, both the quantity consumed and the actual marginal price observed are endogenous. This is true in spite of the fact that the entire set of marginal prices for traits are beyond the influence of the individual consumers. That is, the hedonic price function is exogenous to the resident, but the actual marginal price is determined simultaneously.

This problem is easily demonstrated in the context of the earlier grocery illustration. Assume that the marginal price of ounces of beans is $.10 when large cans are purchased and $.20 when smaller cans are purchased. Although the consumer cannot alter these marginal prices of large and small cans, it is clear that he or she can affect the marginal price paid by his or her level of consumption. Further, since one of the key determinants of the consumer's demand for beans is the marginal price structure for beans, a correction for simultaneity is required to identify the demand structure.

A second source of simultaneity is the traditional demand and supply simultaneity described by Working (1927). This type of simultaneity exists even if the marginal price structure is linear. However, as with traditional market demand studies, this source of simultaneity is only problematic when the unit of demand observation is sufficiently large enough to have an impact on market prices. For analyses using microdata this does not pose a serious problem, but for aggregate data studies where cities or census tracts are the unit of observation, this looms as a significant source of simultaneity bias.

Straszheim (1975) develops methodology for dealing with simultaneity problems. He first estimates hedonic functions for a number of geographic submarkets and then calculates the price implied by the appropriate hedonic function evaluated at a common quality level. These predicted constant quality prices are utilized in place of the actual prices in estimating the demand functions for a number of locational traits. This methodology reduces the information contained in the nonlinear price functions to a single exogenous parameter that varies cross-sectionally and hence solves simultaneity problems.

In an attempt to utilize more price function information, Linneman (1981) suggested that actual prices be purged of their simultaneity by an instrumental variable technique. Specifically, he estimates an instrumental variable system for actual trait prices and utilizes the predicted trait prices in the estimation of the trait demand functions. This approach has the advantage of utilizing more than one parameter to describe the set of prices that face consumers. However, its empirical usefulness critically depends upon the availability of valid instruments. In contrast, the single parameter approach developed by Straszheim is not dependent on the availability of good instrument variables in the data set.

Another potential methodology for dealing with these simultaneity issues is to evaluate the appropriate hedonic function at a variety of quality levels. Each of these constant quality price levels could then be included as a separate independent variable in the location-specific trait's demand function. For example, the demand for rooms could be specified as a function of income, family size, age of the household, the marginal price of the first room, the marginal price of a second room, and the marginal price of a third room. The inclusion of multiple price parameters for a trait would allow a more complete specification of the exogenous price function that the consumer faces than has been previously been implemented. A final merit of this type of methodology is that it does not require the presence of valid instruments.

Another type of simultaneity bias present when estimating locational trait demand functions is that between personal characteristics such as the age and number of children and the location decision. Straszheim (1975) and others note the important role of children and other life-cycle variables under the assumption that family size is exogenous with respect to locational demands. Using an instrumental variable approach in conjunction with the Wu (1974) test, Linneman (1981) expands the examination of the impacts of children to incorporate the simultaneity of family size and residential choice. The most important finding in this regard is that family size exhibits a simultaneous relationship with respect to many important components of the location decision. This work presents a fruitful avenue for empirical study in the context of the timing and dynamics of the residential migration decision.

In conclusion, it is noteworthy that the literature has not implemented this trait demand approach to industrial location decisions. However, the demand for locations by firms can be modeled in a manner similar to that outlined in this section for households. Specifically, firms can be viewed as demanding various location-specific traits (such as access to highways or shoppers), with the demand for these traits being a function of production function parameters and the marginal prices of these traits. A hedonic price function for firms could be estimated by regressing the value of industrial properties as a function of various traits of value to firms. The marginal trait prices could then be utilized to estimate the demand equations for these traits. This approach would clearly enrich our understanding of industry location decisions. However, it is currently difficult to implement due to the paucity of data on industrial consumers.

V. THE USE OF IMPLICIT MARKET HOUSING MARKET MODELS

The two major uses of the location trait demand equations are (a) to evaluate the benefits associated with various public projects (such as pollution abatement or neighborhood improvement); and (b) to predict residential location patterns. Prior to the implicit market demand models, the procedure for calculating the benefits of an urban project was to directly use the hedonic price of the trait. For example, if the hedonic function indicated that the presence of abandoned buildings in a neighborhood reduced the property values by $1000 per dwelling, the benefit of a program removing such structures would be estimated as $1000 times the number of residences in the neighborhoods. Rosen (1974) demonstrates that the use of market prices tends to overestimate the benefit from the program because market prices reflect the highest successful bid for a trait.

This point is clearly demonstrated in the following example. Suppose one wanted to know the benefit associated with giving a Rolls-Royce Silver Cloud to every reader of this article. To determine the benefit of this program one could use the market price of this car to measure its value, so that if the price of a Rolls-Royce is $100,000, the benefit of providing this automobile to every reader this article would be $100,000 times the number of readers of the article. Clearly this measure overestimates the true benefit that the readers of this article would derive from receiving a Rolls-Royce because the income and tastes of the typical reader of this article are such that, given the current prices of substitutes and complements, they are willing to pay far less than $100,000 to obtain a Rolls-Royce Silver Cloud.

To more accurately measure a reader's valuation of the car one could evaluate the bid curve for automobile quality at the quality level of a

Rolls-Royce and the income and taste levels relevant to the reader. The total benefit is then the sum of these individual valuations. In this example, it is likely that the use of the market price rather than the bid curve leads to a substantial overestimate of the project's benefits. In the context of public projects, such as improving neighborhoods with abandoned buildings, this analysis suggests that the use of the prices obtained from the hedonic function may similarly overestimate the value of the project. Just as in the Rolls-Royce example, this is because the price paid for neighborhoods without abandoned buildings reflects the valuation of this trait by those who find it worth paying the price of living in a neighborhood without abandoned buildings. This point has been noted and trait bid curves have been used to estimate the benefits of various projects by Blomquist and Worley (1980), Harrison and Rubinfeld (1978) and Nelson (1978).

Although the conceptual superiority of the implicit market models of residential choice is easily appreciated, it is not clear that this superiority translates into a practical advantage in terms of predicting residential patterns. These models specify residential decisions as a system of demand (or bid) equations that are functions of a variety of variables such as income, family size, and the prices of substitutes and complements. They provide detailed insights as to why families desire various locational traits, but they fail to provide simple location rules such as those present in the Alonso model. In fact, many of the residential demand influences generated by the implicit market models operate in conflicting directions. For example, higher income may mean greater demand for access, school quality, residential space, and more neighborhood excitement. The increased demand for school quality and residential lot space suggest that higher income families will tend to live in suburban neighborhoods whereas the demands for neighborhood excitement and access suggest that high income residents will reside in the central city areas. In fact, a major contribution of these models is that distance and income are not sufficient statistics for predicting residential location patterns. They must therefore develop a method for analyzing the divergent locational incentives derived from the locational trait bid functions.

The simplest method to achieve this goal is to assume that the supply distribution of location-specific traits is spatially exogenous. With this assumption one can utilize the equilibrium condition that in the long-run, supply will equal demand. If it is assumed that the joint distribution of personal characteristics and the functional forms of the bid and offer curves are known, one can explicitly solve for the hedonic function. This market clearing price function can then be used in conjunction with the bid curves to determine which families are the highest bidders for each location site available. In this case, the locations will go to the highest bidder as revealed by the bid curves.

The short-run residential equilibrium is distinguished from the long-run equilibrium in that the hedonic trait prices need not adjust to make supply equal demand. Once again, if it is assumed that the spatial distribution of residential sites is exogenously determined along with the joint distribution of personal traits and that the hedonic prices do not adjust in order to eliminate excess supply, a simple residential allocation algorithm is possible. The estimated trait demand functions are evaluated for each family to obtain the family's optimal consumption of each locational trait, and then a search across all possible locations and families is done to determine the residential pattern that minimizes the welfare loss due to the divergence between desired and actual trait levels.

This methodology is simply summarized using a two-trait example. Assume that the demand for rooms is known and is a function of income I, family size FS, the price of a room P_{rm}, the price of access P_{acc}, and a vector of demand parameters $(\hat{b})$

$$\text{Rooms} = f(I, FS, P_{rm}, P_{acc}, \hat{b}). \tag{3.9}$$

Similarly, the demand for access is stated as shown in Eq. (3.10), where the demand parameter vector for access is indicated by $\hat{a}$

$$\text{Access} = g(I, FS, P_{rm}, P_{acc}, \hat{a}). \tag{3.10}$$

With these functions the optimal demand by the jth household for rooms (Rooms*) and access (Access*) is obtained by evaluating Eqs. (3.9) and (3.10) at the income and family size of the jth household and the prices of rooms and access indicated by the hedonic function

$$\text{Rooms}_j^* = f(I_j, FS_j, P_{rm}, P_{acc}, \hat{b}) \tag{3.9'}$$

$$\text{Access}_j^* = g(I_j, FS_j, P_{rm}, P_{acc}, \hat{a}). \tag{3.10'}$$

One expects higher income families to exhibit higher optimal demands for rooms (Rooms$_j^*$) and access (Access$_j^*$). Given traditional spatial locations, the former demand suggests that higher income families would tend to live in relatively suburban areas whereas the latter suggests that higher income families would be attracted toward the center city. In order to determine which of these two influences dominates, a loss function is required that specifies the utility loss associated with consuming nonoptimal amounts of the various location-specific traits. A general loss function is

$$L_{ji} = k[\text{Rooms}_j^* - \text{Rooms}_i), (\text{Access}_j^* - \text{Access}_i)], \tag{3.11}$$

TABLE 3.1
Family and Residential Site Descriptions

	Income		Number of children		Age difference between oldest and youngest child	
	Period 1	Period 2	Period 1	Period 2	Period 1	Period 2
Family 1	$20,000	$25,000	0	0	0	0
Family 2	$ 5,000	$ 6,250	2	2	3	3
Family 3	$15,000	$18,750	3	1	6	0
Family 4	$10,000	$12,500	2	0	7	0
Family 5	$30,000	$37,500	3	2	6	6

	Number of rooms	Access to CBD	Structural neighborhood homogeneity
Site 1 (City	6	Very good	No
Site 2 (City)	4	Good	Yes
Site 3 (City)	5	Good	No
Site 4 (Suburb)	6	Fair	Yes
Site 5 (Suburb)	7	Poor	Yes

where L_{ji} is the loss of the jth family associated with living in the ith location, Rooms$_i$ is the number of rooms available at the ith location, Access$_i$ is the access associated with residing in the ith location, and k is the functional form of the loss function. The location pattern is then determined by minimizing L_{ji} over possible locations. For example, if it is assumed that utility loss is described by a quadratic loss function, the location pattern that minimizes the sum of square deviations between the optimal trait demand and actual trait consumption will arise.

Using a quadratic loss function (with weights equal to average trait prices) and the three-trait demand model reported in Linneman (1981), it is possible to analyze the residential location patterns of different families and the impacts of changing income and demographic characteristics on residential location patterns. Assume that there are two time periods and that in each period there are the five family types and residential sites as described in Table 3.1. The primary differences between Period 1 and Period 2 are that income is 25% higher for all families in Period 2 and family size is notably smaller in the second period. The spatial distribution of residences is the same in both periods and includes a central city location (Site 1), two other city locations (Sites 2 and 3), and two suburban locations (Sites 4 and 5). The residential demand equations specified in Linneman (1981) yield the optimal trait demands reported in Table 3.2 for a white family that anticipates no new children in the next 12 months. A search over the possible residential location patterns, given the optimal

TABLE 3.2
Predicted Optimal Trait Demands

	Number or rooms		Access to CBD[a]		Structural neighborhood homogeneity[b]	
	Period 1	Period 2	Period 1	Period 2	Period 1	Period 2
Family 1	5.16	5.24	.5867	.5897	.5069	.5421
Family 2	5.19	5.21	.5718	.5725	.4988	.4900
Family 3	5.31	5.44	.5736	.5846	.3936	.4487
Family 4	4.89	5.04	.5696	.5823	.4746	.5597
Family 5	5.55	5.41	.5825	.5872	.2880	.2782

[a] This is an index of access to CBD. Higher values indicate greater accessibility.
[b] This is a dichotomous variable where 0 indicates No and 1 indicates the presence of structural neighborhood homogeneity.

trait demands shown in Table 3.2, yields the location patterns displayed in Table 3.3 as the loss minimizing patterns. In both periods the location pattern with respect to income is nonmonotonic. In the first period the highest income family (5) lives in Suburban Area 5, which provides large dwellings in a homogeneous neighborhood but with poor access. However, in Period 2 this family moves to the nicest central city area. This is due to the rise in income increasing the demand for access while the reduction in family size reduces the demand for dwelling space.

The homogeneous central city area is inhabited in both periods by the fourth family type. This is because the income increase in the second period is offset by the reduction in family size. The other inner-city area is inhabited in Period 1 by Family 3 (middle income, large family), whereas in the second period this area becomes populated by the lowest income families. Also, in the second period Family 3 moves to the farthest suburbs as its rising income increases its demand for dwelling space in a manner that more than offsets the increased demand for access.

TABLE 3.3
Optimal Residential Location Patterns for a Quadratic Loss Function

	Period 1					Period 2				
	Site 1	Site 2	Site 3	Site 4	Site 5	Site 1	Site 2	Site 3	Site 4	Site 5
Family 1	*								*	
Family 2				*				*		
Family 3			*							*
Family 4		*					*			
Family 5					*	*				

This model can be expanded to include an iterative process that yields the long-run price structure for housing as well as the long-run equilibrium housing pattern. This can be accomplished by repeated iterations in which the prices of the traits respond to an excess supply price adjustment function. Similarly, endogenous supply considerations could be added to arrive at a more sophisticated analysis of residential location patterns.

Although this example indicates that the new models are capable of predicting nonmonotonic residential locations patterns with respect to income and distance, it does not answer the critical question as to whether the results from the new models are sufficiently superior to the simple bid-rent models at predicting residential patterns to warrant the higher cost associated with their implementation. To date no one has examined this question. Instead, the developers of the implicit market models have assumed that the theoretical superiority of their modeling efforts is proof that these models provide sufficiently superior predictive insights to warrant their use. However, this conclusion depends on the error structure of these models. At a minimum, an analysis of the sensitivity of the residential location patterns predicted by the implicit market models should be conducted in terms of the various specification issues discussed in this Chapter. Specifically, it would be useful to know how the residential location patterns predicted by these models differ depending upon the type of market definition utilized, the functional specification of hedonic equation, which variables are included or omitted from the hedonic function and demand specification, and the nature of the loss function used in the residential allocation algorithm. Until it is determined how sensitive the residential location predictions are from the new models in terms of these issues, some caution about their use in this regard would seem appropriate.

VI. CONCLUSION

This chapter has indicated both the promise and problems of the implicit market models of residential choice. It is necessary to establish the robustness of these models over a variety of specification issues. Future work should also develop in more detail the predictions of residential location patterns implied by the system of demand equations yielded by this system.

ACKNOWLEDGMENTS

The author is indebted to Douglas Diamond for comments and suggestions on earlier drafts of this chapter.

REFERENCES

Alonso, W. *Location and Land Use*. Cambridge, Mass.: Harvard University Press, 1964.
Bailey, M. "Effects of Race and Other Demographic Factors on the Values of Single-Family Homes." *Land Econ.* 42 (May 1966): 215–220.
Blomquist, G., and Worley, L. "Hedonic Prices, Demands for Urban Housing Amenties, and Benefit Estimates." Unpublished manuscript, 1980.
Butler, R. *Hedonic Indexes of Urban Housing: Theory and Problems of Cross-Sectional Estimation*. PhD dissertation, Massachusetts Institute of Technology, 1978.
Diamond, D. "The Relationship Between Amenities and Urban Land Values." *Land Econ.* 51, (February 1980): 1–32.
Domencich, T., and McFadden, D. *Urban Travel Demand: A Behavioral Analysis*. Amsterdam: North-Holland Publ., 1975.
Edel, M., and Sclar, T. "Taxes, Spending, and Property Values: Supply Adjustments in a Tiebout-Oates World." *J. Polit. Econ.* 82, (September–October 1974): 941–954.
Freeman, A. "The Hedonic Price Approach to Measuring Demand for Neighborhood Characteristics." In *Studies in Urban Economics*, edited by D. Segal. New York: Academic Press, 1979.
Goodman, A. "Hedonic Prices, Price Indices and Housing Markets." *J. Urban Econ.* 5 (October 1978): 471–484.
Griliches, Z., "Hedonic Price Indexes for Automobiles." In *Price Statistics of the Federal Government*, Report to the Office of Statistical Standards, Bureau of the Budget, Prepared by the Price Statistics Review Committee of the National Bureau of Economic Research. New York: National Bureau of Economic Research, 1961.
Griliches, Z. "Hedonic Price Indexes Revisited: Some Notes on the State of the Art." In *Price Indexes and Quality Change*, edited by Z. Griliches. Cambridge, Mass.: Harvard University Press, 1971.
Harris, R., Tolley, G., and Harrell, C. "The Residence Site Choice." *Rev. Econ. Stat.* 50 (February 1968): 241–247.
Harrison, D., and Rubinfeld, D. "Hedonic Housing Prices and the Demand for Clean Air." *J. Environ. Econ. Manag.* 5 (March 1978): 81–102.
Heckman, J. "The Common Structure of Statistical Models of Truncation, Sample Selection, and Limit Dependent Variables and a Simple Estimator for Such Models." *Ann. Econ. Soc. Measurement,* 5 (Fall 1976): 475–492.
Kain, J., and Quigley, J. *Housing Markets and Racial Discrimination*. New York: National Bureau of Economic Research, 1975.
King, A. "The Demand for Housing: Integrating the Roles of Journey-to-Work, Neighborhood Quality, and Prices." In *Household Production and Consumption*, edited by N. Terleckyj. New York: National Bureau of Economic Research, 1975.
King, A., and Mieszkowski, P. "Racial Discrimination, Segregation, and the Price of Housing." *J. Polit. Econ.* 81 (May–June 1973): 590–606.
Linneman, P. *The Demand for Residence Site Characteristics*. Ph.D. dissertation, University of Chicago, 1977.
Linneman, P. "An Empirical Methodology for Analyzing the Properties of Public Goods." *Econ. Inq.* 18 (October 1980a): 600–617.
Linneman, P. "Some Empirical Results on the Nature of the Hedonic Price Function for the Urban Housing Market." *J. Urban Econ.* 8, (June 1980b): 47–68.
Linneman, P. "The Demand for Residence Site Characteristics." *J. Urban Econ.* 9 (March 1981): 129–149.
Madden, J. "Urban Land Use and the Growth of Two Earner Households." *Amer. Econ. Rev.* 70, (May 1980): 191–197.

Mieszkowski, P., and Saper, A. "An Estimate of the Effects of Airport Noise on Property Values." *J. Urban Econ.* 5 (October 1978): 425–440.

Nelson, J. "Residential Choice, Hedonic Prices, and the Demand for Urban Air Quality." *J. Urban Econ.* 5 (July 1978): 357–369.

Oates, W. "The Effect of Property on Property Values: An Empirical Study of Tax Capitalization and the Tiebout Hypothesis." *J. Polit. Econ.* 77 (November–December 1969): 957–971.

Pollard, R. *Topographics, Amenities, and Building Height in an Urban Area.* PhD dissertation, University of Chicago, 1977.

Quigley, J. "Housing Demand in the Short Run: An Analysis of Polytomous Choice." *Explor. in Econ. Res.* 3 (1976): 76–102.

Ridker, R., and Henning, J. "The Determinants of Residential Property Value with Special References to Air Pollution." *Rev. Econ. Stat.* 44 (May 1967): 147–157.

Rosen, H., and Fullerton, D. "A Note on Local Tax Rates, Public Benefit Levels, and Property Values." *J. Polit. Econ.* 85 (April 1977): 433–440.

Rosen, S. "Hedonic Prices and Implicit Markets: Product Differentiation in Pure Competition." *J. Polit. Econ.* 82, (January–February 1974): 34–55.

Schaffer, R. "Racial Discrimination in the Boston Housing Market." *J. Urban Econ.* 6 (April 1979): 176–196.

Smith, B., and Campbell, J. "Aggregation Bias and the Demand for Housing," *Internat. Econ. Rev.*, V1N2, (June 1978): 495–505.

Straszheim, M. "Estimation of the Demand for Urban Housing Services From Household Interview Data." *Rev. Econ. Stat.* 55 (February 1973): 1–8.

Straszheim, M. "Hedonic Estimation of Housing Market Prices: A Further Comment." *Rev. Econ. Stat.* 56 (August 1974): 404–406.

Straszheim, M. *An Econometric Analysis of the Urban Housing Market.* New York: National Bureau of Economic Research, 1975.

Tiebout, C. "A Pure Theory of Local Expenditures." *J. Polit. Econ.* 64 (October 1956): 416–425.

Vaughn, R. *The Residential Demand for Urban Parks.* Ph.D. dissertation, Univeristy of Chicago, 1974.

Working, E. "What Do Statistical 'Demand Curves' Show." *Quart. J. Econ.* 41 (November 1927): 212–235.

Wu, D. "Alternative Tests of Independence Between Stochastic Regressors and Disturbances: Finite Sample Results." *Econometrica* (May 1974): 529–546.

4

Specifying the Demand for Housing Characteristics: The Exogeneity Issue

GLENN BLOMQUIST   LAWRENCE WORLEY

I. HEDONIC PRICES AND DEMAND FOR HOUSING CHARACTERISTICS

The rapidly growing literature on the demand for housing characteristics has begun to take into account the complex and subtle nature of the
implicit market for these characteristics.[1] Although early research attempted to infer demand directly from the hedonic housing equation, it is
now more common to interpret the equation as a market-clearing price
function. As such, it is influenced by the suppliers as well as the demanders of housing. Thus, the standard practice is to estimate the demands employing a two-step procedure.

Following Rosen (1974), housing is viewed as a bundle of characteristics and estimating the demand for characteristics involves (*a*) estimating a hedonic housing equation and determining the implicit prices of
the characteristics; and (*b*) using these implicit prices along with information about the consumers and producers of housing to estimate and, if
necessary, identify the demand equations for these characteristics.
Freeman (1979) observes that in only two special cases is there agreement
concerning demand estimation. One case is where the hedonic is linear.
There is no variation in the prices of characteristics, and demand (at least
as we usually define it) cannot be estimated. The other case is where the
hedonic is nonlinear and where all consumers have the same utility func-

[1] For a critical review of this research on housing markets see Smith (1980).

THE ECONOMICS OF
URBAN AMENITIES

89

tion and have equal values of all arguments in the utility function. In this second case, the demand can be obtained directly from the hedonic equation. The demand is the marginal function obtained from the total willingness-to-pay function—the hedonic housing equation.

The treatment of housing supply particularly lacks harmony. Harrison and Rubinfeld (1978) and Bender, Gronberg, and Hwang (1980)—investigating the demand for the amenity, clean air in the neighborhood—assume that the supply of houses with some specified air quality is completely inelastic and that it is completely inelastic at any specified air quality. Using this assumption, they estimate the inverse demand for clean air. Linneman (1977)—investigating the demands for rooms, access, and neighborhood homogeneity—and Blomquist and Worley (1981)—investigating the demands for several neighborhood amenities and rooms—assume that the supply of houses with some specified quantity of a characteristic is perfectly elastic and that this holds for any quantity of the characteristic. Accordingly, they estimate the ordinary (quantity is the dependent variable) demand for various housing characteristics. Nelson (1978) and Witte, Sumka, and Erekson (1979) assume that the supply is neither completely inelastic nor perfectly elastic and estimate demand and supply simultaneously.[2] Which specification is appropriate depends upon the housing characteristic whose demand is being estimated and the supply mechanism for the characteristic. Misspecification will lead to biased estimates since the regressor that is assumed to be independent is, in fact, correlated with the error term. Unnecessary estimation of a simultaneous system may introduce problems associated with the choice of instrumental variables.

Freeman (1979, p. 166) argues that the correctness of each assumption depends on the speed of adjustment in supplying housing characteristics relative to the speed at which housing prices adjust to supply. He emphasizes that additional housing amenities, such as clean air, can be supplied through either additional amenities for existing houses or additional houses in areas with a higher level of amenities. If demand adjusts relatively more quickly, then the quantities of the particular bundle of housing characteristics can be assumed to be exogenous and demand can be estimated inversely. If supply adjusts relatively more quickly, then the

---

[2] To some extent, most of the studies that estimate the value of housing amenities do consider the importance of the supply assumption. Harrison and Rubinfeld do check for simultaneous equation bias by estimating the demand for clean air using 2SLS. Linneman uses a Wu test to check for endogeneity and, where appropriate, employs instrumental variables. Blomquist and Worley estimate benefits of increased housing characteristics under several assumptions. An exception is Brown and Pollakowski (1977), who assume fixed supplies and estimate the value of shoreline from the hedonic housing equation.

implicit prices can be assumed to be exogenous and demand can be estimated in the usual way (i.e., with quantity consumed as a function of price). If the speeds of adjustment are approximately equal, then demand must be estimated in a way that accounts for the simultaneity. Freeman's conclusion, which is the point of departure for this chapter, is that the question of appropriate specification is essentially an empirical one.

In Section II we estimate the hedonic housing equation for a particular housing market using a maximum likelihood search procedure to determine the best functional form of the hedonic and whether or not it is linear. After calculating the implicit prices for the housing characteristics, we proceed in Section III to estimate the demand for each characteristic, again determining the best functional form using a maximum likelihood search procedure. In Section IV we test for the relative exogeneity of implicit prices and quantities of the housing characteristics. We present our conclusions about the supply conditions for each housing characteristic, the nature of the implicit market, and implications for measuring the value of housing amenities in Section V.

II. THE HEDONIC HOUSING EQUATION

In this section we estimate for residences (bundles of housing described by the vector of characteristics $\mathbf{Z}$), the hedonic price function $P(\mathbf{Z})$ and calculate the implicit prices (P_{Z_i}) for each housing characteristic (Z_i). The data are composed of observations from the 1970 U.S. Census for Springfield, Illinois. The hedonic equation is estimated using block data (Third Count) for housing prices and housing traits. The demand equations are estimated for block groups (Fifth Count) using an average of the implicit prices for the blocks within the group as well as income and taste variables for the block group.[3] In our sample there are 199 blocks and 38 block groups. Table 4.1 reports the summary statistics for housing prices, housing characteristics, and income and taste variables for the southern section of Springfield.

Given the interest in the functional form of the hedonic equation (with respect to variation in the first partial derivatives), we follow the statistical model of Box and Cox, which permits investigation of the functional specification through search for the best fit as measured by the log likelihood function. The search is limited to power transformations of the

---

[3] Suppression of block data for income and taste variables for reasons of confidentiality prevents estimating the demand equations using block data. We are limited to owner-occupied housing for the same reason.

TABLE 4.1
Summary Statistics for 1970 Housing Data for Springfield, Illinois, by Block

Variable	Definition	Mean[a]	Standard deviation[a]
PHOUS	Reported property value (median)	$19,670	9,013
ROOM	Rooms per house	5.020 rooms	.689 rooms
HBAS	Houses with basement	66.31%	25.57%
HPLB	Houses with adequate plumbing	98.09%	4.943%
DPP	Distance from electric power plant	12,140 ft	5,412 ft
NLAK	Proximity to Lake Springfield[b]	6,182 ft	4,065 ft
NPK	Proximity to the closest park[b]	26,193 ft	4,668 ft
DSS	Distance from Highway 66	4,808 ft	5,221 ft
NFF	Proximity to Interstate 55[b]	10,680 ft	3,789 ft
WHOS	Houses with nonblack occupants	92.39%	12.95%
INC	Income per adult	$6,076	$3,538
FAMSZ	Family size	3.410 persons	.425 persons
AGE	Age	31.35 years	5.556 years
GSPER	Grade school population	1.805%	.891%
HSPER	High school population	.782%	.789%
PROF	Professional population	24.25%	13.27%
SMHOS	In same house 5 years	29.12%	26.69%

[a] These are the summary statistics for 199 census blocks for PHOUS down to WHOS and average values for 38 census block groups for INC down to SMHOS.

[b] These proximity variables are calculated by substracting the distance from the amenity source from the maximum distance in the sample. For Lake Springfield the maximum is 12,710 ft.; for parks, the maximum is 27,010 ft.; and for Interstate 55, the maximum is 17,100 ft.

variables. Thus the hedonic equation is

$$\frac{P^\lambda - 1}{\lambda} = b_0 + b_1 \frac{Z_1^{\gamma_i} - 1}{\gamma_1} + \cdots + b_n \frac{Z_n^{\gamma_n} - 1}{\gamma_n} + e, \qquad (4.1)$$

where λ is the power transformation of housing price, γ_i is the power transformation of each housing site trait, the b_i are constant coefficients and e is an error term that is assumed to be normally distributed with zero mean and constant variance. It should be noted that the linear functional form is the special case where the transformation factor for each variable equals 1 and the natural logarithmic form is the special case where the transformation factor for each variable equals zero.

Table 4.2 reports the constrained maximum likelihood estimates for the hedonic equation. To simplify a complex, costly search, the γ_i are constrained to equal λ. By varying λ in increments of 0.1, we determined that the preferred functional form is that where λ equals 0.1. Construct the statistic $-2 \ln(L_0/L_a)$, where ln indicates logarithm, L_0 is the likelihood under the null hypothesis and L_a is the likelihood under the alternative hy-

TABLE 4.2
Hedonic Equations for Housing Price,
PHOUS is the Dependent Variable

Housing trait	Coefficient[a] (absolute t value)		
	$\lambda = \gamma_i = 1.0$	$\lambda = \gamma_i = .1$	$\lambda = \gamma_i = 0.0$
ROOM	86.095	2.9833	2.147
	(14.09)	(13.04)	(13.62)
HBAS	.2747	.03457	.02321
	(2.50)	(2.02)	(1.93)
HPLB	1.0774	.1768	.2907
	(1.83)	(1.73)	(3.62)
DPP	.2476	.001553	.01477
	(1.44)	(.30)	(.32)
NLAK	.6303	.06763	.04745
	(3.70)	(3.04)	(2.78)
NPK	.2881	−.01359	−.003634
	(1.61)	(.34)	(.13)
DSS	.2968	.08429	.05963
	(1.86)	(3.33)	(3.00)
NFF	.1532	.02898	.02670
	(.84)	(.86)	(.98)
WHOS	−2.747	.004009	.002727
	(1.12)	(.40)	(.44)
R^2	.8172	.7768	.7704
F	93.86	73.48	70.85
ln L	−1008.7	−988.0	−988.6

[a] Since the coefficients are for different transformations, the values cannot be compared directly, but the signs and t values can.

pothesis. This statistic is approximately distributed chi-square (Mood, Graybill, and Boes, 1974) and can be used to test whether or not the preferred form is significantly different from other forms. The estimate of .1 (ln $L = -988.0$) is significantly different from that λ for the linear form, 1.0 (ln $L = -1008.7$) at the 1% level. It is not significantly different from that λ for the logarithmic form, 0.0 (ln $L = -988.6$) at the 5% level.

The results based on our data indicate that the linear form of the housing price equation, used in earlier studies such as Ridker and Henning (1967), is inferior to a nonlinear form such as the transformation where λ equals .1 or the logarithmic form. Using different data, Linneman (1980) does a constrained search over Box–Cox transformations and finds the best λ ranges from .2 to .4. He also does not find them to be significantly different from the log form. For our hedonic equation, .2 and .4 are not significantly different from .1 at the 5% level. Goodman (1978) finds the

TABLE 4.3
Marginal Trait Prices Calculated from the
Hedonic Equation, Where $\lambda = \gamma_i = .1$

Variable	Average evaluated price[a]	Average price[b]	Standard deviation[c]
PROOM	$8100/room	$8264/room	$2128/room
PHBAS	$9.20/%	$74.17/%	$24.39/%
PHPLB	$33.07/%	$35.42/%	$12.26/%
PDPP	$.002378/ft	$.003196/ft	$.002038/ft
PNLAK	$.1916/ft	$.5865/ft	$1.391/ft
PNPK	$-.01244/ft	$-.06273/ft	$.3024/ft
PDSS	$.2995/ft	$.5723/ft	$.5873/ft
PNFF	$.07939/ft	$.1346/ft	$.1103/ft
PWHOS	$.7916/%	$149.5/%	$107.1/%

[a] Trait price evaluated at the mean of PHOUS and Z_i for the 199 census blocks.

[b] Average prices of the 38 census block groups. The averages of the marginal prices exceed the average evaluated prices because of some extreme values of marginal prices among the block groups. The average evaluated price is the marginal price evaluated at the means of the characteristics.

[c] Standard deviation of the price of the 38 census block groups.

best λ is .6, which is significantly different from the linear form and for our hedonic equation is significantly different from .1 as well.

The functional form is of special interest because the nonlinear form of the hedonic equation implies that trait prices do indeed vary across the southern section of Springfield. The marginal trait price of any particular trait is given by the partial derivative of the hedonic equation with respect to the quantity of the trait. For the unconstrained Box–Cox hedonic form we have: $\partial P/\partial Z_i = b_i P^{(1-\lambda)} Z_i^{(\gamma_i - 1)}$. For our constrained case where γ_i equals λ, we have: $\partial P/\partial Z_i = b_i (P/Z_i)^{(1-\lambda)}$. Averages of the marginal trait prices are given in Table 4.3 for λ equals 0.1. All of the traits, which are defined to be "goods," have positive trait prices except for NPK. The unexpected sign on NPK can be explained by measurement error. Air distance to the nearest park was used—a measure that is probably a highly inaccurate measure of the effective distance to a park. In addition, no weighting was assigned to parks with differing facilities. (The prices for DPP, NFF, NPK, and WHOS are based on hedonic coefficients that are not significant at any of the usual levels.)

Using the implicit prices calculated from the hedonic housing equation, demands are estimated for the neighborhood amenities and the most important structural characteristic—ROOM.

III. DEMANDS FOR HOUSING CHARACTERISTICS

In keeping with our concern for proper specification, preliminary demand equations for housing characteristics were estimated, first assuming that the implicit prices of characteristics are taken as given by consumers and then, as an alternative, assuming that quantities of characteristics are fixed. The best functional form for the demand equation is determined by using a constrained Box–Cox procedure similar to that used for the hedonic equation. Table 4.4 shows the demand equations under both assumptions concerning the relative speed of adjustment of the supply of characteristics.

For each of the five demands for characteristics that is estimated, chi-square tests indicate that the "best" (λ) functional form is significantly different from the linear at the 1% level. Comparing the "best" functional form to the log–log form, we find that log–log is the "best" for NLAK and DSS (as dependent variables). Chi-square tests indicate that the log–log form could not be rejected for DPP (as a dependent variable) and NLAK (as an independent variable) but could be rejected for NFF (as a dependent variable) at the 10% level and ROOM (as a dependent variable) at the 5% level. All others could be rejected at the 1% level.

In the demand equations we observe several patterns. First, the coefficients for own-price are negative and significant at the 1% level for 4 of the 5 housing characteristics. For the fifth, ROOM, the coefficient is negative in the standard specification and positive in the inverse demand. (The results of the Hausman tests reported later suggest an explanation for the contradictory coefficients for ROOM.) Second, the structural characteristic ROOM appears to be a substitute for each of the locational amenities. The coefficient for PROOM is positive and significant at the 5% level for NLAK, DSS, NFF, and DPP in both the standard and inverse demand equations. Third, the income effect appears to be positive in that all 10 coefficients are positive. Only 4 of the income coefficients are significant at the 10% level, but this is not surprising with the number of other demand factors included in the demand equation. Age of family head appears to increase the demand for housing in that 4 of the coefficients are positive and significant at the 10% level and 4 of the remaining 6 are positive. There is a weak indication that family size increases the demand for housing in that 9 of the 10 coefficients are positive. There is some evidence that professional status decreases demand. Given these mixed but reasonable results for the demand equations, we turn our attention to determining the appropriate demand specification: standard, inverse, or one that accounts for simultaneity with supply.

TABLE 4.4
Demands and Inverse Demands for Housing Characteristics Using the Best Functional Form[a]

Regressors[b]	Dependent variable, best λ									
	(1) NLAK 0.0	(2) PNLAK[c] -.2	(3) DSS 0.0	(4) PDSS[c] -.1	(5) NFF .1	(6) PNNF[c] .2	(7) DPP .1	(8) PDPP[c] -.4	(9) ROOM -.3	(10) PROOM[c] -.4
PNLAK	*-.8585[d] (18.44)	*-1.8326 (16.25)	-.0438 (1.11)	.0634 (.76)	.0078 (.16)	.0068 (.44)	.0209 (.63)	1.2896 (1.13)	.0043 (1.18)	.0076 (.73)
PDSS	-.0286 (.41)	-.0947 (.52)	*-.9176 (15.43)	*-1.6390 (12.55)	*-.1515 (2.01)	.0298 (1.28)	-.0687 (1.34)	-1.4081 (.68)	—	—
PNFF	.0614 (.63)	-.3160 (1.04)	*-.1943 (2.36)	.1601 (.75)	*-1.7707 (14.99)	*-.2877 (8.22)	-.1223 (1.51)	-.2758 (.08)	—	—
PDPP	.1559 (.98)	*1.8302 (2.64)	*.2431 (1.80)	.0553 (.13)	*.6281 (2.19)	-.0411 (.85)	*-2.2623 (11.54)	*-40.025 (4.10)	*.0045 (2.66)	*.0896 (1.67)
PROOM	*.8279 (2.23)	*9.1286 (5.78)	*1.3314 (4.23)	*5.0675 (5.04)	*.8700 (3.73)	*1.3955 (4.83)	*1.5393 (9.64)	*84.541 (7.65)	*-.4554 (2.09)	*.5250 (7.30)
PNPK	.0275 (.42)	-1.3845 (.75)	.0925 (1.64)	.6028 (.69)	.0850 (1.09)	-.0002 (.00)	.0422 (.79)	*63.579 (2.78)	—	.3285 (1.58)
PWHOS	.0053 (.13)	.8209 (.43)	-.0171 (.50)	-.6024 (.64)	.0485 (1.04)	.0862 (.79)	.0232 (.73)	11.256 (.48)	-.0027 (1.60)	.0108 (.26)
PHBAS	—	—	—	—	—	—	—	—	*.0041 (1.78)	—
PHPLB	—	—	—	—	—	—	—	—	*.1740 (6.30)	*.7521 (2.91)
INC	.0771 (.47)	*1.3205 (1.99)	.0929 (.67)	.3000 (.94)	.1358 (1.29)	*.0659 (1.96)	*.1042 (1.45)	10.061 (1.31)	.0106 (.18)	*.1198 (1.69)

96

FAMSZ	.0091	1.4067	.1532	.5903	.2135	.1446	.2639	*8.8788	-.0677	.0412
	(.02)	(1.61)	(.39)	(.91)	(.51)	(.79)	(.92)	(1.82)	(1.48)	(1.00)
AGE	.1726	*2.0444	-.0734	.7436	.2461	*.2024	.0994	*24.189	-.0907	*.2290
	(.42)	(1.72)	(.21)	(1.09)	(.80)	(1.90)	(.47)	(2.19)	(1.12)	(2.52)
GSPER	.0039	*.1303	.0053	.0009	-.0080	-.0188	-.0011	*1.1622	-.0085	*.0143
	(.26)	(1.88)	(.42)	(.04)	(.38)	(.98)	(.08)	(1.77)	(1.42)	(2.53)
HSPER	.0060	-.0941	.0075	-.0215	.0200	.0127	*.0087	*-.5911	*.0040	*-.0046
	(.68)	(2.95)	(1.00)	(1.57)	(1.58)	(.98)	(2.70)	(2.56)	(1.91)	(2.37)
PROF	.1051	*-.3933	-.0316	-.1370	-.0428	-.0299	-.0633	*-2.3103	*.0218	-.0130
	(1.54)	(2.22)	(.55)	(1.28)	(.77)	(1.28)	(1.66)	(1.75)	(1.99)	(1.11)
SMHOS	-.0060	.1506	-.0015	.0122	.0044	*.0144	-.0056	2.6566	.0006	.0069
	(.53)	(1.18)	(.16)	(.34)	(.34)	(2.65)	(.64)	(1.26)	(.05)	(.39)
Constant	-.9465	-13.513	-1.8560	-8.3632	-2.2226	-4.7946	-13.592	-280.47	2.9204	-1.7626
R^2	.9756	.9612	.9792	.9550	.9718	.9742	.9672	.9452	.9756	.9214
F	65.61	40.73	77.16	34.90	56.63	62.07	48.48	28.33	41.73	21.65
SEE	.2052	.3200	.1744	.2425	.2131	.1072	.1456	1.6138	.0173	.0141
ln L	-132.68	56.09	-120.14	45.21	-127.79	105.84	-136.11	243.96	25.77	-123.41

Note: Absolute t values are shown below each coefficient.

a The sample consists of 38 census block groups.

b In none of the demand equations does the best λ equal one, the transformation that is perhaps the most easily interpreted. To compare the coefficients reported in this table to those in the linear (λ = 1.0) equations, the values of the retransformed variables can be plotted using the Box–Cox coefficients, and the slope calculated at the mean. For example, for NFF where λ = .1, the own-price coefficient is approximately equal to a linear coefficient of −416.78, which can be compared to the estimated linear coefficient of −223.1.

c In each regression where the price is the dependent variable, all regressors are quantities. For example, PNLAK is regressed on NLAK, DSS, NFF, DPP, ROOM, NPK, WHOS, INC, FAMSZ, AGE, GSPER, HSPER, PROF, and SMHOS.

d The asterisk indicates significance for α = .10 for a two-tail test except for own-price and INC where a one-tail test is performed.

IV. THE RELATIVE EXOGENEITY OF PRICES
   AND QUANTITIES

The question of the appropriate specification can be posed in terms of exogenity. If supply adjusts slowly, then the quantities of housing characteristics are, in a sense, exogenous to consumers and the implicit prices are endogenous. If supply adjusts rapidly, then the implicit prices are, in a sense, exogenous to the consumer and the quantities are endogenous. If supply adjusts at a moderate pace, then both quantities and prices are endogenous.

Although theoretical arguments may be sufficiently convincing for some housing characteristics, it is not always clear which specification is appropriate. As Freeman noted, the question of whether quantities and–or prices are endogenous is an empirical one, with the answer depending upon the relative speed of supply-side adjustment.

An implication of the endogeneity of a regressor is that the regressor is correlated with the error term. This correlation results in OLS yielding biased estimates of the model's parameters and will exist even for large samples. Hence OLS estimates are inconsistent in this case. Hausman (1978) derived an asymptotic test of the null hypothesis that the regressor is uncorrelated with the error term; the test may be used in this context. It tests whether or not the regressor of interest—say, price of the housing characteristic—is correlated with the error term in the demand equation. If the null hypothesis is not rejected, it indicates that the regressor is exogenous and that OLS can yield consistent estimates of demand. If the null hypothesis is rejected, then endogeneity of a regressor is one possible explanation.[4]

Since it is contradictory to maintain that we have a demand system in equilibrium and at the same time accept H_0: $E(Z_i\epsilon) = 0$ and H_0: $E(P_{Z_i}\epsilon) = 0$, a relative test of significance is employed. If exogeneity of both quantity and price can be accepted at the standard significance levels, the decision is made to reject the null hypothesis for the variable with the higher significance. If the null hypothesis is rejected at the standard significance levels for quantity and price, it indicates simultaneity.

A strong case can be made for using significance levels that are lower than standard levels. Given that 2SLS and IV estimation procedures are consistent in the presence or absence of an endogenous explanatory variable and that OLS is consistent only in the absence of endogenous explanatory variables, one would prefer to minimize the probability of Type II

---

[4] Endogeneity of a regressor is not the only circumstance that will result in rejection of the null hypothesis. Errors in variables and the omission of a relevant regressor are other possible causes of correlation between the regressors and the error term.

error, even if this means allowing more Type I errors. This is the case here. If we reject H_0 when it is actually true (Type I error), all we will have lost is some efficiency of estimation. However, if we do not reject H_0 when it is actually false (Type II error), our estimation will no longer be consistent.

A Hausman test is performed on the best functional form of the demand equation under the two alternative assumptions concerning exogeneity. Let X_j be the variable (either P_{Z_j} or Z_j) to be tested for endogeneity and $\mathbf{X}$ be the vector of either price or quantity variables other than P_{Z_j} or Z_j. Let Y_j be the demand variable opposite to X_j, that is, Z_j if $X_j = P_{Z_j}$. Let $\mathbf{W}$ be the vector of additional variables used to estimate the instrumental variable for the Hausman test. Following Hausman, the alternative estimator should be consistent under both the null and alternative hypotheses but inefficient under the null hypothesis. $\mathbf{W}$ will include the average price of housing $\bar{P}$ in the block group and the population of the block group.[5] We regress:

$$X_j = c + b\mathbf{X} + a\mathbf{W} \tag{4.2}$$

to obtain $\hat{X}_j$. Then to test H_0: $E(X_j\epsilon) = 0$ we regress:

$$Y_j = c + B(\mathbf{X}X_j) + \alpha\hat{X}_j. \tag{4.3}$$

The significance of $\hat{\alpha}$ is then tested, with significance being taken as reason to reject the H_0: $E(X_j\epsilon) = 0$.

The results of the Hausman tests are shown in Table 4.5, where we see evidence that the appropriate specification of demand varies from one housing characteristic to another. The most striking results are for ROOM, where the null hypotheses are rejected at the .01% level for each price and quantity. The supply of houses with more rooms appears to adjust at a rate similar to that of housing prices. At least these speeds are close enough that estimation of the demand for rooms must take account of the simultaneity with supply (e.g., 2SLS, IV, or estimating a simultaneous system).

For NFF, proximity to Interstate 55, there is a clear indication that quantity is more exogenous than price. The null hypothesis that price is exogenous can be rejected at the 11% level, whereas that for quantity can be rejected only at the extreme 98% level. This means that the supply of housing with quick access responds slowly relative to housing prices and that the inverse demand shown in Column 6 of Table 4.4 is the more appropriate demand equation.

[5] The results subsequently reported are robust with respect to using $\bar{P}$ alone and $\bar{P}$ and population together but may be sensitive to the choice of other alternative estimators or other forms of the Hausman test.

TABLE 4.5
Relative Exogenity of Prices and Quantities of Housing Characteristics

Characteristics	Assumption		*t* value on α	Level at which H_0 is rejected	Appropriate exogenous variable
	Exogenous variable	Dependent variable			
Proximity to	PNLAK	NLAK	−.21	84	PNLAK
Lake Springfield	NLAK	PNLAK	1.04	31	
Distance from	PDSS	DSS	−.31	76	PDSS
Highway 66	DSS	PDSS	−.59	44	
Proximity to	PNFF	NFF	1.64	11	NFF
Interstate 55	NFF	PNFF	.03	98	
Distance from	PDPP	DPP	1.21	24	PDPP
electric power plant	DPP	PDPP	3.39	.3	
Rooms per house	PROOM	ROOM	11.18	.01	Simultaneous
	ROOM	PROOM	32.45	.01	

For NLAK, proximity to Lake Springfield, and DSS, distance from Highway 66, and DPP, distance from the power plant, it appears that prices are relatively exogenous, meaning that supplies of these locational characteristics respond quickly relative to housing prices. This might occur through new housing developments on open land in these areas. For NLAK the null hypothesis can be rejected at the 31% level, whereas that for the price, PNLAK, can be rejected only at the 84% level. The standard demand equation shown in Column 1 of Table 4.4 is the more appropriate of the two. For DSS neither null hypothesis can be rejected at anything close to a usual level, and the difference between the levels is smaller than that for NLAK. Nonetheless it appears that the standard demand shown in Column 3 is the more appropriate. For DPP, the difference in rejection levels for the null hypothesis is approximately the same as that for DSS. Again the evidence is that the price is the relatively more exogenous variable and that the standard demand equation shown in Column 7 is the more appropriate. The levels of significance hint that one might consider a simultaneous estimation procedure.

For each housing characteristic the results are indicative of relative exogeneity–exogeneity of implicit characteristic prices compared to the exogeneity of the quantities of the characteristics.[6] It appears that the results are not an indication of errors in variables or stochastic regressors.

[6] It should be recognized that the evidence on relative exogeneity is based on equations in which either all implicit prices of complements and substitutes or all quantities of housing characteristics are regressors. More extensive testing might entail consideration of specifications with various combinations of prices and quantities of characteristics.

The relative exogeneity results are not sensitive to the functional form of the demand equation in that the list of appropriate exogenous variables reported in Table 4.5 is the same for the best (λ*), log(λ = 0) and linear (λ = 1) functional forms.

The variables for the implicit prices are clearly stochastic since they are derived from the estimated hedonic price function, and it would seem that we have a built-in bias for rejecting H_0 when testing the exogeneity of price variables. However, in three cases we accepted H_0 for price variables, which gives some indication that this effect is minor.

Generally the results indicate there is little simultaneity in the implicit market for the four locational housing characteristics. However, they strongly indicate that one must carefully consider the appropriate specification of the demand function, that is, the standard or inverse demand. In particular, our results are inconsistent with specifying that all markets have either completely inelastic supply or perfectly elastic supply.

V. CONCLUSIONS

In this chapter we have addressed the issue of proper specification of the demand function for housing characteristics. After estimating the hedonic equation for housing prices using a limited Box–Cox search to determine the best functional form and calculating the implicit marginal prices for various housing characteristics, the demands for these characteristics were estimated under alternative assumptions about the supply conditions. First it was assumed that supply adjusted slowly relative to demand prices, and then it was assumed that supply adjusted relatively quickly. The purpose was to provide information on whether demands for characteristics should be estimated inversely, ordinarily, or simultaneously and also on the nature of the supply of each characteristic. The same constrained Box–Cox procedure was used to determine the best functional form of the demand equations.

A Hausman test was employed in its instrumental variable form, first to test the exogeneity of characteristic prices when demand is estimated with price as a regressor and then to test the exogeneity of quantity when the inverse demand is estimated. For the locational amenities—lakeside proximity (NLAK), distance from busy commercial area (DSS) and distance from an electric power plant (DPP)—there is evidence that demands can be estimated using OLS, assuming prices are exogenous. For access to a major interstate highway (NFF), demand can be estimated by OLS, assuming quantities are exogenous. For the structural characteristic, rooms per house (ROOMS), there is strong evidence of simultaneity.

Perhaps the most useful result is that proper specification of demands depends upon the particular housing characteristic and that alternatives to initial assumptions warrant at least some investigation. Caution should be exercised in applying these results to other housing markets since they may be quite sensitive to the instrument used in the exogeneity test and possibly relevant housing characteristics omitted (because of data limitations) from the hedonic and demand equations. Nonetheless, the results illustrate the advantages of using an empirical test along with theoretical arguments concerning the supply of housing characteristics in estimating the demand for housing amenities and the benefits of amenity provision.

ACKNOWLEDGMENTS

We gratefully acknowledge the constructive comments of Douglas Diamond, Jr., Peter Linneman, Rati Ram, and David Spencer. The authors take sole responsibility for any errors.

REFERENCES

Bender, B., Gronberg, T. J., and Hwang, H.-S. "Choice of Functional Form and the Demand for Air Quality." *Rev. Econ. Stat.* 62 (November 1980): 638–643.

Blomquist, G., and Worley, L. "Hedonic Prices, Demands for Urban Housing Amenities, and Benefit Estimates." *J. Urban Econ.* 9 (March 1981): 212–221.

Brown, G. M., Jr., and Pollakowski, H. O. "Economic Value of Shoreline." *Rev. Econ. Stat.* 59 (August 1977): 272–278.

Freeman, A. M., III, "Hedonic Prices, Property Values and Measuring Environmental Benefits: A Survey of the Issues." *Scandinavian J. Econ.* (1979): 154–173.

Goodman, A. C. "Hedonic Prices, Price Indices and Housing Markets." *J. Urban Econ.* 5 (October 1978): 471–484.

Harrison, D., Jr., and Rubinfeld, D. L. "Hedonic Housing Prices and the Demand for Clean Air." J. Environ. Econ. Manag. 5 (March 1978): 81–102.

Hausman, J. A. "Specification Tests in Econometrics." *Econometrica* 46 (November 1978): 1251–1270.

Linneman, P. "An Analysis of the Demand for Residence Site Characteristics." Ph.D. dissertation, University of Chicago, 1977.

Linneman, P. "Some Empirical Results on the Nature of the Hedonic Price Function for the Urban Housing Market." *J. Urban Econ.* 8 (July 1980): 47–68.

Mood, A. M., Graybill, F. C., and Boes, D. C. *Introduction to the Theory of Statistics.* 3 ed. New York: McGraw-Hill, 1974.

Nelson, J. "Residential Choice, Hedonic Prices and the Demand for Urban Air Quality." *J. Urban Econ.* 5 (October 1978): 357–369.

Ridker, R., and Henning, J. "The Determinants of Residential Property Values with Special Reference to Air Pollution." *Rev. Econ. Stat.* 49 (May 1967): 246–257.

Rosen, S. "Hedonic Prices and Implicit Markets." *J. Polit. Econ.* 82 (January–February 1974): 34–55.

Smith, B. "Demand for Housing: A Reexamination of Methodological Issues." Paper presented at the Conference on Urban Economics held June 24–25, 1980, at the University of Chicago, Chicago, Illinois.

Witte, A. D., Sumka, H. J., and Erekson, H. "An Estimate of a Structural Hedonic Price Model of the Housing Market: An Application of Rosen's Theory of Implicit Markets." *Econometrica* 47 (September 1979): 1151–1173.

III

URBAN AMENITY MARKETS

5

View Amenities, Building Heights, and Housing Supply*

ROBERT POLLARD

I. INTRODUCTION

A key assumption in urban land-use models such as those of Alonso (1964), Mills (1967), and Muth (1969) is that the city lies on a featureless plain. Although this assumption leads to simple yet powerful analytical models, it precludes the possibility of explaining the substantial impact of a city's topography on land-use patterns. For example, the city of Chicago lies on an essentially featureless plain; yet it is impossible to explain the pattern of housing prices and density within the city without taking into account the pervasive influence of Lake Michigan. In this chapter, I develop and test an urban land-use model that incorporates topographic features. It assumes that some topographic features, such as lakes or parks, may be regarded as location-specific amenities and that housing units with a view of or accessibility to these amenities provide additional housing services.

Another novel feature of the model developed here is the method by which the supply of housing is measured. In conventional models it is measured by the value of output per unit of land or the capital–land ratio. In this model the most important determinant of the supply of housing is the height of buildings. The two measures are actually quite similar since

* Originally published as "Topographic Amenities, Building Height, and The Supply of Urban Housing." *Reg. Science Urban Econ.* 10(1980, 181–199). Elsevier-North Holland Publishing Company, New York. Reprinted with permission.

THE ECONOMICS OF
URBAN AMENITIES

ISBN 0-12-214840-1

variations in the value of output per unit of land, or the capital–land ratio, are usually achieved by variations in building height.

The use of building height as a direct measure of housing output offers a number of advantages. Since building height is directly observable, all pitfalls associated with the measurement of the physical stock of housing are avoided. In addition, the inclusion of building height as a determinant of housing output allows one to satisfactorily treat the value of visual amentities.

In the next section a housing supply model is developed in which housing producers respond to housing prices that are determined not only by accessibility to the Central Business District (CBD) but by accessibility to and views of location-specific amenities. A production function is employed that incorporates the effect of building height on the productivity of inputs in producing housing. Assuming profit maximization by competitive housing producers yields equilibrium conditions for the optimal height of buildings. The equilibrium conditions are used to analyze the effects of amenities on the optimal height of buildings.

In the following section the model is applied to estimate the effect of the Lake Michigan amenity on housing in the city of Chicago. Parameters of the model are estimated and discussed and the predictions of the model concerning building height are compared with a direct measure of building height.

In the final section the quantitative importance of amenities on housing expenditures and the supply of housing is discussed.

II. THE BASIC MODEL

The predominant uses of urban land are for residential, industrial, or commercial purposes. According to traditional theory, competitive bidding among potential users will assure that land is allocated to the activity commanding the highest rent. The model developed here deals only with residential land use; therefore it implicitly assumes that the most productive use of all land considered is in housing.

The underlying purpose of the model to be developed is to generate empirically testable propositions concerning the effects of amenities on residential building heights. Since it would be necessary to eventually adopt specific functional forms in order to derive empirically testable propositions, these specific forms will be introduced directly into the theoretical derivation of the model.

A. The Price of Housing Services

Since the principal focus of the chapter is on the supply of housing, a formal model of the demand for housing will not be developed. Instead, a price function for housing will be assumed that is somewhat more specific, though entirely consistent with those common in the literature.

In conventional models, where all employment takes place in the CBD, the price of a unit of housing services depends only on the distance to the CBD k, that is, $P = P(k)$. In this present study it will be assumed that individuals are willing to pay not only for accessibility to the CBD but also for accessability to and a view of a location-specific amenity, that is, $P = P(k, s, z, v)$, where s is the distance of a housing unit from a location-specific amenity; z is the floor of a particular housing unit, designed to capture the idea that the higher the floor the better the view afforded; and v is the zero–one variable indicating the absence or presence of a view of an amenity from the housing unit.

The specific housing price function employed in this model is:[1]

$$P = P_0^* \exp(-\delta_k k - \delta_s s + \gamma v) Z^\alpha \qquad \delta_k, \delta_s, \gamma, \alpha > 0. \qquad (5.1)$$

This formulation assumes that the price of a unit of housing services declines exponentially with distance from the CBD and amenity.[2] The remaining terms in the price equation are intended to capture the effects of views. The breadth of view[3] increases with the height of a housing unit. A constant elasticity α will be assumed between the price of housing and the floor of the unit. In addition to breadth of view, housing units that provide a view of the amenity are assumed to command a premium of γ per cent.

B. The Production Function for Housing

In conventional models housing services are produced by structures that combine land and nonland inputs. The intensity of factor use in producing housing is measured by the ratio of nonland to land inputs. In actuality, most of the variation in factor intensity is accomplished by variation

---

[1] Equation (5.1) implies that as distance from the amenity s becomes large, the price of housing services approaches zero. A more precise formulation would be

$$P = P_0^* \exp[-\delta_k k - \delta_s \max(s, s_0) + \gamma v]Z^\alpha, \qquad (5.1')$$

where s_0 defines the maximum distance over which accessability to the amenity influences the price of housing. Empirical results suggest that the influence of the amenity extends over most of the sample area under consideration; therefore the use of Eq. (5.1) may be justified.

[2] Muth (1969, pp. 71–72) derives the necessary conditions for an exponentially declining rent gradient.

[3] Breadth of view, caused here, refers to the scope of the view, not its composition.

in the height of buildings, although height per se is not explicitly treated in these models. Since the primary concern of this chapter is the height of buildings, a production function will be employed that treats height explicitly.

The output of housing services Q measured in units of housing services per floor, is a function $Q = Q(L, N, H)$ of the land input L, the nonland input N, and the height of buildings H. The marginal products of land and nonland inputs are assumed positive; the marginal product of height is discussed later. It will simplify matters, with only a slight loss in generality, to assume that the height component of the production function is separable from the land and nonland components. The production function may then be written $Q = G(L, N) F(H)$. Given the possibility of replicating buildings, it seems reasonable to further simplify matters by assuming constant returns to scale for land and nonland inputs for buildings of a given height. These modifications permit the production function to be expressed as a function of the ratio of nonland to land inputs n, or $Q = Lg(n)F(H)$. The assumption of constant returns to scale implies that $g'(n) > 0$ and $g''(n) < 0$. The specification of the height component of this production function requires a further explanation.

An apparent feature of multistory buildings is that the construction costs per square foot of living space increase with height. This is plainly illustrated in the case of a two-story building. The addition of a second story requires a stairway that reduces living space on both floors as well as entails a capital expenditure. For high-rise buildings the incremental cost of additional floors is not so clear. Foundation costs and window–wall costs do not increase in proportion to the number of floors. The heterogeneity of buildings and the rapid technological change in construction techniques makes it difficult to provide firm estimates. The available evidence suggests that after the few initial floors, additional floors can be added at constant cost.[4] However, the cost of living space increases with the number of floors because additional space must be devoted to structural supports, elevator shafts, and mechanical equipment.[5]

To incorporate these properties into the production function, the height component will be written as $H^{-\beta}$, where β is an elasticity (assumed constant) that measures the rate of change of the proportion of usable floor area with respect to changes in the height of buildings. Using these assumptions, the complete production function can now be written as

$$Q = g(n)LH^{-\beta}. \tag{5.2}$$

[4] In a computer simulation study of a hypothetical high-rise building, Thompsen (1966, p. 50) found that construction costs per floor remained almost constant.
[5] Hoch (1969, p. 90)

C. The Supply of Housing

Using Eq. (5.2) a supply function for housing services can now be derived by considering the production decision of an entrepreneur in a competitive housing market. At any location the entrepreneur must decide how tall a building to construct, its floor area, and the level of non-land inputs per floor. The total profit π^* from a building is, of course, equal to total revenue less total cost. The total revenue from a building can be found by summing the revenue for each floor. (It will simplify matters to treat building height as a continuous variable so that the summation process can be done by integration.) The revenue function is then given by

$$R = \int_0^H P(k,s,z,v) \cdot Q(L,N,H)\, dz.$$

Substituting in the specific functional forms for P and Q given by Eqs. (5.1) and (5.2) into Eq. (5.3) yields

$$R = \int_0^H P_0^* \exp(-\delta_k k - \delta_s s + \gamma v)\, Z^\alpha g(n) L H^{-\beta}\, dz$$

$$= P_0 \exp(-\delta_k k - \delta_s s + \gamma v)\, Z^\alpha g(n) L H^{1+\alpha-\beta}, \tag{5.3}$$

where $P_0 = (1 + \alpha)^{-1} P_0^*$. The total cost for a building at any location is the sum of the land and nonland costs. Land is assumed to sell for r per unit. The price of nonland inputs P_N is assumed constant throughout the city and equal to unity. The profit from a building can then be written as

$$\pi^* = P_0 \exp(-\delta_k k - \delta_s s + \gamma v)\, g(n) L H^{1+\alpha-\beta} - P_N N H - rL. \tag{5.4}$$

As will be noted from Eq. (5.4), total profits are directly proportional to the land area used in the building; thus the optimal area of a building is indeterminant. However, the primary concern here is with the height of buildings, and this does not require a determination of building area. By recasting the profit function in terms of profits per unit of land π, it is possible to solve for the optimal level of land and nonland per floor:

$$\pi = \pi^*/L = P_0 \exp(-\delta_k k - \delta_s s + \gamma v)\, g(n) H^{1+\alpha-\beta} - nH - r. \tag{5.5}$$

The first-order conditions for a maximum to Eq. (5.5) are that,[6]

$$\pi_n = g'(n) P_0 \exp(-\delta_k k - \delta_s s + \gamma v)\, H^{1+\alpha-\beta} - H = 0 \tag{5.6a}$$

$$\pi_H = (1 + \alpha - \beta) P_0 \exp(-\delta_k k - \delta_s s + \gamma v)\, g(n) H^{\alpha-\beta} - n = 0. \tag{5.6b}$$

---

[6] Equation (5.6a) is the first-order condition for optimal investment in nonland inputs per floor. The first term on the left-hand side of Eq. (5.6a) is the marginal revenue product from

The second order condition for a maximum requires that

$$\Delta = (\alpha - \beta)\left[\frac{g''(n)n}{g'(n)} - (\alpha - \beta)\right] > 0.$$

By rearranging this second order condition additional insights into the model are possible. The assumption of constant returns to scale implies that

$$g''(n)n/g'(n) = (\alpha - \beta)/\sigma_{NL}$$

where σ_{NL} is the elasticity of substitution between land and nonland inputs. The second order conditions can then be rewritten

$$\Delta = (\alpha - \beta)^2(\sigma_{NL}^{-1} - 1) > 0.$$

Thus, the second-order condition for a maximum reduces to the condition that the elasticity of subsitution be less than unity.[7]

For the purpose of subsequent manipulations, it will be useful to rearrange the first-order conditions. First, by dividing the left- and right-hand sides of Eq. (5.6a) by the left- and right-hand sides of Eq. (5.6b) and then rearranging terms, Eq. (5.7a) can be obtained,

$$g'(n)n/g(n) = 1 + \alpha - \beta. \tag{5.7a}$$

Second, by solving Eq. (5.6b) for H, Eq. (5.7b) can be obtained,

$$H = [(1 + \alpha - \beta)P_0 \exp(-\delta_k k - \delta_s s + \gamma v)\,[g(n)/n]]^{-1/(\alpha-\beta)}. \tag{5.7b}$$

An idea of the numerical value of the elasticity of the proportion of hous-

---

adding a unit of nonland input to each floor. That is, it is the marginal product of nonland input per floor, $g'(n)H^{-\beta}$ times the number of floors H, times the average price per floor,

$$P_0 \exp[-\delta_k k - \delta_s s + \gamma v]H^\alpha.$$

The second term is the marginal cost of adding nonland inputs; it is the price of a unit of nonland inputs (taken to be unity) times the number of floors H.

Similarly, Eq. (5.6b) provides the first-order conditions for the optimal number of floors. The first term on the left-hand side is the marginal revenue product of adding a story, holding constant nonland inputs per floor. This consists of two parts. The first is the revenue received on the extra story from adding an additional story with $g(n)H^{-\beta}$ units of housing services that can be rented at a price

$$P_0^* \exp[-\delta_k k - \delta_s s + \gamma v]H^\alpha = (1 + \alpha)P_0 \exp[-\delta_k k - \delta_s s + \gamma v]H^\alpha.$$

The second is the loss of revenue from the first H stories given by the change in services per floor $-\beta g(n)H^{-\beta-1}$, times the number of floors H, times the average price per floor,

$$P_0^* \exp[-\delta_k k - \delta_s s + \gamma v]H^\alpha.$$

The second term is the marginal cost of an additional floor n.

[7] The elasticity of substitution defined previously differs slightly from conventional measures. It is the elasticity between land and nonland inputs along a given floor of housing rather than for housing in general.

ing space that is usable with respect to height β can be obtained from the formula for factor shares. The factor share accruing to land can be expressed as:

$$1 - \frac{HN}{R} = 1 - \frac{Hn}{P_0 \exp(-\delta_k k - \delta_s s) \, g(n) \, H^{1+\alpha-\beta}}$$

$$= 1 - \frac{1}{P_0 \exp(-\delta_k k - \delta_s s) \, [g(n)/n] H^{\alpha-\beta}} = \beta - \alpha. \quad (5.8)$$

Assuming for example, a factor share for land of 10% and, as estimated results presented later will suggest, a value of .07 for α, the implied value for β is .17.

D. Implications of the Model

The implications of the model for building height may be demonstrated by examining the properties of the equilibrium conditions expressed in Eqs. (5.7a) and (5.7b). In particular, height gradients, height differentials due to a view, and height differentials due to a view of an amenity will be considered.

1. Height Gradients for Housing

The height gradient for housing structures may be found by taking the differential of Eq. (5.7b).

$$dH/H = (\alpha-\beta)^{-1}(\delta_k \, dk + \delta_s \, ds). \quad (5.9)$$

Height gradients are seen to be proportional to price gradients. Since price gradients are assumed to be exponentially declining with distance from the CBD, this result is analogous to the standard result that the value of output per unit of land declines exponentially with distance from the CBD. Note that the factor of proportionality between height and price gradients depends on $\alpha - \beta$, a term that reflects the marginal revenue and marginal cost of an additional floor.

In this formulation, the presence of a view of the amenity has no influence on height gradients. This result is a consequence of the particular functional form assumed and will be tested later.

2. Height Differentials due to View Premia

In this model the influence of a view on the price of housing services is captured in two separate terms: (a) α, the elasticity of the price of housing services with respect to height captures the effect of the breadth of view; and (b) γ is the premium offered for a view of a specific amenity regardless

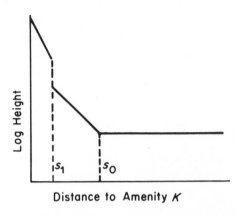

Log Height

s_1 s_0

Distance to Amenity K

FIGURE 5.1. Building heights as a function of distance to a view amenity.

of height. The presence of either premium increases the optimal height of buildings.

The effect of the height premium on optimal building height can be demonstrated by differentiating Eq. (5.7a) with respect to α:[8]

$$dH/d\alpha = [-H/(\alpha - \beta)]$$
$$\{\log H + (1 + \alpha - \beta)^{-1} + [(\alpha - \beta)/n](dn/d\alpha)\} > 0. \quad (5.10)$$

Equation (5.7b) implies that buildings with a view of the amenity will be

$$\exp \gamma^{-1/(\alpha-\beta)} = \exp[-\gamma/(\alpha - \beta)] \quad (5.11)$$

times as tall as those without such a view.

3. The Pattern of Building Heights

The combined effects of accessability to and a view of an amenity can be illustrated by examining building heights along a street that emanates from a location specific amenity. See Figure 5.1.

The tallest buildings are those located adjacent to and offering a view of the amenity. Moving away from the amenity, building heights decline at a rate of $\delta_{s/(\alpha-\beta)}$. At the point designated s_1, view of the amenity is no longer possible, and there is a discrete decline in building height of $(\exp[-\delta/(\alpha - \beta)] - 1)$ percent. Buildings continue to decline at a rate of $\delta_{s/(\alpha-\beta)}$ until the point at which accessability to the amenity ceases to exert any influence on the price of housing. Beyond this point, designated s_0, the height gradient is flat.

[8]

$$\frac{dn}{d\alpha} = \left(\frac{g''(n)n}{g(n)} + \frac{g'(n)}{g(n)} - \left[\frac{g'(n)}{g(n)}\right]^2 n\right)^{-1} = \frac{n(\alpha - \beta)}{(1 + \alpha - \beta)\Delta} < 0.$$

III. EMPIRICAL RESULTS

The model just presented yields explicit predictions about the relation of price and height gradients for housing and price and height differentials due to a view of an amenity. In this section these parameters are estimated using data collected from the city of Chicago, and the predictions of the model are tested.

A. The Sample

The sample of apartments and buildings that provide the data for this paper was selected from rental vacancies advertised in Chicago newspapers during the months of April and May of 1975. A total of 232 apartments in 154 buildings were used for the sample.[9] The sample area was bounded on the south by the Loop, on the east by Lake Michigan, and on the north by the city boundary with Evanston. The sample area was extended westward until single family homes predominated.

Each building in the sample was visited and data were collected on the height and age of the building. In addition, the distances to the Loop, Lake Michigan, and Lincoln Park were recorded. For each apartment, the monthly rent and size were recorded as well as whether it has a view of the Loop or Lake Michigan. In some cases, air-conditioning, heat, utilities, and carpeting were included in the rent, whereas in others, they were not. It was necessary therefore to adjust rents for the services included.[10]

B. Basic Results

Equation (5.1) specifies how the price of a unit of housing services is affected by accessibility to the CBD and accessibility to and a view of amenities. The parameters of this price equation are the basis for the predicted height gradients in Eq. (5.9) and the predicted height differentials due to a view in Eq. (5.11). Before this price equation can be estimated, a number of modifications are necessary. In particular, the empirical counterpart of a unit of housing services must be defined, and consideration must be given to the presence of multiple amenities.

[9] There was a maximum of four observations per building.

[10] The cost of carpeting was estimated to be 1¢ per square foot per month. The following costs in terms of square foot per month were determined on the basis of data provided by Commonwealth Edison: heat 2¢, utilities 2¢, air conditioning ½¢.

The observations described above consist of apartment rents, which are, of course, the product of price times quantity of housing services. To determine the price of housing services, it is necessary, therefore, to have a measure of the quantity of housing services provided by an apartment.

The simplest assumption that could be made is that the quantity of housing services yielded by an apartment is proportional to its area, that is, $Q_{APT} = k(SQFT)$. However, upon reflection this seems to be an over-simplification. Apartments are not just living space. Every apartment, regardless of size, must contain a kitchen and bathroom that produce services in addition to mere living space. Therefore, it seems reasonable to assume for apartments as a whole that the quantity of housing services increases less than in proportion to the area of the apartment. To incorporate this assumption, the quantity of housing services flowing from an apartment may be written as $Q_{APT} = k(SQFT)^{\nu}$, where $\nu < 1$ is the elasticity of housing services with respect to apartment size.

Another factor to be considered is that buildings are capital goods whose flow of services declines over time. Therefore, it is necessary to adjust the flow of services emanating from an apartment for the age of the structure. One of the many possible assumptions is that buildings depreciate at a constant percentage per year.[11] The quantity of housing services yielded by an apartment may now be written as

$$Q_{APT} = k(SQFT)^{\nu}e^{-\rho(\text{age})}. \qquad (5.12)$$

Having defined the measure of housing services, it is necessary now to specify how the presence of multiple amenities will affect its price. The dominant amenity in the sample area is, of course, Lake Michigan. However, casual empiricism suggests that two other important amenities are a view of the Loop and accessibility to Lincoln Park, an extensive city facility located along the lakefront. Since the effects of amenities are captured in the exponential terms of the price equation, it can be easily modified to account for additional amenities.[12]

$$P = P_0 Z^{\alpha} e^A, \qquad (5.13)$$

where $A = -\delta_k \text{Dist-Loop} - \delta_s \text{Dist-Lake} + \delta_1 \text{Loopview} + \delta_2 \text{Lakeview} + \delta_3 \text{LincPark}$

The rent of any apartment may now be written as the product of Eqs.

[11] Several other specifications of the age term were considered, but the goodness-of-fit test suggests that this form is the most appropriate.

[12] There is a slight asymmetry in the treatment of the Lincoln Park amenity. The form of the data made it impossible to distinguish those apartments with a view of the park from those without, therefore a single variable was defined. Apartments located within one block of the park were defined as having access.

(5.12) and (5.13). The resulting equation (in log form) is

$$\log R = \log(PQ) = C - \delta_k\text{Dist-Loop} - \delta_s\text{Dist-Lake}$$
$$+ \delta_1\text{Loopview} + \delta_2\text{Lakeview} + \delta_3\text{LincPark}$$
$$+ \rho_R(\text{Age}) + \alpha \log \text{FLOOR} + \nu \log \text{SQFT}. \qquad (5.14)$$

Using the modified price Eq. (5.13), the equation for building height [Eqs. (5.10) and (5.11)] may be written (in log form)

$$\log H = C - \delta_k{}^H\text{Dist-Loop} - \delta_s{}^H\text{Dist-Lake} + \gamma_1{}^H\text{Loopview}$$
$$+ \gamma_2{}^H\text{Lakeview} + \gamma_3{}^H\text{LincPark} + \rho_H\text{Age} \qquad (5.15)$$

where

$$\delta_i{}^H = \frac{\delta_i}{\alpha - \beta} \quad \text{and} \quad \gamma_i{}^H = \frac{\gamma_i}{\alpha - \beta}.$$

These equations were estimated by ordinary least squares.

The estimated coefficients of the rent regression are shown on the left side of Table 5.1. The coefficients of the Dist-Loop and Dist-Lake terms are estimates of the two price gradients. The coefficients imply that rents decline about 4% per mile with distance from the Loop and 8.5% per mile with distance from the lake.

The coefficients of the Loopview and Lakeview terms, δ_1 and δ_2, imply that a view of the Loop increases rents by 3% and a view of the lake increases rents by 7%. However, the Loopview coefficient is not significant at the 5% level. The coefficient of the Lincoln Part term implies that accessibility to the park increases rents by 5%.

The coefficient of the floor variable is an estimate of α, the elasticity of the premium paid for height. The results imply that a 1% increase in the floor of an apartment leads to an increase in rent of about 7%. For example, moving from the twentieth to the twenty-first floor is an increase in height of 5%; rents increase, therefore, by $.07 \times .05 = .0035\%$, or, using the mean monthly rent in the sample—$257.50, about 90¢ a month.

The remaining coefficients in the rent regression are concerned with the quantity of housing services yielded by an apartment. The coefficient of the SQFT term is an estimate of the elasticity of the flow of housing services with respect to the area of an apartment. As assumed, it has an estimated value substantially smaller than unity. The coefficient of the age term, although significant, is only .3%, suggesting that the decline in services flowing from an apartment takes place very slowly.

The results of the height regression appear on the right side of the Table 5.1. The building height gradients from the Loop and lake, $\delta_1{}^H$ and $\delta_2{}^H$ are estimated to be 12% and 85%, respectively. The coefficients of the Loopview and Lakeview terms imply that buildings with a view of the

TABLE 5.1
Rent and Height Regressions

Variable	Rent equation		Height equation	
	Coefficient	t Statistic	Coefficient	t Statistic
DIST-LOOP	−.038	(−11.2)	−.123	(−7.8)
DIST-LAKE	−.085	(−2.2)	−.854	(−5.2)
LOOPVIEW	.029	(0.8)	.581	(4.3)
LAKEVIEW	.070	(2.7)	.565	(5.1)
LINC.PARK	.049	(2.4)	.409	(4.0)
Age	−.0029	(−4.2)	−.011	(−4.1)
log FLOOR	.067	(6.2)		
log SQFT	.616	(18.7)		
CONSTANT	1.590	(7.1)	3.063	(19.1)
R^2	.858		.772	
N	232		154	

Loop are $e^{.58} = 1.79$ times and those with a view of the lake are $e^{.57} = 1.77$ times as tall as those without a view. Buildings with accessibility to Lincoln Park are $e^{.41} = 1.51$ times as tall as those lacking accessibility.[13]

C. A Test of the Model

Height gradients and view differentials have been directly estimated in the height regressions. In addition, the model shows how these gradients and differentials can be inferred from the price equation. Hence a test of the predictive ability of the model is provided by a comparison of the height gradients and view differentials predicted by the model with those directly estimated in the height regression. Due to the nonlinearity of the

[13] The residuals of the rent and height regressions were examined for evidence of violations of the basic assumptions of the linear regression model. A Goldfield–Quandt test, with observations ordered according to distance to the Loop, did not provide evidence for a rejection of the homoscedasticity assumption in either the rent or height regressions. A test for spatial autocorrelation along lines suggested by Cliff and Ord (1972) revealed no evidence of autocorrelation in the height regression, but revealed the presence of a slight positive autocorrelation in the rent regression. This positive autocorrelation may be attributable to the fact that in some instances there were multiple rent observations from a single building. A test for correlation of the residuals of the rent and height regression did not provide evidence for a rejection of the independence assumption.

Tests were also performed on the specification of the model. A test to determine the extent of the lake's influence on building heights and rents supported the assumption that the effect of the lake extends over the entire sample area. An interaction term was included to investigate the possibility of differential rent and height gradients in the presence of a view. The interaction terms were not statistically significant nor did their inclusion significantly increase the explanatory power of the mode. Finally, alternative functional forms, including the linear and logarithmic were considered for the Loop and lake gradients. Using the residual sum of squares as a measure of goodness-of-fit, they proved inferior to the exponential formulation.

estimating equation, large-sample statistical theory must be used to provide an appropriate test. The test statistic is derived in Appendix B.

The Z statistic, which provides the basis for the test of the gradients and differentials predicted by the model with those directly estimated, includes the parameter β. Since there is a considerable range in the estimates of the factor share of land, and consequently the value of β, the test statistic is computed for values of β corresponding to a factor share for land of 10, 15, and 25%.[14] Test results appear in Table 5.2.

For an assumed factor share for land of 10%, the assumption of equality can be rejected only for the Loop gradient at the 5% confidence level. If the share of land is 15%, only the assumption of the equality of the Lakeview differential can be maintained. If the share of land is as large as 25%, the assumption of equality can be rejected in all instances. Consequently the test for the equality of the measured and predicted height gradients and view differentials yields inconclusive results. With the exception of the height gradient from the Loop, the test hinges upon the actual factor share of land in housing, a magnitude that unfortunately is not known with a sufficient degree of certainty.

IV. THE IMPORTANCE OF TOPOGRAPHIC AMENITIES

Using the regression results presented, it is possible to make some statements about the quantitative importance of topographic amenities. Specifically, the effects of Lake Michigan on housing prices and expenditures and on the supply of housing will be considered.

The effects of amenities on housing prices can be illustrated by considering two housing units that are identical except for their amenity components.

Consider two apartment units that are 16 years old and contain 658 sq. ft. of living area—the mean values in the sample. Both units are located 8 miles from the Loop. The first unit is located on the first floor of an apartment located 1 mile from the lake and consequently does not provide a lake view. It has a predicted monthly rent of $173. A similar apartment with a lakeview, located on the tenth floor of a lakefront building, has a predicted monthly rent of $235.

In this example the residents of the lakefront apartment are paying $62 per month or 26% of their housing expenditure for consumption of ameni-

[14] Muth (1971, p. 25) estimates the factor share of land to be 10%, whereas Smith (1976, p. 403) estimates the share to be 15–20%, and Mills (1972, p. 110) cites evidence placing the share between 10 and 25%.

TABLE 5.2
Tests for Equality of Height Gradients and Differentials

Hypothesis tested	Assumed value for land's share	Value predicted by model	Value directly measured	Difference of predicted and measured	Variance of difference	Z statistic
Equality of height gradients from Loop	.10	−.380		−.257	.00084	−13.1
	.15	−.253	−.123	−.130	.000071	−15.4
	.25	−.152		−.029	.000005	−13.0
Equality of height gradient from lake	.10	−.850		.004	.0367	0.02
	.15	−.566	−.854	.288	.0060	3.7
	.25	−.340		.514	.0023	10.7
Equality of height differential due to Loopview	.10	.290		−.291	.0052	−1.2
	.15	.193	.581	−.388	.0127	3.4
	.25	.116		−.465	.00022	31.7
Equality of height differential due to lakeview	.10	.700		.135	.022	0.91
	.15	.467	.565	−.098	.0036	−1.6
	.25	.280		−.285	.00011	−27.2
Equality of height differential due to Lincoln Park	.10	.490		.081	.012	0.74
	.15	.327	.409	−.082	.0014	−2.19
	.25	.196		−.213	.00031	−12.1

ties. Assuming families spend 20% of their income on housing, this expenditure for amenities represents 6% of annual income. Since there are numerous buildings along the lake in excess of 50 stories, this example cannot be regarded as extreme.

The effect of amenities on the supply of housing—as measured by building height—can be demonstrated by considering building heights predicted by the height regression.

At the Loop, buildings without a view of the Loop or lake have a predicted height of 17 floors, those with a view of the Loop or the lake have a predicted height of 30 floors, and those with a view of both Loop and lake have a predicted height of 54 floors. Eight miles from the Loop, a lakefront building without a view has a predicted height of 6 floors. A building at the same location with a lakeview has a predicted height of 11 floors. A building equidistant from the Loop but 1 mile from the lake has a predicted height of only 3 floors. Consequently, the presence of either a lakeview or accessability to the lake leads to a doubling of the predicted height of buildings. These results for Lake Michigan are indicative of the substantial impact of topographic amenities on the height of buildings, the supply of housing, and the structure of cities.

APPENDIX A. VARIABLE DEFINITIONS AND SAMPLE STATISTICS

Variable		Mean	SD	Minimum	Maximum
	RENT SAMPLE				
RENT—	Adjusted monthly apartment rent in dollars	257.50	84.3	124	481
DIST-LOOP—	Distance to Loop in miles	5.2	2.9	1.0	10.9
DIST-LAKE—	Distance to lake in miles	.41	.26	0	1.6
SQFT—	Size of apartment in square feet	656.8	189.3	300	1300
FLOOR—	Floor of apartment	10.5	11.6	1	65
AGE—	Age of building in years	16.4	14.6	1	55
LAKEVIEW—	Dummy variable for apartments with a view of lake	.147		0	1
LOOPVIEW—	Dummy variable for apartments with a view of Loop	.07		0	1
LINC-PARK—	Dummy variable for apartments with accessibility to Lincoln Park	.26		0	1
	HEIGHT SAMPLE				
HEIGHT—	Height of building in floors	12.5	13.0	1	70

Appendix A. (*continued*)

Variable		Mean	SD	Minimum	Maximum
DIST-LOOP—	Distance to Loop in miles	5.2	3.0	1.0	10.9
DIST-LAKE—	Distance to lake in miles	.45	.28	0	1.6
	HEIGHT SAMPLE				
AGE—	Age of building in years	20.1	15.3	1	55
LAKEVIEW—	Dummy variable for buildings with a view of the lake	.26		0	1
LOOPVIEW—	Dummy variable for buildings with a view of the Loop	.15		0	1
LINC-PARK—	Dummy variable for buildings with accessibility to Lincoln Park	.20		0	1

APPENDIX B

The model predicts that height gradients δ_i^H will be equal to $\delta i/(\alpha - \beta)$ and that height differentials due to a view γ_i^H will be equal to $\gamma i/(\alpha - \beta)$. The estimated coefficients of the height gradients $\hat{\delta}_i^H$ and height differentials due to a view $\hat{\gamma}_i^H$ provide unbiased estimates of the actual height gradients and differentials due to a view. Similarly, $\hat{\delta}_i$, $\hat{\gamma}_i$, and $\hat{\alpha}$ provide unbiased estimates of their respective parameters. β is determined from the factor share of land in the value of housing. Owing to the nonlinearity of the functions $\hat{\delta}_i/(\hat{\alpha} - \beta)$ and $\hat{\gamma}_i/(\hat{\alpha} - \beta)$, large sample theory will be used to create a test.[15]

Here, $\hat{\delta}_i/(\hat{\alpha} - \beta)$ can be said to have a limiting normal distribution with mean $\delta_i/(\alpha - \beta)$ and variance

$$\left(\frac{\delta_i}{\alpha - \beta}\right)^2 \left[\frac{\sigma_{\delta_i}}{\delta_i} - 2\rho \left(\frac{\sigma_{(\alpha-\beta)}}{\alpha - \beta}\right)\left(\frac{\sigma_{\delta_i}}{\delta_i}\right) + \left(\frac{\sigma_{(\alpha-\beta)}}{\alpha - \beta}\right)\right]$$

where σ denotes the standard errors and ρ is the correlation coefficient between δ_i and α.[16]

The hypothesis of the equality of the height gradients predicted by the model with those directly measured may now be written

$$\delta_i/(\alpha - \beta) - \delta_i^H = 0. \tag{5.B1}$$

Since $\hat{\delta}_i/(\hat{\alpha} - \beta)$ and $\hat{\delta}_i^H$ are asymptotically normally distributed, the test

---

[15] The test statistic will be derived for the case of height gradients; the statistic for height differential due to a view is identical.

[16] Theil (1971, pp. 372–384, especially Problem 3–6).

statistic will be

$$Z = \frac{\hat{\delta}_i/(\hat{\alpha} - \beta) - \hat{\delta}_i{}^H}{\text{var}[\hat{\delta}_i/(\hat{\alpha} - \beta) - \hat{\delta}_i{}^H]}. \tag{5.B2}$$

Assuming a value for β, the coefficients of the rent and height regressions in Table 5.1 provide all the information necessary to compute the numerator. Calculation of the denominator is slightly more complicated.

The variance of the difference in the gradients may be written as

$$\text{var}[\hat{\delta}_i/(\hat{\alpha} - \beta)] + \text{var}(\hat{\delta}_i{}^H) - 2 \text{ cov}[\hat{\delta}_i/(\hat{\alpha} - \beta), \hat{\delta}_k{}^H].$$

The variance of $\hat{\delta}_i/(\alpha - \beta)$ has been defined above, and the variance of $\hat{\delta}_k{}^H$ is available directly from the variance–covariance matrix in Appendix C. Owing to the unequal sample sizes, the covariance of $\hat{\delta}_i/(\hat{\alpha} - \beta)$ and $\hat{\delta}_i{}^H$ is not easily estimated. As an alternative, the covariance is assumed to take on its maximum value, even though this may lead to an underestimate of the true variance. When $\hat{\delta}_i/(\hat{\alpha} - \beta)$ and $\hat{\delta}_i{}^H$ are perfectly correlated, their covariance will be a maximum and equal to

$$\{[\text{var}(\hat{\delta}_i/(\alpha - \beta))][\text{var}(\hat{\delta}_i{}^H)]\}^{1/2}.$$

The test statistic may now be written as

$$Z = \frac{\hat{\delta}_i/(\alpha - \beta) - \hat{\delta}_i{}^H}{\{\text{var}[\hat{\delta}_i/(\alpha - \beta)] + \text{var } \hat{\delta}_i{}^H - 2[\text{var}(\hat{\delta}_i{}^H/((\alpha - \beta))][\text{var}(\hat{\delta}_i{}^H)]\}^{1/2}} \tag{5.B3}$$

APPENDIX C. VARIANCE–COVARIANCE MATRICES

Rent Regression (×10⁻³)

$$\text{Rent Regression} \ (\times 10^{-3})$$

	DIST-LOOP	DIST-LAKE	LOOPVIEW	LAKEVIEW	LINCPARK	FLOOR	AGE	SQFT
DIST-LOOP	.0114							
DIST-LAKE	.0538	1.46						
LOOPVIEW	-.00648	-.0542	1.42					
LAKEVIEW	-.00356	.0478	.234	.702				
LINCPARK	.000632	.0130	.0843	.124	.427			
FLOOR	.0123	.161	-.135	-.0491	.0426	.120		
AGE	.00309	.00422	.0208	.0227	.00924	.0350	-.0830	
SQFT	.0171	-.239	-.173	-.128	.0737	.0154	.0499	1.07

Height Regression (×10⁻³)

$$\text{Height Regression} \ (\times 10^{-3})$$

	DIST-LOOP	DIST-LAKE	LOOPVIEW	LAKEVIEW	LINCPARK	FLOOR	AGE	SQFT
DIST-LOOP	.246							
DIST-LAKE	1.29	26.7						
LOOPVIEW	.828	4.34	18.5					
LAKEVIEW	.0900	.245	6.81	12.2				
LINCPARK	.348	2.40	3.31	3.88	10.4			
AGE	.00873	.129	.0375	.0523	.00523	.00773		

REFERENCES

Alonso, W. A. *Location and land use*. Cambridge, Mass.: Harvard University Press, 1964.

Cliff, A. D., and Ord, J. K. "Testing for spatial autocorrelation among regression residuals." *Geograph. Analy.* 4, (July 1972) 267–284.

Hoch, I. "The three-dimensional city." In *In the quality of the urban environment*, edited by Harvey S. Perloff. Baltimore, Md.: Johns Hopkins Press, 1969.

Mills, E. S. "An aggregative model of resource allocation in a metropolitan area." *Am. Econ. Rev.* 57 (May 1967) 197–210.

Mills, E. S. *Studies in the structure of the urban economy*. Baltimore, Md.: Johns Hopkins Press, 1972.

Muth, R. F. *Cities and housing*. Chicago, Ill.: University of Chicago Press, 1969.

Muth, R. F. "The derived demand for urban residential land." *Urban Stud.* 8 (Oct. 1971) 234–253.

Smith, B. "The supply of housing." *Quart. J. Econ.* 90 (Aug. 1976) 389–405.

Theil, H. T. *Principles of econometrics*. New York: Wiley, 1971.

Thompsen, C. "How high to rise." *Appraisal J.* 12 (Oct. 1966) 386–391.

6

The Costs of Urban Expressway Noise[1]

ROGER J. VAUGHAN   LARRY E. HUCKINS

Unwanted sound, or noise, has been a disamenity in urban areas for as long as cities themselves have existed. This problem has been of sufficient magnitude to have provoked attempts to control and limit it directly. In ancient Rome, imperial edict forbade the riding of chariots through residential districts at night; in Chaucer's London, street vendors were prevented from hawking their wares after dark; and in New York, an ordinance in 1930 forbade junkmen to use bells weighing more than 6 oz. For the most part, however, unwanted sound has been accepted as one of the costs of city life. Moreover, it is likely that land prices and location patterns have adjusted to the presence of persistent noise.

The industrial revolution has greatly extended man's capacity to make noise and the concentration of a large proportion of the population in urban areas has increased what we here will call the *nuisance value* of noise. A late 1960s Federal Housing Authority study showed that 60% of all city dwellers are bothered by noise. Following the widespread and well-publicized campaigns against air and water pollution, there has been a rapid increase in public concern about noise. This concern has yet to lead to the kind of extensive economic research that air and water quality have received.[2] However, order-of-magnitude estimates of the cost of

---

[1] The research was completed while the authors were graduate students at the University of Chicago. They are indebted to Professor George Tolley for comments on earlier drafts of this chapter.

[2] Most of the economic research has been on aircraft noise (e.g., Walters, 1974, and McMillan, Reid, and Gillen, 1978). This disamenity is not a particularly pervasive urban problem.

THE ECONOMICS OF
URBAN AMENITIES

noise are essential to the efficient control of externalities in the urban environment. For example, controlling noise damages through changes in the location and construction of urban expressways involves vastly greater costs and benefits than did the tinkling of the junkmen's bells.

Fortunately, one of the methodologies developed by economists to estimate the costs of air pollution is directly applicable to the noise pollution problem. Viewing the ambient noise level as a relatively clearly defined disamenity, we would anticipate that the cost that additional noise imposes on households will be reflected in their equilibrium prices for comparable residences with different noise levels. This chapter applies this methodology of hedonic price analysis to the problem of estimating the costs of urban freeway noise.

We begin with a detailed examination of how noise levels are measured. There is sometimes a tendency for analysts of disamenities and property values to ignore the detailed characteristics of the amenity (or disamenity). This neglect leaves unclear the answer to the question of how the measures they use of good (or bad) are related to ordinary experience and what other amenities and disamenities these may be correlated with.

We define two indices of noisiness that relate the neighborhood noise level both to the background noise level over a period of time and to the level and duration of intermittent noises during that period. The indices are based upon the energy and pressure levels of the background and intermittent noise levels. The former corresponds to the Equivalent Sound Level used by the Environmental Protection Agency. Measures of noise were taken at 233 locations in the city of Chicago, using a weighing network that closely corresponds to that of the human ear.

In the second section a theoretical model of the relationship between property values and the determinants of housing prices, including neighborhood amenities and disamenities, is presented. In Section III, data for property in the city of Chicago are used to estimate this model. The results indicate that an increase in the level of noise in a neighborhood significantly decreases the value of a residential property. The greater the selling price of the house, the greater the cost of a given percentage increase in the noise level. From this an order of magnitude estimate of the total damages due to expressway traffic noise in Chicago is computed. Conclusions and policy implications are discussed in Section IV.

I. THE MEASUREMENT OF NOISE

Air and water pollutants, either in particulate or chemical form, lend themselves fairly easily to measurement, but noise pollution is difficult to measure because it leaves no residuals and is highly unstable over time. In addition, the nuisance value attached to a sound depends upon the tastes of the people who hear the noises. At the present state of the art, an exact measure of the degree of noise pollution is impossible. All that can be hoped for is an index that approximates the relationship between sound and nuisance.

Sound is a pressure wave transmitted through mass and has an intensity of pressure and a frequency of wave.[3] The magnitude of the pressure fluctuations in the air generated by a source (such as a truck or auto) producing vibration (sound waves) is expressed in terms of the amplitude of the pressure fluctuation measured either through the energy level or the pressure level. The basic unit of noise measurement is the decibel (dB), and the sound pressure level (SPL), or noise intensity, is defined as

$$\text{SPL} = 10 \log(W/W_0) \text{ dB} = 20 \log (P/P_0) \text{ dB}, \qquad (6.1)$$

where W is the energy of the sound pressure wave, W_0 is the reference energy level, P is the pressure of the sound wave, and P_0 is the reference pressure level.

The human ear distorts the sound it receives, screening out and responding less to low (and very high) frequency noise. It is possible to duplicate this discrimination by measuring noise through a weighing network. Three such networks are built into soundmeasuring equipment: (a) A, which approximates the human ear and is generally used for measuring sound levels as perceived by human beings; (b) B, which discriminates less than A; and (c) C, which discriminates hardly at all.[4] Other weighing schemes that might eventually provide a better method of evaluating environmental noise are being developed but have not yet become standardized and available in commercial instrumentation. Thus, all objective noise measurements in this study were made through the A network, the A-weighed decibel units being signified dBA.

One difficulty that noise analysts face is that it is not possible to attach a specific nuisance value to sounds. The roar of distant traffic may be more irritating than the sound of wind through the trees, even when both are at the same decibel level and the same frequency. Before such distinctions can be explained and refinements made in measuring them, further improvements in our understanding of the way human beings perceive and respond to sound must be made.

Sound fluctuates considerably over time. A simple measure of the background noise level would not reflect the irritation caused by passing vehicles, trains, or over-flying aircraft. A noise index must include a way

[3] For a more detailed discussion see U.S. Environmental Protection Agency (1974).
[4] This issue is discussed more fully by Peterson and Gross (1967).

of evaluating the whole sound profile of a given locale over a period of time and reducing it to a single number. Because of the logarithmic scale, it is impossible to add noise levels to calculate a representative index. It is necessary to reduce the sound decibel measures to nonlogarithmic form by using either the appropriate energy or pressure levels, weighing the results, and then reconverting the resultant number to decibels. For ease of calculation, environmental noise can be divided into two components: (*a*) background noise, which is relatively stable between rush hours (Caccavari and Schechter 1973), for there is evidence to show that the neighborhood that is relatively noisy by day is also relatively noisy by night (Bonvallet 1950 and 1951); and (*b*) intermittent noise from specific sources (usually related to transportation). Since there was no strong a priori reason for selecting either pressure or energy levels as the best reflector of the irritation value of noise, both levels are used. The definitions of the two noise indices as formulated by the Argonne National Laboratories are

$$\text{NOISE1} = \text{dBA} + 10 \log_{10} \left[1 + \sum_{i=t}^{t_i} (W_i/W - 1) \right] \qquad (6.2)$$

and

$$\text{NOISE} = \text{dBA} + 20 \log_{10} \left[1 + \sum_{i=t}^{t_i} (P_i/P - 1) \right] \qquad (6.3)$$

where W_i, P_i, and t_i are, respectively, the energy, pressure, and time duration of the ith intermittent noise, and W and P are the energy and pressure levels of the background noise level; t is the total length of time over which readings are taken, and dBA is the background noise level in decibels. Since each provides a slightly different weighing for intermittent noise and we had no prior way of choosing between them, both measures were used in the analysis.

The Environmental Protection Agency (1974) has chosen an energy equivalent noise level, called the Equivalent Sound Level, for the purpose of identifying levels of environmental noise. This measure is mathematically equivalent to the energy level index NOISE1.

Noise readings were taken with a portable sound meter at 233 locations in the city of Chicago over 5-min time intervals. The average background sound level was noted, and the level and time duration of the principal intermittent noises were also recorded. From these measurements, the noise indices defined in Eqs. (6.2) and (6.3) were calculated. In addition to the objective measurement, a subjective estimate of the noisiness of the area was made (SURV9), in which a very quiet neighborhood scored 5 and a very noisy one scored 1, with intermediate values indicating intermediate noise levels.

For NOISE1—the index computed from energy levels—the mean

TABLE 6.1
Sound Levels [dBA] and Human Response[a]

Level	Equivalent	Effect
140	Carrier deck jet operation	
130	Hydraulic press at 3 ft	
	Large pneumatic riveter at 4 ft	
120	Jet take-off at 200 ft	
	Discotheque	
110	Jet take-off at 2000 ft	
	Unmuffled motorcycle at 20 ft	
100	Loud power mower at 10 ft	
	New York subway station	
90	Heavy truck at 50 ft	
	Inside automobile in heavy traffic	
80	Pneumatic drill at 50 ft	
	Freight train at 50 ft	
70	Freeway traffic at 50 ft	
	Loud conversation at 3 ft	
60	Air-conditioning unit at 20 ft	
	Average urban residential street	
50	Light auto traffic at 100 ft	
	Living room	
40	Bedroom	
	Library	
30	Soft whisper at 15 ft	
	Broadcasting studio	
20		
10	Just audible	
0	Threshold of hearing	

The Effect column reads (bottom to top): Contribution to hearing damage → Pain.

[a] SOURCE: *Noise Pollution,* U.S. Environmental Protection Agency, Washington, D.C., 1972.

value was 54.1 dBA, with a standard deviation of 4.85, whereas for NOISE—the index computed from pressure ratios—corresponding figures were 53.6 dBA and 4.50. The quietest neighborhood had an index value of 46.0 dBA, and the noisiest, 70.0 dBA. The subjective noise measure, SURV9, had a mean value of 3.07 and a standard deviation of 0.52. Some familiar equivalents to various dBA levels are shown for comparison in Table 6.1.

II. MEASURING THE IMPACT OF A DISAMENITY

Having constructed an index of noise, the next step is to attach a dollar value to the costs associated with each level. One way would be to add up all the individual damages that noise causes—the spoiling of leisure time, the sleeplessness and loss of labor productivity, the damage to buildings, and even the harm done to animals and plants. Such an approach would be conceptually similar to the approach used by Ridker in estimating the damages of air pollution.[5] Three distinct stages are necessary:

1. Identification of all the possible areas where noise might have a harmful effect
2. Determination of the functional relationship between the level of noise and the extent of the damages for each of the areas
3. Placement of a dollar value on the damages

Even where damages are readily apparent, the difficulties inherent in such a detailed approach are obvious. With environmental noise, at least at the current state of knowledge, they are insuperable. Although the major impact of a noisy neighborhood is undoubtedly upon the inhabitants rather than upon the structures, there is little scientific evidence to allow the accurate prediction of the effects of different levels of neighborhood noise on either.[6] After an extensive review of a large number of experiments, Kryter (1970) concluded that there was no significant impact of noise levels below 75 dBA on either health or human operational efficiency.

An alternative approach is to use the value that individuals place on noise by observing market behavior. If a consumer is well informed about the product that he or she purchases, then the price paid for that product must be at least equal to the value placed upon it. Therefore, when a buyer purchases a home, the purchase price reflects the dollar value placed on living in that particular home in that neighborhood.

There have been a few attempts to use property prices to determine the impact of urban noise. In a study of apartment rents in Portland, Oregon, a slight negative influence was discerned, but it was neither consistent nor statistically significant.[7] The sample was small, however, and no detailed noise measures were taken. In a study in Toledo, Ohio, results showed that prices of property near a freeway fell.[8] Both studies were based upon small samples and did not explore very carefully the conceptual problems involved in such measurement. In addition, the quantity of data available for each observation was not great.

Property values are an attractive source of information on the value placed upon urban amenities for two reasons. First, the residential prop-

---

[5] See Ridker (1967).

[6] See Cohen (1968), Jansen (1968), and Teichner, Arees, and Reilly (1963).

[7] U.S. Department of Commerce, Bureau of Public Affairs, 1966.

[8] U.S. Department of Transportation, Bureau of Public Roads, 1967. The actual drop in value was slight, and the study concluded that noise was not a serious issue and that the advantages of accessibility probably outweighed the nuisance value of the noise.

erty market is highly competitive, so prices are not distorted by individual actions. Second, because of the high price of altering consumption, buyers invest time and effort in finding out about the amenities available at a prospective site. Because 9 out of 10 buyers are moving from elsewhere in the area, they can gain a great deal of information at low cost (Zimmer, 1973).

The market price of a house is a "two-dimensional" figure in that it reflects not only the price of housing but also the "quantity" purchased. It represents *total expenditure* on housing by a family and can be derived using the traditional utility maximization procedure.[9] Assume that a consumer's level of welfare depends upon the characteristics or location of housing that he or she consumes H and the quantity of all other goods X. Then,

$$U = U(H, X) \qquad \text{where } U_h, U_x > 0. \tag{6.4}$$

The consumer also faces a budget constraint such that the total expenditure on housing $P(H)$, plus the total expenditure on all other goods X (where X has a unit price) must equal income Y. Therefore,

$$P(H) + X = Y \tag{6.5}$$

Utility is maximized where, for each of the j structural and locational characteristics,

$$U_{H_j} = \lambda(\partial P / \partial H_j) \tag{6.6}$$

$$U_x = \lambda \tag{6.7}$$

where λ is the Lagrange multiplier.

There has been some debate over the choice of a functional form for the hedonic price function. We adopted a common and simple-to-analyze form, the log-linear, after finding that it had the best fit of all simple nonlinear forms.

$$\log(\text{Price}) = C + \sum_j \alpha_j H_j + \mu, \tag{6.8}$$

where μ is a random disturbance term. Equation (6.8) provides a model from which the benefits of quiet (or the damages due to noise) may be approximately estimated and quantified in dollar terms from the data described in the next section.[10]

---

[9] This exposition is similar to that of Rosen (1974).

[10] The specification does not incorporate Rosen's (1974) two-step procedure for estimating the willingness-to-pay function for quiet. This is because data were not available on the shifters of such a function. However, this specification does permit the marginal damage from noise to vary with the level of the noise and the value of the dwelling. Inasmuch as the value of the dwelling is closely related to the permanent income of the household, the error introduced by not including income as a demand shifter may not be serious.

III. THE DAMAGES FROM EXPRESSWAY NOISE

Data concerning attributes of individual residences, locational factors, and attributes of the blocks and census tracts in which the houses were located were assembled to analyze factors influencing property prices in the city of Chicago. The variables used in the empirical analysis are discussed here.

First, data on a large number of residences in the city of Chicago, sold between March 1971 and June 1972, were obtained from the Society of Real Estate Appraisers. These data included information on the selling price of the residence (PRICE), the age of the structure (AGE), the square feet of living area (AREA), the type of structure (BRICK, entered as a dummy variable having the value 1 if the interior had only average or no interior modernization), the number of garages (GARAGE), and the width of the lot (WIDTH). Each of these residences was then located on a large-scale map, and certain locational information was computed— including the weighted travel-time distance to the Central Business District, which was measured as twice the distance to the nearest expressway entrance added to the distance to the CBD from the freeway entrance (DSCBD)—and the direct distance to Lake Michigan in thousands of feet (DISLAK). Other data were collected concerning zoning, land use, and neighborhood characteristics, including the total number of lots on the block (TOTLOT) and the number of visible broken windows (SURV13). A subjective measure of the noisiness of the block was rated on a scale of 1–5 (1 for very noisy and 5 for very quiet). Finally, two objective noise indices were computed from measurements taken at 233 locations. Table 6.2 summarizes this list of variables.

In estimating the model derived in Section II, a standard ordinary least squares regression procedure was used. This approach assumes that the disturbance term in the estimating equation has a zero mean and a constant variance and is successively uncorrelated. Since the problem of heteroscedasticity can be encountered in cross-sectional studies, it is necessary to test the properties of the disturbance term. This was done by plotting the disturbance term U against the estimated value of PRICE. The resulting plot indicated that U had the appropriate properties.

A more serious problem, one that must be faced in all analyses of property prices, is multicollinearity. This arises because of the large number of possible determinants of house values and the complex interactions between them and is compounded by the limitations of the data available. The various measures of building and neighborhood quality are no more than approximations of the actual factors that determine the value placed upon a structure and its neighborhood by the purchaser. Multicollinearity

TABLE 6.2
Description of Data Used for Analysis of the Impact of Noise on Property Values

Name	Description	Source
PRICE	Market price of structure when sold	Real Estate company data
AGE	The age of the structure	Real Estate company data
AREA	Living area in square feet	Real Estate company data
BRICK	Dummy variable having the value 1 if the structure is brick, 0 otherwise	Real Estate company data
MOD	Dummy variable having the value 1 if there was no, or only average, interior modernization; 0 otherwise	Real Estate company data
GARAGE	The number of garages	Real Estate company data
WIDTH	The width of the lot	Real Estate company data
RRSPAC	Millions of square feet in the census tract used for recreational purposes	Location on large-scale map
DISCBD	Weighted distance to the CBD, the weighting reflecting relative travel time	Location on large-scale map
DISLAK	Direct distance to Lake Michigan	Location on large-scale map
TOTLOT	Total number of structures on block	Street survey
SURV13	Number of broken windows observable on block	Street survey
NOISE1	Noise index based on energy ratios	Street survey
NOISE	Noise index based on pressure ratios	Street survey

does not affect the best linear unbiased characteristics of the estimated coefficients if the model is correctly specified. However, even when properly included, the variable may not be statistically significant. Therefore, it is not possible to choose the correct variables to include by their significance. Instead, the decision must be based upon intuitive reasoning and some prior expectations about the sign and magnitude of the coefficient.

Because the object of this chapter is to determine the nature of the impact of noise, the possibility of "harmful" multicollinearity between the measures of noise and other variables had to be investigated. For simple "pairwise" multicollinearity, there is a simple rule-of-thumb test proposed by Klein (1962). Such collinearity can be tolerated if the simple correlation coefficient between the two variables is less than the square root of the coefficient of multiple determination. Both objective measures of noise, NOISE and NOISE1, are generally not highly correlated with the other variables in the study. In contrast, the subjective measure of noise, SURV9, has correlations of greater than .5 with several other variables. The greater degree of multicollinearity of SURV9 with other variables makes this measure of noise less reliable than the objective measures of noise.

The performance of the sound pressure level index NOISE was always better than that of the sound energy level index NOISE1, both in the overall R^2 and also in terms of the confidence that could be placed in the estimated coefficient. Both indices were transformed by setting all noise measures below a certain threshold value equal to that value and then entering them into the model to determine at what level noise starts to reduce property values. For both indices, the threshold level that resulted in the highest R^2 (and the greatest level of significance) was 50 dBA, with higher or lower thresholds performing less satisfactorily.

Several specifications of the basic model were estimated, varying the exogenous variables that were included. The estimates from these different specifications are shown in Table 6.3. Model 3 in Table 6.3 was determined to be the best model for the objective measures of noise. The coefficient of NOISE (with a base level of 50 dBA, NOISE50) is significant at the 5% level and the model explains 55.4% of the variation in log(Price). In models using other base levels of the sound pressure level index or using the sound energy level index, less of the variation in price was explained and less confidence could be placed in the coefficient. Only the results for NOISE are used to develop damage estimates.

In model 3, the log of property prices, as would be expected, is inversely related to the noise level, the number of lots on the block, the lack of extensive interior modernization, the distance to the lake, the distance to the CBD, the age of the building, and the number of broken windows. The square feet of living area, the number of garages, the width of the lot, and the amount of residential and recreational land available per person are directly related to the log of property prices, all with the expected sign. These estimates of the coefficients in Table 6.3 can be used

TABLE 6.3
Regression on the Log of Price

Variables	Model 1		Model 2		Model 3	
NOISE50	−.0080	(−2.019)[a]	−.0074	(−2.031)	−.0065	(−2.002)
AREA	.00014	(5.103)	.000097	(3.842)	.00018	(6.928)
BRICK	.1845	(5.321)	.1738	(5.436)	.0850	(2.512)
GRG	.0327	(1.846)	.0249	(1.522)	.0317	(2.085)
TOTLOT	−.0087	(−5.173)	−.0079	(−5.079)	−.0053	(−3.637)
MOD			−.0735	(−1.810)	−.0845	(−2.364)
WIDTH			.0107	(6.179)	.0069	(4.235)
RRSPAC					53.53	(2.023)
DISLAK					−.8226	(−1.983)
DSCBD					−.0022	(−2.240)
AGE					−.0057	(−5.687)
SURV13					−.2050	(−3.403)
Constant	5.669		5.055		5.378	
R^2	.2891		.4032		.5541	

[a] The t Statistic is shown in parentheses.

to compute the damages that environmental noise creates by determining the impact on property values of noise levels above the 50-dbA base.

To estimate the damages to property values caused by various noise levels, the observed property price is compared to what the price would be if the noise level were reduced to the threshold level at which noise does not affect property prices. To illustrate this, let P_0 be the observed property price and P be what the property valuation would be in the absence of noise levels above the base level. Then,

$$D = P - P_0 \quad \text{where } D = \text{damages.} \tag{6.9}$$

For a linear model this simply equals the coefficient of the noise variable times the noise level minus the threshold level, BASE, or

$$D = b_3(\text{NOISE-BASE}). \tag{6.10}$$

This estimate is independent of the actual property price. However, it is likely that the amount of damage would depend on whether the property were worth \$5000 or \$30,000. High-income groups can afford to have more concern with the environment and, thus, given that quietness is a normal good, will be prepared to spend more to abate noise. The better performance of the logarithmic is justified by this insight. Damages are therefore a function of both the noise level and property value. Therefore, from Eq. (6.9)

$$\log(P_0) = a + b_1(\text{DSCBD}) + b_2(\text{DISLAK}) + b_3(\text{NOISE}) + \cdots . \tag{6.11}$$

The coefficient b_3 is estimated with the appropriate noise index centered as NOISE-BASE, with values less than 0 set equal to 0 called just NOISE. With noise levels at or below this base, Eq. (6.11) becomes

$$\log(P) = a + b_1(\text{DSCBD}) + b_2(\text{DISLAK}) + \cdots , \tag{6.12}$$

since the NOISE term drops out. Subtracting Eq. (6.12) from Eq. (6.11), gives

$$\log(P) - \log(P_0) = -b_3(\text{NOISE}), \tag{6.13}$$

or

$$\log(P/P_0) = -b_3(\text{NOISE}), \tag{6.14}$$

so,

$$P/P_0 = \exp[-b_3(\text{NOISE})] \tag{6.15}$$

or

$$P = P_0 \exp[-b_3(\text{NOISE})] \tag{6.16}$$

Thus,

$$D = P - P_0 = P_0 \exp[-b_3(\text{NOISE})] - P_0$$
$$= P_0\{\exp[-b_3(\text{NOISE})] - 1\}. \tag{6.17}$$

Using coefficients estimated in model 3, and shown in Table 6.3, damages caused by different levels of noise are calculated and presented in Table 6.4. These damage estimates are attributable to the transportation noise from expressways if it is these noises that raise the noise level above the 50-dBA threshold (measured using the NOISE index). Traffic is the dominant source of noise in most urban residential areas (exceptions occur, of course), and this is especially true in neighborhoods bordering major traffic arteries such as expressways. The average value of a home bordering these expressways was $17,600 in 1970.

Having assessed the level of noise damages to a particular residence, it is necessary to estimate the total level of damages in order to evaluate the cost-effectiveness of alternative policies aimed at noise abatement. The simplest approach, the one employed here, is to multiply the number of affected properties by an estimate of the average level of damages per unit. This was the approach used by Ridker and Henning (1967) to measure the total cost of air pollution in St. Louis.

A number of objections to this approach have been raised. The summing of damages in this way may violate certain general conditions of equilibrium and omit consumer-surplus components of total damages. The issue is too complex to enter into this context.[11] However, the extent of noise pollution in Chicago is much more limited than the extent of air pollution—only 1% of the dwellings in Chicago are seriously affected. Thus, the importance of the unmeasured consumer surplus is reduced.

To obtain an estimate of the total number of residences affected by noise from Chicago's expressways, the block statistics of the 1970 Census of Population and Housing were used. The number of residences estimated to lie within 500 ft. of the expressways were summed over a sample of 20 miles of the system, and then this figure was extrapolated over the entire system. The expressway system is comprised of the Dan Ryan, the Eisenhower, the Kennedy, the Edens, the Skyway, and the first 2 miles of the Stevenson.[12] It was estimated that there were about 5500 owner-occupied dwellings with an average value of $17,600 and 16,000 rental units with an average monthly rent of $105 affected.[13] The reduction in the

---

[11] For a thorough discussion see Freeman (1979).

[12] The remainder of the Stevenson Expressway within the city of Chicago is bordered by manufacturing land.

[13] There are 1.2 million housing units in the city of Chicago, 422,000 of which are owner-occupied.

TABLE 6.4
Noise Damages as a Function of Noise Levels and
Property Values (in Dollars)

Dwelling unit value in dollars	Sound pressure level noise index in dBA										
	50	52.5	55	57.5	60	62.5	65	67.5	70	72.5	75
5000	0	82	165	250	336	423	512	602	694	787	882
7500	0	123	248	375	504	635	768	904	1041	1181	1323
10,000	0	164	330	500	672	846	1024	1205	1388	1575	1764
12,500	0	205	413	624	840	1058	1280	1506	1735	1969	2206
15,000	0	246	495	749	1007	1270	1536	1807	2082	2362	2647
17,500	0	287	578	874	1175	1481	1792	2108	2429	2756	3088
20,000	0	328	661	999	1343	1693	2048	2409	2777	3150	3529
22,500	0	369	743	1124	1511	1904	2304	2711	3124	3543	3970
25,000	0	410	826	1249	1679	2116	2560	3012	3471	3937	4411
27,500	0	451	908	1374	1847	2328	2816	3313	3817	4331	4852
30,000	0	492	991	1499	2015	2539	3072	3614	4164	4725	5293
32,500	0	532	1074	1624	2183	2751	3328	3915	4512	5118	5735
35,000	0	573	1156	1748	2351	2963	3584	4217	4859	5512	6176
37,500	0	614	1239	1873	2519	3174	3840	4518	5206	5906	6617
40,000	0	655	1321	1998	2686	3386	4096	4819	5553	6299	7058

value of these properties caused by the average noise level in the vicinity is shown in Figure 6.1. If the average noise level is 62.5 dBA and if the threshold level is 50 dBA, then the total cost of noise to these affected properties is $24 million.

These estimates are very imprecise. A more accurate measure of total damages would be possible if the actual noise level experienced by residents adjacent to the expressway system were known. There are two methods to estimate total damages. First, a detailed survey can be taken of noise levels bordering expressways. Second, engineering algorithms relating noise levels to the design of the expressway, the average vehicle speed, and the volume of traffic can be utilized. Since it was possible to take only a small sample of actual noise readings, the second method was employed to estimate neighborhood noise levels along Chicago's expressways. The small sample was used to check the reasonableness of the predictions derived through the use of the algorithms. The National Cooperative Highway Research Program (NCHRP) Report No. 117 presented comprehensive models for estimating neighborhood noise levels.[14] The median noise level L_{50} near a level roadway is related to the volume of

[14] Gordon, C., Galloway, W., Kugler, C. A., and Nelson, D. for Bolt, Beranek, and Newman, *Highway Noise: A Design Guide for Highway Engineers*, National Cooperative Highway Research Program, Report No. 117, Los Angeles, California, 1971.

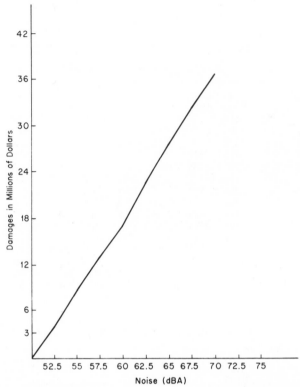

FIGURE 6.1. Estimated total damages along Chicago expressways as a function of average noise level.

traffic per hour V, the distance to the center of the roadway D, and the average speed of the traffic S. The functional relationship can be defined as

$$L_{50} = 20 + 10 \log V \; 10 \log D + 20 \log S \qquad (6.18)$$

or

$$L_{50} = 20 + 10 \log V - 10 \log D + 20 \log S \qquad (6.19)$$

where L_{50} is the median noise level, V is the vehicle in vehicles per hour, D is the distance measured between the observer and the nearest point to the center line of the roadway in feet, and S is the speed measured as the average speed of vehicular flow in miles per hour with the qualification that "for a 20 percent mix of diesel trucks the average noise level would be 8 dBA higher than that predicted [Gordon, Galloway, Kugler, and Nelson, 1971, p. 38]." The same report also presents a detailed model for calculating noise levels that takes into account the vehicle flows of trucks and autos, their respective vehicle speeds, barriers impeding noise radiation, the width of the highway, the distance from the highway, the gradient of the road, the elevation or depression of the highway relative to the surrounding land, and the smoothness of the road surface. Given the characteristics of the contours of the expressways and vehicle flow figures, it is possible to plot noise contours along the expressways.

To test some hypothetical sample computations, actual noise readings were taken along the Kennedy Expressway with a portable sound meter. Noise readings were taken over 10-min intervals and at various distances from the highway at various locations where the highway had various elevation or depression levels. Given the estimates, it is possible to estimate with some confidence the total noise damages by taking into account the elevation and depression of the highway.

It was assumed that 5% of the dwelling units within 500 ft. of a depressed expressway were within the 72.5-dBA contour lines and 10% of the dwelling units were within 62.5-, 60-, 57.5-, 55-, and 52.5-dBA contours, respectively. For a level section of highway, 5% of the dwellings were assumed to be within the 72.5-dBA contour, and an additional 10%, within the 70-, 67.5-, 65-, 60-, 57.5-, 55-, and 52.5-dBA contours. Finally, along the sections of elevated highway, 5% were assumed to be within 70 dBA. An estimate of total damages in which at least some confidence may be placed is reached by estimating the damages for each of the various noise levels associated with various sections of highway, summing for each section, and then weighting by the proportion of the highway that was elevated, level, or depressed, and summing again.

A brief "windshield" survey of all expressways in Chicago was carried out in order to determine their elevation. This survey revealed that about 60% of the expressways is depressed (usually 15–25 ft. below the level of the adjacent land). Also, it was estimated that about 35% of the expressway system was elevated (about 12% 5–15 ft.; 14%, 15–25 ft.; and 10%, 25 ft. or more), whereas less than 5% was within 5 ft. of being level.

Based on these assumptions, the total damages due to traffic noise from the expressways in Chicago were estimated to be about $11,250,000. Varying the assumptions about the densities of the housing and the noise contours caused by the traffic noise will, of course, cause the total damage estimate to vary. This damage estimate assumes that the noise level *actually* declines with distance to the expressway border three times faster than it would if distance were the only factor. This is because of the effects of barriers and buildings that block or attenuate the traffic noise. Alternate assumptions of four and two times the rate of attenuation give total damage estimates of $8.0 million and $18.5 million, respectively (with damages of the latter extending beyond 500 ft.). The noise contours corresponding to the first total damage estimate are considered to be superior to the alternate estimates because the noise contours of this estimate are close to those measured in the tests along the Kennedy Expressway. It is interesting to note that although depressed sections of the expressways account for 60% of expressway mileage in Chicago, they contribute only 44% of the total damages.

IV. CONCLUSION AND IMPLICATIONS

One conclusion is clear. High levels of expressway noise seem to create a significant disamenity for those urban residents who bear the brunt of them. Of course, this much is evident to anyone who has lived near an expressway and from the traditional concern for regulating urban noise. The real usefulness of the application of the amenity model of urban land prices and the hedonic model of dwelling prices to the expressway noise problem is the potential that the damage estimates have for cost–benefit analysis of noise control policies.

Although the analysis of specific policies is beyond the scope of this chapter, certain general conclusions can be supported. For example, it is clear that sources of roadway noise that can be modified cheaply (e.g., tire design, mufflers) are worthy candidates for control policies. Similarly, the design and location of new expressways should take account of the costs of noise, at least when the costs of quieter designs are not very different from that of high-noise ones. Third, the case for compensation for loss of quiet may be strong in many situations. In fact, ideally, the inclusion of such compensation (properly calculated) as a cost of the project would lead to optimal design decisions. On the other hand, the order-of-magnitude of the total costs of expressway noise, as estimated here, does not seem to support sweeping revisions in highway design or the halt of most highway proposals that merit construction on other grounds.

REFERENCES

Bonvallet, G. L. "Levels and Spectra of Traffic, Industrial, and Residential Area Noise." *J. Acoustical Soc. Am.* 23 (1951): 435–439.
Bonvallet, G. L. "Levels and Spectra of Transportation Vehicle Noise." *J. Acoustical Soc. Am.* 22 (1950) 281–295.
Caccavari, C., and Schechter, H. *Background Noise Study in Chicago.* Chicago, Ill.: Department of Environmental Control, City of Chicago, 1973.
Cohen, A. *Noise and Psychological State.* Washington, D.C.: U.S. Department of Health, Education and Welfare, 1968.

Freeman, A. M., III, *The Benefits of Environmental Improvement: Theory and Practice.* Baltimore, Maryland: John Hopkins, 1979.

Gordon, C., Galloway, W., Kugler, C. A., and Nelson, D. for Bolt, Beranek, and Newman. *Highway Noise: A Design Guide for Highway Engineers,* National Cooperative Highway Research Program, Report No. 117. Los Angeles, California, 1971.

Jansen, G. "The Effects of Noise on Physiological State." In *Proceedings of the Conference on Noise as a Public Health Hazard,* Washington, D.C.: National Academy for the Advancement of Sciences, 1968.

Klein, L. R. *An Introduction to Econometrics.* Englewood Cliffs, New Jersey: Prentice Hall, 1962.

Kryter, K. D. *The Effects of Noise on Man.* New York: Academic Press, 1970.

McMillan, M. L., Reid, B. D., and Gillen, D. W. "An Approach Toward Improved Estimates of Willingness to Pay for Public 'Goods' from Hedonic Price Functions: The Case of Aircraft Noise." Unpublished manuscript, University of Alberta, 1978.

Peterson, A., and Gross, E. (eds.). *Handbook of Noise Control,* West Concord, Mass.: University of Mass., 1967.

Ridker, R. G. *Economic Costs of Air Pollution: Studies in Measurement.* New York: Praeger, 1967.

Ridker, R. G., and Henning, J. A. "Determinants of Residential Property Values with Specific Reference to Air Pollution." *Rev. Econ. Stat. 44* (1967): 246–256.

Rosen, S. "Hedonic Prices and Implicit Markets: Product Differentiation in Pure Competition." *J. Polit. Econ. 82* (January 1974): 35–55.

Teichner, W. H., Arees, E., and Reilly, R. "Noise and Human Performance, A Psychophysiological Approach." *Ergonomics* 6 (1963).

U.S. Environmental Protection Agency. *Information on Levels of Noise Requisite to Protect Public Health and Welfare with an Adequate Margin of Safety.* Washington, D.C., 1974.

Walters, A. A. *Noise and Prices.* Oxford: Clarendon Press, 1974.

Zimmer, B. G. "Residential Mobility and Housing." *Land Econ. 39* (1973): 193–207.

7

The Influence of Urban Centers on Recreational Land Use[1]

ORVILLE F. GRIMES, JR.

I. INTRODUCTION

The rapid growth in outdoor recreation in recent years has attracted wide attention. Less attention has been paid to the fact that the very areas experiencing the most significant increases in demand for outdoor recreation (major centers of population) are also the ones relatively most deficient in supply. Extreme crowding is common at recreation sites in many large cities. For this reason and also because of increases in family income and mobility, much of the demand for urban recreation has come to involve day-long or weekend trips to sites located near urban centers. Parcels of land formerly given over to agriculture have been transformed into public parks or sold as sites for vacation homes. As the cost of travel and travel time has risen, the demand of urban residents for land with high-quality recreational amenities also within a short driving radius of large population centers has risen particularly rapidly.

How is the use of land for recreation surrounding urban areas determined? One approach to answering this question is to view land as an input used by families in producing recreation and to consider demand and supply for this input. The demand for outdoor recreation, from which the demand for recreational land is derived, has received much attention.

---

[1] Portions of the results of this study were reported in Grimes (1974). The views expressed in this chapter are the author's and should not be interpreted as reflecting the views of the World Bank.

Although not analyzed in the context of proximity to urban centers, the role of distance traveled as a part of the costs of recreation has been emphasized.[2]

The supply of recreational land is more difficult to analyze and in fact has received virtually no attention. Relevant supply characteristics of recreational land are its amenity attributes, such as natural water features, and its nearness to urban centers where demanders reside. In a situation where nearness acquires residential scarcity value (i.e., there is positive residential demand), supply prices are influenced by the savings in cost of not having to travel to sites farther away. The consumer of recreation faces not a given supply price but a schedule of prices for close substitutes, varying with distance from the city and recreational features. Thus the analysis of demand and supply for recreational land requires a framework in which accessibility is a key element.

Accessibility has been featured in models explaining land use inside of urban areas. Since travel cost figures prominently in the price paid for recreation, distance traveled to use a recreation site would appear to play a role analogous to daily commuting to employment in explaining recreational land values. Complications arise, however, when travel to use recreation sites is undertaken from more than one urban center, as is usually the case. Most urban land-use studies have described the effects of accessibility to only one center. However, where land has access value to more than one center, the effect on land value is less clear. There is some question as to whether residents of different centers will intermingle or group themselves according to center of origin. A further uncertainty is whether competition between centers will result in residents of a large center living beyond localized land price peaks at locations around smaller centers. An important feature of a model of recreational land use near urban centers should thus be to explain the interactions of demand for land emanating from more than one center.

Another needed departure from conventional land-use models is the inclusion of amenity attributes. The assumption that urban land extends outward from a city center along the traditional flat featureless plain has little applicability to recreational land, whose very essence is heterogeneity because of quality differences imparted by amenities. The price of recreational land at any given level of accessibility will be influenced by differences in the level of recreational amenity features associated with it. Amenities include natural features, such as proximity to water and quality of water. Other, nonrecreational amenities, such as public services and exclusiveness of neighborhoods, will also enter in.

---

[2] See, for example, Clawson and Knetsch (1966); Boyet and Tolley (1966); Cesario and Knetsch (1970); and Smith (1975).

The purpose of the study discussed here was to develop and apply a model capable of explaining recreational land use near urban areas.[3] Private access recreation, whose study has been neglected relative to public access recreation, was examined. Specifically, vacation homesites, rather than public parks or lakes, was the focal point.

In the following section a model of the market for recreational land near urban areas will be presented, and testable implications will be derived. Section III will present empirical findings obtained from a sample of recreational homesites located along the Lake Michigan shoreline within access of Chicago residents. These results indicate that access to a major metropolitan area as well as the level of specifically recreational amenities are strongly reflected in land values. Thus such land is drawn out of agricultural or urban residential use and into recreational use.

II. A MODEL OF THE DEMAND FOR RECREATIONAL LAND

Analysis of the spatial pattern of demand for private access recreation in urban areas initially involves derivation of the demand for land for recreational use located beyond the margin of full-time residences for one urban center. Let the utility of each urban household be

$$U = U(R, Z), \tag{7.1}$$

where R is the quantity of recreation consumed per household and Z is per household expenditure on all other commodities.

The production function for recreation is

$$R = R(L, B, A_1 \cdot \cdot \cdot A_n), \tag{7.2}$$

where L is the space occupied by the recreational property, B is building input, and $A_1 \cdot \cdot \cdot A_n$ are amenities, that is, inputs other than space and buildings affecting recreation, the use of which is acquired by purchase of the recreational property.[4]

The household devotes its income to expenditures on recreation inputs, all other commodities, and transportation:

$$Y = PL + B + Z + tD, \tag{7.3}$$

where P is recreational land price, B is expenditure on recreational housing structure, t is the price of transportation per mile, and D is distance

---

[3] See Brown and Pollakowski (1977) for a similar study of the value of water recreation amenities within an urban area.

[4] Inputs other than L, B, and $A_1 \cdot \cdot \cdot A_n$, such as boating equipment, fuel, and other current purchase inputs, are not considered in this study.

traveled to use the recreation site. The price per unit of recreational housing structure, whose value is unity, is assumed to be determined by construction costs and is exogenous. Note that, since space and amenities are both purchased in a single transaction, household expenditure on land PL includes outlays for amenities as well as for space.

The price of land used by residents of a city for recreation depends in part on the value of the land in alternative uses. If the land is within daily commuting distance to a center, it has a value based on these commuting savings and not just the recreational commuting value. On the other hand, land located at the recreational margin, that is, at the distance where value for recreational use has declined to the value for other uses, will command a price reflecting its opportunity value in agricultural use. For all inframarginal recreational land not used for full-time commuter residences there is a travel saving premium, which results from the willingness of households to pay to avoid traveling extra distance to consume recreation. This premium is an aggregative consequence of the individual recreation production behavior explained by the present model. As will be shown later, the model itself determines how, through competition for land in the aggregate, this premium must vary with distance. In addition to distance considerations, amenity features influence the price of land at each location. Thus, for purposes of developing the model, the equation for recreational land price as a function of distance and amenities may be written

$$P = P(D, A_1 \cdot \cdot \cdot A_n). \qquad (7.4)$$

Households maximize utility subject to the production constraint [Eq. (7.2)], the expenditure constraint [Eq. (7.3)], and the land price constraint [Eq. (7.4)]. Solution of the resulting Lagrange expression indicates that the marginal rate of substitution between recreation and all other goods must equal the marginal contribution to recreation of dollars spent on the factors L, B, and A_1-A_n. Distance traveled to consume recreation is chosen so that the disutility resulting from traveling an extra mile to a recreation site just equals the added expenditure on land associated with the site.

Solution of this system may be briefly summarized. Into the differential of Eq. (7.4) may be substituted the first order condition $L \, \partial P/\partial D = -t$, which determines household choice of distance. Since L can be shown to depend uniquely on P and D, solving the resulting differential equation under the assumption of constant marginal transport cost produces the expression for land price given by Eq. (7.4). According to Eq. (7.4), the price of recreational land depends on distance and amenity characteristics. It is the basis for the empirical analysis presented later.

III. LAND USE AROUND MULTIPLE
URBAN CENTERS

It has been assumed so far that households travel from one large urban center to their recreational properties. If we now allow for the fact that residents of more than one center may be bidding for the same recreational land, the pattern of changes in urban land values with distance will be considerably modified. This is particularly the case when the land is located close enough to be used for full-time residences. In this case, it becomes subject to the much steeper bid gradients of full-time commuters.

The empirical portion of this research was conducted in a region containing a dominant metropolitan center and several smaller secondary centers. The interaction between dominant-center and secondary-center land price functions could have three different results for recreational land. First, prices bid for land by dominant-center residents could be everywhere as high as those bid by secondary-center residents. This could only occur when subcenter employment was very small or dispersed or subcenter residents had much lower demands for recreation. The second and third cases involve residents of smaller centers bidding recreational land prices up beyond what dominant-center residents are prepared to pay at that distance. In one instance the size of the premium over the dominant-center bids would reflect recreational commuting savings based on distance to the secondary center. In the other the premium would reflect the costs of full-time commuting to the dominant center. Whether the second or third case predominates depends on the distance of the land from the subcenter, the size of the subcenter population, the rate of decline of land prices from the dominant center, and the demands for recreation by the residents of each center.

The spatial distribution of recreational housing by city of origin of users will correspond to whichever pattern of changes in land price with distance is observed. Land price functions indicate the prices that residents of a given city are willing to pay at each distance. However, if residents of another city are willing to pay more, these residents are bid out of the market for recreational land around their own city. Thus, in the first case, where secondary centers do not exert an influence strong enough to raise land prices above what dominant-center residents are willing to pay, most homesites will be owned by dominant-center residents. Otherwise, recreational sites under the influence of the subcenter will be acquired primarily by subcenter residents. However, a certain number of dominant-center residents who place premiums on urban amenities will be willing to pay the higher subcenter prices.

The case of clustering of residents is shown in Figure 7.1. The

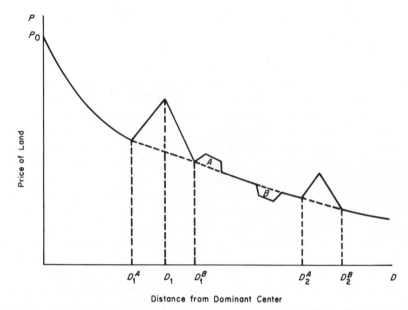

Distance from Dominant Center

FIGURE 7.1. Influence of secondary center submountains and amenities on dominant center land rent function.

dominant-center land price function, originating at P_0 on the vertical axis, is interrupted by demands for recreational land emanating from two secondary centers. At the point of intersection of land price bids with another center, a household no longer enjoys a discount for consuming recreation at a greater distance. This will likely eliminate its participation in the market.

Thus, at a given distance one and only one land price function will prevail. This discussion underscores the point that within submountains, the secondary centers will be the ruling influences on land values, whereas at locations outside submountains, value will be determined by the dominant center. If only one city exerted an influence on land values, the land price function might be determined by regressing land price against distance of all properties from this city. However, in the case of influence from more than one center, distance must be measured from the appropriate ruling center.

Although land is divided into zones within which a single ruling center prevails, the price of recreational land within each zone will be affected by competition for land from different centers. In the case of multiple centers there will be many land price margins, each dependent on demand for recreational land from intersecting centers. For the secondary center at D_1 in Figure 7.1, for example, the price at the margin is the price at D_1^A on the near side and at D_1^B on the far side of D_1. For the dominant center, the price at the margin lies at the point (not shown in Figure 7.1) where value of land for dominant-center recreation declines to value in agricultural use or, conceivably, to zero.

The dominant-center land price function will also be cut by concentrations of amenity features, the value of which will be reflected in the price of recreational land at these locations. Areas such as A in Figure 7.1 represent local quality maxima, such as prestige locations, whereas troughs such as area B reflect the adverse effects of dilapidated or otherwise undesirable residential areas as well as pockets of industrial or other nonrecreational use of land.

IV. EMPIRICAL EVALUATION

A. Data

Estimation of the theoretical relationships was undertaken using a sample of 294 recreational properties. The sample extended from the western edge of Porter County, Indiana to a point 20 miles north of the Muskegon-Muskegon Heights (Michigan) SMSA, a distance of 166 miles. Only transactions involving property located 1 mile or less from Lake Michigan were selected.

Empirical studies of urban land prices have traditionally suffered from a lack of adequate price data. Analysts have often had to rely on essentially judgmental estimates of land values, such as tax assessments or appraisals by the Federal Housing Authority of independent appraisers.[5] Such estimates, however carefully arrived at, may be biased in a number of ways. The present study attempts to avoid these difficulties by using only actual market transactions in land. The market price of each parcel was determined by consulting the Documentary Tax stamps of the Internal Revenue Service on the purchase deed. In Indiana and Michigan in 1966, stamps totaling $1.10 for every $1000 of sale price were required on deeds indicating transfer of ownership of property.

The upper and lower distance limits of the sample were determined in part by adherence to conventional notions of urban land-use theory and in part by data limitations. Properties within the city limits of Chicago were excluded so as to focus more fully on the influence Chicago residents have

[5] Tax appraisals were used by Brigham (1965), FHA appraisals by Sirmans, Kau, and Lee (1979), and independent appraisals for purposes of mortgage approval by Diamond (1980).

on the price of recreational land outside the city. For the same reason, properties located within the city limits of other urban centers along the Lake Michigan shoreline were also omitted. The Lake County, Indiana, shoreline was eliminated because of the extremely small number of recreational homesites located 1 mile or less from Lake Michigan. The upper distance limit, that is, the point of conversion of land from urban to nonurban uses, was determined by examining the pattern of addresses of buyers on the purchase deeds and extending the sample in distance until only 5% of buyers were found to come from the Chicago metropolitan area.[6]

To standardize for seasonal effects in the purchase and sale of land, an equal number of transactions occurring before and after June 1, 1966 were obtained. The year 1966 was chosen because it was the most recent complete year for which comparable data for the Indiana and Michigan counties were available. Indiana discontinued the Documentary Tax stamps in July 1967 and inaugurated a similar state tax only in April 1969. Michigan dispensed with the Federal Stamps in January of 1968 but replaced them immediately with a state real estate transfer tax stamp at the same rate of $1.10 per $1000 of sale price.

B. Treatment of Subcenters

The proposition was tested that all urbanized areas with populations of at least 5000 would exercise an independent influence on local land values. On this basis seven secondary urban centers, all but one located on Lake Michigan and thus directly on the sample ray from Chicago, were identified: Michigan City-Long Beach, Indiana; and Benton Harbor-St. Joseph, South Haven, Holland, Grand Rapids, Grand Haven-Spring Lake, and Muskegon-Muskegon Heights, Michigan.[7] Upper and lower distance bounds for the submountains of these centers were determined

---

[6] To provide a check on data reliability and for a variety of other reasons, in some counties more than one data set was collected. For Muskegon County, a confirmation of the upper distance limit of the main sample was furnished by a second sample of 45 properties, which yielded an almost identical percentage of buyers from the Chicago area. The two data sets were not combined, however, because only assessed valuation of land, not market value, was available for the latter. For counties where two or more sets of market value data were obtained, Chow F tests were performed on each pair of sets to determine whether or not pooling of the data was justified.

[7] Special problems arose with the secondary center of Grand Rapids, located not on Lake Michigan but 29 miles inland. Theory suggests that the greatest impact of Grand Rapids on land price would be at the point on the shoreline where distance to Grand Rapids was a minimum. Accordingly, the intersection of the shoreline from Grand Rapids was chosen as the midpoint of the Grand Rapids submountain. It was from this point that Chicago-based distances for the submountain were measured.

by ordering the observations simultaneously by city of buyer and distance and examining the spatial pattern of buyers emanating from secondary centers.

The distance bounds of the submountains, along with the fraction of submountain residents residing in the secondary center, in Chicago, and elsewhere, are given in Table 7.1. Secondary-center residents were found to predominate up to a distance of about 10 miles or less from each center. In the case of South Haven, a very small community, this influence tapered off at a distance of only 2 miles. Furthermore, the locational distribution of purchasers given in Table 7.1 lends credence to the hypothesis that no dominant-center resident would choose to live within a secondary-center submountain. Only about 25% of all Chicago-area residents in the sample were found to have located within the confines of a secondary center, despite the fact that submountains comprise 67% of the total shoreline. Conversely, less than 5% of the residents of areas outside submountains came from secondary centers, but 44.4% were from Chicago.

Although, as previously indicated, there is little intermixing between Chicago and secondary-center residents, two instances should be noted in which dominant-center residents might conceivably locate within submountains. First, the spatial pattern of amenities found within submoun-

TABLE 7.1
Secondary-Center Submountains, Chicago Distance Bounds, and Distribution of
Purchasers of Recreational Land by Place of Origin

	Distance from Chicago (miles)			Percentages of purchasers from		
Submountain	Lower	Upper	1966 population of center[a]	Sec. center	Chicago	Other
Michigan City– Long Beach	52	61	38,823	78.9	18.4	2.7
Benton Harbor– St. Joseph	82	98	28,861	60.0	30.0	10.0
South Haven	110	114	6,257	59.3	18.5	22.2
Holland	136	150	25,597	56.7	6.7	36.6
Grand Rapids	151	159	188,787	57.2	7.1	35.7
Grand Haven– Spring Lake	160	169	11,527	66.7	0.0	33.3
Muskegon–Musk. Heights	175	193	45,026	83.8	0.0	16.2
Rest of shoreline (excl. above)	37	203	—	4.2	44.4	51.6

[a] Interpolation from 1960 and 1970 (preliminary) estimates, U.S. Bureau of the Census.

tains can affect household decisions to locate on the basis of distance alone. For example, dominant-center residents purchasing retirement homes might locate within submountains to take advantage of easy access to shopping facilities. Second, the expansion of submountains with population growth may envelop nearby dominant-center residents, who might not relocate if moving costs were prohibitive.

Estimation of a dominant-center land price function modified to include submountains was undertaken in the following manner. As discussed in the preceding section, at any given distance from Chicago either the Chicago land price function or a secondary-center function will be the ruling influence on land price. Accordingly, a distance variable, *Distance from Ruling Center,* was defined for which distance of all properties located outside submountains was measured from Chicago and distance of all properties located within submountains, regardless of origin of buyer, was measured from corresponding secondary centers. To allow for differences in land price intercepts among the eight urban centers, that is, differences in the height of submountains, zero–one variables were constructed for each of the seven secondary-center submountains.

C. The Problem of Functional Form

The abovementioned clustering of sample households by place of origin suggests that secondary centers exert only a local influence on land price. If this is the case, dominant-center residents will be found on the far side as well as on the near side of secondary centers. The data, showing Chicago influences predominating on both sides of secondary centers, lend support to this proposition. By the familiar expression $P_D = -t/L < 0$, land price declines with distance from city center. A functional form for this expression should thus be consistent with intersections between dominant-center and secondary-center land price functions, at points such as D_1^A, D_1^B, D_2^A, and D_2^B in Figure 7.1.

There is evidence that the behavior of urban land prices with distance is linear in the logarithms.[8] Provided their slopes are equal, log linear dominant-center and secondary-center land price functions can be shown to intersect. Consider a log linear dominant-center land price function $V = A_0 D^{-B_0}$ and secondary-center land price function $V = A_1 |(D - D_1)|^{-B_1}$. Setting the functions equal to each other and solving for distance D yields two points of intersection summarized by

$$D = \frac{D_1}{1 - (A_0/A_1)^{-(1/B)}} \tag{7.5}$$

[8] See, for example, Mills (1969, p. 246).

where $B = B_0 = B_1$. If $A_0 \neq A_1$, as expected with different sizes of centers, D is finite. When values of D corresponding to locations of secondary centers are inserted into (7.5), points of intersection occur at locations slightly beyond the centers. In general, the log linear function is finite at any nonzero distance, and A is the value of land at a distance of 1 mile from the center, giving a measure of the height of the function.

Studies by Mills (1969) and Muth (1969) have also suggested that declines in land price in urban areas may be of the negative exponential form $V = A \exp^{-BD}$, or $\log V = \log A - BD$, where A is land price at the center of the city and B is the percentage rate of change of land price per unit of distance. The negative exponential form can also be shown to be consistent with the configuration of land prices depicted in Figure 7.1. Thus, if the dominant-center land price function is given by $V = A_0 \exp^{(-B_0 D)}$ and the secondary center function by $V = A_1 \exp^{(-B_1|(D-D_1)|)}$, setting the functions equal and solving for D produces

$$D = \frac{\log A_0 - \log A_1 - B_1 D_1}{B_0 - B_1}, \qquad (7.6)$$

where B_0 and B_1 are now percentage rates of change of land price per unit change in distance. The slopes, or the incremental change in land price per unit change in distance, are $B_0 P$ and $B_1 P$. Equation (7.6) indicates that, providing that B_0 and B_1 are not equal, the dominant-center and secondary-center land price functions intersect.

The true function relating urban land price to distance may be neither log linear nor negative exponential, but one that exhibits very steep declines near the city center and much smaller declines farther away. Nevertheless, the precipitous fall in land price near the dominant center would probably be more accurately represented by a log-linear than by a negative-exponential form. For these reasons and also because the empirical results were slightly more reasonable, the log-linear form, using a single distance variable, was used to estimate the equations of the model.[9]

Based on these considerations of ruling centers and functional forms, the regression equation for (7.4) was of the form

$$\log Y = a + bD_{RC} + \sum_{i=1}^{7} y_i R_i + \sum_{j=1}^{13} \delta_j A_j + u, \qquad (7.7)$$

where Y is land price per square foot,[10] D_{RC} is the logarithm of distance

[9] The relationships of the model were also estimated using negative exponential regressions with different distance variables for dominant and secondary centers, as suggested by Eq. (7.6).

[10] Price-per-square-foot rather than price-per-front-foot was used as the dependent variable because the effects on land price of distance and many amenities can be regarded as dis-

from ruling center, the R_is are zero–one variables, and the A_js are amenity features. Each of the seven R_is takes on the value of unity for properties located within a particular submountain. The coefficients of the R_is are indicators of submountain height, and their antilogs give the value of land at a distance of 1 mile from a secondary center relative to land identical in all other respects at a distance of 1 mile from Chicago.

D. Distance from Urban Centers

The results obtained from applying (7.7) to the 294 sample observations are given in Table 7.2. The coefficient of distance from ruling center is of the expected sign and statistically significant at the two-tailed .01 level. It indicates that land prices decline from dominant and secondary centers by .77% per 1% increase in distance from these centers.

The coefficients of the seven ruling center zero–one variables represent the difference between Chicago and secondary-center land price intercepts. All seven are negative and significant at the .05 level or higher, indicating, as expected, that land prices at a distance of 1 mile from each secondary city are below those at a distance of 1 mile from Chicago.

The fact that land prices 1 mile from secondary centers are below those 1 mile from Chicago lends only partial support to the analysis of land price and distance depicted in Figure 7.1. If the submountains of the seven secondary centers rise above the Chicago function, as Figure 7.1 indicates, prices bid for land by secondary-center residents will be higher than those bid by Chicagoans at the same distance. Land prices 1 mile from secondary centers should therefore not only be lower than those 1 mile from Chicago but also higher than the prices Chicago residents would be willing to pay at secondary centers.

Estimates of prices bid by secondary-center residents may be obtained using the ruling center coefficients.[11] As mentioned, these coefficients measure the difference between the logarithm of land price 1 mile from a secondary center and the logarithm of land price 1 mile from Chicago. For example, the ruling center coefficient for Holland is -1.63. The logarithm of land price 1 mile from Chicago is given by the constant term in the regression equation presented in Table 7.2; its value is 1.07. The logarithm of price bid at Holland is thus $(1.07 - 1.63)$ or $-.56$.

---

tributed over the entire lot. However, the effects of water-oriented amenities, such as proximity to water and quality of water, are likely to be concentrated along property frontage. In general, amenities can affect land price on a per-square-foot, per-front-foot, or even a once-for-all basis. Given this problem, the more reasonable course of action seemed to be to use price-per-square-foot in estimation of Eq. (7.4), as shown in Table 7.2, and to further investigate, using price-per-front-foot, those amenities likely to be clustered along frontage.

[11] These comparisons pertain to land values holding amenities constant.

TABLE 7.2
Determinants of Price of Recreational Land,
Indiana and Michigan, 1966[a]

Explanatory variable	Coefficient
Distance from ruling center (D_{RC})	$-.77$***
Ruling centers (R_1)	
Michigan City–Long Beach	-1.05**
Benton Harbor–St. Joseph	-1.84***
South Haven	-2.33***
Holland	-1.63***
Grand Rapids	-3.32***
Grand Haven–Spring Lake	-2.25***
Muskegon–Muskegon Heights	-1.79***
Amenities (A_j)	
Distance from Lake Michigan	$-.14$***
Beach accessibility	.10
Water quality	.08***
Homeowners' council	.42***
Prior approval	.58***
Covenant	.74***
Topography	
Hilly/Dry/Wooded	.61**
Hilly/Dry/Unwooded	.58*
Level/Dry/Wooded	.28
Level/Dry/Unwooded	.64**
Hilly/Wet/Wooded	$-.03$
Hilly/Wet/Unwooded	-1.82**
Level/Wet/Wooded	.63*
R^2	.44
df	271

[a] Dependent variable: Logarithm of sale price of land less value of improvement per square foot.
  * $p \leq .10$, one-tailed.
 ** $p \leq .05$, one-tailed.
*** $p \leq .01$, one-tailed.

An estimate of prices bid by Chicago residents at Holland may be obtained using the Chicago land price function (log V_c = log A_0 − B_0 log D_c), where V_c is land price bid by Chicago residents, A_0 is land price 1 mile from Chicago, and D_c is distance from the secondary center to Chicago. Log A_0 = 1.07, and from Table 7.2, B_0 = .77. Using these values for D = 139 miles, the logarithm of the price Chicagoans are willing to pay for land at Holland is −2.726. The difference between −.56 and −2.726 is statistically significant at the two-tailed .05 level. Therefore, the land price peak around Holland does appear to rise above the Chicago land price function.

This procedure was repeated for the six other secondary centers. Differences between actual and Chicago bid prices were significant at the two-tailed .05 level for all centers except Grand Rapids. In larger centers, such as Michigan City-Long Beach and Muskegon-Muskegon Heights, land prices were seven to nine times greater than those Chicagoans would have been willing to pay at those distances.

To provide a check on these results, land prices were regressed on the ruling center zero–one variables and on distance of all properties in the sample, including those within submountains, from Chicago. In this case, the distance variable measures the Chicago land price function, and if secondary center submountains rise about this function, all ruling center coefficients will be positive and significant. All seven ruling center coefficients proved to be positive, but those for Benton Harbor-St. Joseph and Grand Rapids were not significant at the two-tailed 1% level. This result tends to cast doubt on whether the submountains for these centers emerge above the Chicago function. For Benton Harbor-St. Joseph this was not totally unexpected in view of the fact that all observations were located at the fringes of the city, where prices would not be expected to differ greatly from those paid by Chicago residents. For Grand Rapids, on the contrary, it seems that even though shoreline residents from that center tend to cluster where distance to Grand Rapids is minimized, their collective impact on shoreline recreational land, 29 miles from the center of Grand Rapids, is insufficient to raise land prices above Chicago-based levels.

In the earlier theoretical discussion, two influences on the height of land value submountains were discussed. Competition for recreational land around secondary centers, symbolized by the price at the margin $P(M)$, might affect height of submountains. The Chicago bid value at a secondary-center location gives an estimate of $P(M)$ for the center since, as discussed previously and illustrated in Figure 7.1, secondary-center residents must compete for the land with Chicagoans.

In accordance with the previous discussion, submountain height was regressed on 1966 population of center and on the antilogs of Chicago bid values for each center. The following result was obtained:

$$\text{(Submountain Height)} = 5.07 + .00013 \text{ (Population)}$$
$$ [2.5] [2.7]$$
$$ - 22.2 \text{ (Chicago Bid Value)},$$
$$ [.95] (7.8)$$

where population is in persons and Chicago bid values in dollars per square foot. R^2 was 0.70 for three degrees of freedom. t-values are in brackets below the coefficient.

Indications are that population of center provides a powerful explanation of submountain height. Despite the low number of degrees of freedom, the *t*-value of the population coefficient is significant at the .05 level. The coefficient of Chicago bid value was not significant, indicating that the competition between dominant-center and subcenter residents for recreational land had little effect on central land values in the subcenter.

E. Amenity Influences

1. Proximity to Water

There is wide agreement that the value of a recreation site is enhanced by the presence of water.[12] Of the total of 625 public outdoor recreation areas in the Lake Michigan basin, 536 involve the use of water.[13] Views of water areas are a part of recreation benefits, as are more direct uses of water such as swimming and boating. If proximity to water has value, recreational land on or close to a water resource will command a higher price than comparable land remote from water. Land price would be expected to decline as distance inland increased.

The logarithm of distance, in feet, of properties from Lake Michigan was included in the equation reported in Table 7.2. This specification provided a test not only of the value of proximity to water but also of the relevance of a log-linear form relating land price and distance inland. Distance from Lake Michigan was negative and highly significant in all regressions, for each county and for the aggregated sample.[14] It indicates that land price per square foot falls by an average of about .14% for every 1%-rise in distance inland from the Lake Michigan shoreline. This variable alone explained 19% of the variation in land price for the sample as a whole.

2. Beach Accessibility and Ownership

If portions of recreational shoreline are reserved for use by the public, as is very often the case, the share of beach frontage devoted to private access use will depend on the relative strengths of the demands for private and nonprivate beaches. Shoreline homeowners desiring private beaches will seek out those communities having a high proportion of beach in private ownership. Inland homeowners will opt for communities in which part or all of the beach is owned in common and thus accessible to them.

If beach access has value to all households, even those remote from the

[12] See, for example, Outdoor Recreation Resources Review Commission (1962).

[13] U.S. Department of the Interior, Bureau of Outdoor Recreation, *Water-Oriented Outdoor Recreation: Lake Michigan Basin* (Ann Arbor, Mich., 1965) pp. 6–17.

[14] In regressions for some counties a zero–one variable for properties located 200 ft. or less from a secondary water resource, such as a smaller lake or river, was also included. Though consistently positive, its contribution was marginal, and it was omitted from subsequent regressions.

shoreline, land price will decline continuously up to 1 mile inland, and possibly beyond, to reflect the saving of driving time to beaches. If, however, households located far from the shoreline use public beaches infrequently or not at all, the decline in land price with distance inland would be very steep near the lake and a great deal smaller farther inland, probably even approaching zero at some point. If this is the case, the value of beach accessibility should be measured only for households residing on the shoreline or up to this point, not for the entire sample. Since the negative coefficient of distance from Lake Michigan in Table 7.2 is consistent with either interpretation of land price with distance inland, a more detailed investigation of declines in land price at various distances inland was considered desirable.

The sample was divided into distance zones of 500 ft. in width. The logarithm of land price was then regressed on a series of zero–one variables representing the distance zones. Price-per-front-foot was the dependent variable because effects of water amenities are likely to be concentrated along property frontage. The regression equation was thus of the form $\log Y = a + \sum_{i=1}^{9} y_1 X_i = u$, where Y is price of land per front foot and the X_is are the distance zones. The constant term a will be an estimate of the per-front-foot price of lakefront properties, and the coefficients $(a + y_1, \ldots, a + y_9)$ will be estimates of land price in 500-ft. increments up to 1 mile from the shoreline.

As shown in Table 7.3, all nine regression coefficients of this equation were negative and highly significant. Two-tailed tests were then performed on each pair of coefficients to determine whether and at what point the function indicated a leveling off of land prices. The difference

TABLE 7.3
Coefficients and t Values of Estimated Land
Price–Distance Inland Function

Distance increment[a]	Coefficient	t value
0	4.47	44.4
1–500	−.704	−4.0
501–1000	−1.12	−7.0
1001–1500	−1.47	−8.1
1501–2000	−1.34	−6.3
2001–2500	−1.38	−5.6
2501–3000	−1.53	−7.2
3001–3500	−1.47	−6.0
3501–4000	−1.72	−6.6
4001–5280	−1.48	−5.0
R^2	.33	
df	284	

[a] Number of feet inland from the shoreline.

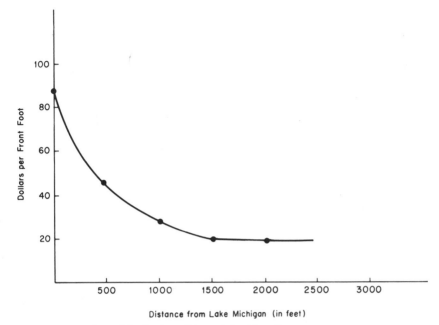

FIGURE 7.2. Estimated land price–distance inland function.

between each successive pair of coefficients up to y_3 was significant, but for succeeding coefficients the null hypothesis of equality could not be rejected. Accordingly, coefficients y_4-y_9 were considered equal to y_3.

The land-price–distance-inland function derived from this procedure is shown in Figure 7.2. The mean 1966 value of Lake Michigan properties in the sample area was $87.60 per front foot. This was more than twice the mean value for properties located just 500 ft. inland, a striking piece of evidence that the land value premium for homesites located directly on a major source of water recreation can indeed be substantial.

The land-price–distance-inland function combined with data on beach ownership was then used to predict the value of beach accessibility to homeowners. Hypothetically, beach use is dependent either upon walking accessibility or driving accessibility. However, the fact that the slope of the land-price–distance-inland function approaches zero at a point 1500 ft. from Lake Michigan strongly suggests that walking accessibility is of greater importance.[15] At an average walking speed of 3 miles per hour, beach accessibility apparently becomes relatively unimportant if a walk to the beach takes longer than about 6 min.

[15] At an average driving speed of 12 miles per hour, surely a conservative figure for a relatively nonurbanized area, it would take a homeowner located 1 mile from the shoreline only 5 min to travel to a lake beach. In this case, though, the function shown in Figure 7.2 would have had a negative slope continually up to 1 mile inland.

The beach accessibility variable in Table 7.2 takes on a value of unity in all situations where beach ownership or accessibility was found to exist. That is, it is defined:

$$\text{for on-lake properties} = \begin{cases} 1 \text{ if beach owned by shoreline homeowners;} \\ 0 \text{ otherwise} \end{cases}$$

$$\text{for off-lake properties} = \begin{cases} 1 \text{ if there is a public beach on} \\ \text{ lake within 1500 feet of property;} \\ 0 \text{ otherwise} \end{cases}$$

Because many beaches in the sample are privately owned in large measure but also contain stretches of shoreline reserved for public use, a single variable, rather than one each for shoreline and nonshoreline properties, was considered appropriate because of possible interaction effects.

Table 7.2 indicates that the value to shoreline homeowners of beach ownership, and to nonshoreline homeowners of beach accessibility, appears to be low. That is, although there is a large benefit—reflected in the land-price–distance-inland function—associated with being located adjacent to a beach, any additional benefits from exclusive use of that beach are small. This result may seem surprising in light of evidence that shoreline residents incur expenditures of real resources to keep their beaches private.[16] The discrepancy may be more apparent than real, however. Many beaches are owned neither by a single individual nor by the general public, but by the homeowners' councils of each community. Road signs, barricades, and inspection by town constables can ensure that beaches are accessible only to residents of the community. To the extent that community residents are similar in tastes, income, and other characteristics, use of a beach by neighbors does not detract from its privacy value, and the beach remains to all intents and purposes private. This effect was not captured in the beach accessibility variable since only properties whose deeds specifically mentioned that ownership of an adjacent beach was included in the sale were assigned a value of unity; all other cases, including that of communal beach ownership, were assigned a value of zero.

3. Water Quality

Water quality has potentially important effects on the rate of participation in, and the duration and magnitude of benefits from, water-based recreational activities. A low level of dissolved oxygen in a stream can destroy its value for fishing. High temperatures may also kill fish but can be beneficial to swimmers. Industrial and municipal discharges may lead

---

[16] Efforts to ensure privacy usually take the form of construction of physical impediments, such as fencing or dense foliage, around the beach itself. Barriers are also placed across access roads.

to more obvious forms of pollution, such as oil spills and floating debris. Combined with agricultural runoffs, these discharges may contribute to the growth of algae, which is harmful to fish as well as unattractive.

Information on levels of total coliform was obtained for 109 sampling points along the Lake Michigan shoreline from Grand Beach, Michigan to north of Muskegon, Michigan, yielding a total of 514 observations.[17] Total coliform is a measure of the potential health hazard posed by water contaminated by fecal or other organic matter and is thus an indicator of the degree to which water is suitable for a variety of uses. However, the levels of this disamenity were apparently not high enough in the sample areas for the negative influence to dominate the correlation between them and the distance to the ruling center.

4. Exclusivity and Neighborhood Characteristics

Unlike natural amenity features such as hilly terrain or a lake view, the supply of which can be altered only through changes in the household's location, quality of neighborhood is an amenity whose supply is influenced by individual and collective actions of households. Restrictive covenants, discriminatory real estate practices, and homeowners' councils are devices designed to enable communities to regulate the socioeconomic characteristics of their populations. A hypothesis is that land values are higher in communities with a greater degree of exclusivity than in those where barriers to entry are low or nonexistent.

The three measures of exclusivity appearing in Table 7.2 are zero–one variables indicating: (a) the existence or absence of a homeowners' council; (b) whether or not the homeowners' council requires that potential buyers be approved by the council prior to purchase; and (c) the presence or absence of a restrictive covenant on the purchase deed.[18] All three are positive, as predicted, and significant at the .01 level or higher. Moreover, the coefficients are quite large. The premium in price per square foot associated with homeowners' councils is 52%, with prior approval, 78%, and with covenants, 109%. This is not to suggest that affixing a restriction, unenforceable in a court of law, onto a purchase deed has any

---

[17] Water quality data for Indiana and Michigan in 1966 were uneven in magnitude and breadth. Indiana reported extensively on a total of 16 water quality parameters—including color, odor, level of dissolved oxygen, turbidity, and temperature—but maintained only two sampling stations along its 33-mile Lake Michigan shoreline. Michigan maintained a large number of sampling points but collected information on only two parameters: total coliform and temperature. Information on dissolved oxygen was not available.

[18] A restrictive covenant stipulates that the buyer may not resell the property at a later date to groups with such racial or other characteristics as are specified in the covenant. Although declared unconstitutional by the U.S. Supreme Court in 1948, many 1966 purchase deeds were found to contain new or renewed covenants.

impact in and of itself on the price of recreational property. Possibly these variables are surrogates either for income of buyer (in which case they simply indicate that higher income homeowners have strong preferences for neighbors of similar income class and are willing to pay premium prices for land to indulge these preferences) or for means by which households exert influence and control in the community other than through income. Note also that the homeowners' council variable may, wholly or in part, reflect activities other than for purposes of exclusivity, such as the achievement of economies of scale in the purchase of public services.

5. Topography

Topographic features of the properties were determined from maps of the U.S. Geological Survey and by inspection. Three sets of characteristics—hilly–level, wet–dry, and wooded–unwooded—were isolated using zero–one variables for each. Seven of the eight interaction variables were included in the regression presented in Table 7.4, the eighth, representing level, wet, and unwooded land, served as reference to avoid collinearity. Coefficients were generally of the expected signs and five were significant at the .10 level or higher.

Table 7.4 presents values of the topography coefficients as departures from the value of level, wet, and unwooded land. With single exceptions, dry properties sell for higher prices per unit than wet properties of similar quality, and wooded land is more expensive than unwooded terrain comparable in other respects. Level properties are generally more valuable than hilly ones, implying that the benefits of a pleasing view from a Lake Michigan dune may be more than offset by increased construction cost per unit of housing. Hilly and wet land, much of which is swamp, is particularly undesirable.

TABLE 7.4
Effects of Topography on Price of Recreational Land,
Indiana and Michigan, 1966

Characteristic	Estimated land price deviation per square foot from price of level, wet, unwooded land ($)	Standard error
Hilly, Dry, Wooded	.84	.34
Hilly, Dry, Unwooded	.79	.42
Level, Dry, Wooded	.32	.34
Level, Dry, Unwooded	.89	.32
Hilly, Wet, Wooded	−.26	.46
Hilly, Wet, Unwooded	−.84	.61
Level, Wet, Wooded	.88	.58

To test for the impact of each recreational community on land values, the logarithm of land prices was regressed on distance from Chicago and on a total of 41 zero–one variables representing each town or community for which two or more observations were available. The results: 35 of the 41 community variables were positive, 15 significantly so, and 6 were negative. Most of the communities contributing positively and significantly to land values were clustered in and near secondary-center submountains. They were not included in the equation reported in Table 7.2 because direct measures of distance and amenity characteristics were desired.[19]

V. CONCLUSIONS

In this study a model was developed to explain the use of private access recreational property near metropolitan areas. The model focused on the urban household maximizing utility from recreation and all other goods subject to constraints pertaining to total expenditure, land price, and a recreation production function. Traditional assumptions about the relation between land price and distance were modified to include demand for land emanating from more than one urban center. Influences of beach accessibility, exclusiveness of neighborhoods, water quality and other amenity features were taken into account. The empirical results strongly support the importance of both access and recreational amenities on recreational land and the general amenity-bid rent model of land use.

REFERENCES

Boyet, W. E., and Tolley, G. S. "Recreation Projection Based on Demand Analysis." *J. Farm Econ.* 48 (November 1966): 984–990.

Brigham, E. F. "The Determinants of Residential Land Value." *Land Econ.* 41 (November 1965): 325–334.

Brown, Jr., G. M., and Pollakowski, H. O. "Economic Value of Shoreline." *Rev. Econ. Stat.* 54 (August 1977): 272–278.

[19] A number of other amenity features were tested and eliminated in early regressions. The contribution of a lake view to recreation was examined using a zero–one variable to denote properties with views, but because of its high (−.83) correlation with distance from Lake Michigan, it was discarded. A surrogate for the supply of public services in each community was constructed by adjusting the 1966 property tax rate for each observation for variations in the ratio of assessed to actual valuation. If recreational households value public services at exactly their cost of production at the margin, variations in the supply of services within each community will have no effect on the price of land. The public service variable was in fact rarely significant and was dropped from the analysis. The distribution of recreational housing by race was examined using percentage of nonwhite population by township. Aside from problems arising from the use of townships rather than communities or census tracts as base populations, the variability of these data was not large enough to permit adequate testing.

Cesario, F. J., and Knetsch, J. L. "Time Bias in Recreation Benefit Estimates." *Water Resources Res.* 6 (June 1970): 700–704.

Cicchetti, C. J. *Forecasting Recreation in the United States*. Lexington, Mass.: Lexington Books, 1973.

Clawson, M., and Knetsch, J. L. *Economics of Outdoor Recreation*. Baltimore, Maryland: Johns Hopkins Press, 1966.

Diamond, Jr., D. B. "The Relationship Between Amenities and Urban Land Prices." *Land Econ.* 56 (February 1980): 21–32.

Grimes, Jr., O. F. "A Land-Use Approach: Private Access Recreation near Urban Centers." *Growth and Change* 5 (April 1974): 1–7.

Gum, R. L., and Martin, W. E. "Problems and Solutions in Estimating the Demand for and Value of Rural Outdoor Recreation." *Am. J. Agric. Econ.* 57 (November 1975): 558–566.

Harris, R. N. S., Tolley, G. S., and Harrell, C. "The Residence Site Choice." *Rev. Econ. Stat.* 50 (May 1968): 241–247.

Mills, E. S. "The Value of Urban Land." In *The Quality of the Urban Environment*, edited by Harvey S. Perloff. Baltimore, Maryland: Johns Hopkins Press, 1969.

Muth, R. F. *Cities and Housing*. Chicago, Ill.: U. of Chicago Press, 1969.

Outdoor Recreation Resources Review Commission, *Outdoor Recreation for America*. Washington, D.C.: Government Printing Office, 1962.

Sirmans, C. F., Kau, J. B., and Lee, C. F. "The Elasticity of Substitution in Urban Housing Production: A VES Approach." *J. Urban Econ.* 6 (October 1979): 407–415.

Smith, V. K. "The Estimation and Use of Models of the Demand for Outdoor Recreation." In *Assessing the Demand for Outdoor Recreation*. Washington, D.C.: National Academy of Sciences, 1975.

U.S. Department of the Interior, Bureau of Outdoor Recreation *Water-Oriented Outdoor Recreation: Lake Michigan Basin*. Ann Arbor, Michigan, 1965.

8

Racial Composition as a
Neighborhood Amenity

BARTON A. SMITH

I. INTRODUCTION

The standard amenity model takes as exogenous the neighborhood characteristics of each location. Given the fixed geographic distribution of these neighborhood amenities, as households bid for housing in each area, a stable equilibrium set of prices emerge such that no household can improve its well-being by moving to an alternative location. An extension of this basic model recognizes that households not only value the standard neighborhood amenities but also the type of households that will be their neighbors. In other words, the characteristics of all individuals living in the same vicinity directly or indirectly affect the utility of each resident. Unlike other amenities, this aspect of the neighborhood environment is endogenous to residential site choices and therefore involves the existence of a type of externality. That is, each household's level of utility is not only affected by its own maximizing choice but by the choices of others as well. In the presence of these interpersonal externalities, the housing market must yield a set of equilibrium prices that both clears the urban housing market in the traditional sense and assures that individual location decisions do not disturb the equilibrium choice of others.[1]

[1] Since in traditional urban models all amenities are assumed fixed and exogenous, a move by one household will leave unaffected the optimum choices of all other households. Where households themselves impose negative or positive externalities upon each other, this is no longer the case. Thus, in this expanded version of the urban model that incorporates externalities between households, much more attention must be given to the conditions that must exist in order for there to be stability in the entire urban housing market.

165

THE ECONOMICS OF
URBAN AMENITIES

For individual households, stability *and* certainty regarding the demographic characteristics of their neighbors is of particular importance. Households will be willing to pay full neighbor-oriented neighborhood premiums only for areas where they can be assured that as all other households make residential site choices, such choices will not adversely affect them. Placed in a dynamic context, households will not only pay higher housing prices for the association of a particular type neighbor but will seek, through choices of housing and location, to obtain various forms of "insurance" that will protect them from the unpleasant consequences of other household's location decisions.[2]

A wide variety of household characteristics might be hypothesized as imposing external effects. These include such demographic attributes as family size or structure, religious preference, ethnic background, and socioeconomic class. Race, in particular, has been given considerable attention in the literature, though a lack of consensus currently persists in both the empirical and theoretical race and housing literature. This may be partially explained by the fact that the analyses of racial impacts on urban housing markets have not been adequately placed within a complete framework of an urban economic model with interpersonal externalities.

The most recent debate involves criticism surrounding the basic housing model of prejudice first proposed by Bailey (1959, 1966) and later popularized by Muth (1974). In general, the arguments reflect the fact that neither Muth, Bailey, nor those who dismiss their models fully considered the unique aspects of location and housing consumption decisions in a world where households value characteristics of their neighbors. As a consequence, they fail to expand their analysis to include household behavior given the presence of uncertainty regarding one's neighbors in long-run equilibrium.

An important issue is whether, in the absence of exclusive neighborhoods that are maintained by direct exclusion of "undesirables," a *stable* market solution can emerge that is consistent with neighbor-oriented preferences. With regards to race, two schools of though exist. Courant and Yinger (1977) argue that, given racial prejudices (preferences), any equi-

---

[2] Of course, it is widely accepted that such instruments as zoning and neighborhood deed restrictions are means to provide household insurance against the imposition of negative externalities associated with conflicting land uses. More recently it has been recognized that both zoning and deed restrictions can effectively "protect" an area from the intrusion of undesirable neighbors, such as low-income households or minorities. However, as will be discussed later in the text, households may also "buy" insurance against the ill effects of many types of neighbor-oriented externalities without the explicit help of such legal institutions as zoning.

librium in the urban housing market is inherently unstable unless buttressed by exclusionary practices of whites to keep blacks out of their neighborhoods. Furthermore, they suggest that current observable patterns of segregation must entail the existence of exclusionary discrimination. This position is in direct opposition to the basic conclusions of prejudice models, of which the Muth–Bailey border model is one type. With prejudice models, segregation and price differentials emerge as a stable equilibrium outcome without the imposition of constraints on the residential mobility of any market participants.

The basic argument presented in this chapter is that the general model of prejudice has been too quickly dismissed by many economists, including Courant and Yinger (1977). This is not to suggest that all exclusionary practices whereby blacks are kept out of white neighborhoods have been eliminated. Rather, as long as preferences regarding the race of one's neighbors continue to exist, the workings of the urban housing market will tend to promote continued segregation, even in the absence of explicit exclusion. This conclusion is based upon a more general treatment of prejudice models that more adequately considers the unique nature of household location decisions involving neighbors.

In the following sections, the basic premises and conclusions of prejudice models are reexamined. The primary intent is to extract a much broader set of hypotheses regarding expected observable housing market outcomes than theretofore developed in the existing literature (see Yinger, Galster, Smith, and Eggers, 1979, for a summarization of the race and housing literature). These hypotheses are then examined in light of new empirical evidence. Although the theoretical models discussed and the empirical ones presented focus almost exclusively on race as the distinguishing characteristic that influences household location decisions, this chapter should be viewed as having general application to housing market behavior and outcomes in most cases where households place a value on who their neighbors are.

II. RACIAL PREJUDICE IN HOUSING MARKETS

For decades explicit racial discrimination involving overt exclusion prevented the movement of black households into white neighborhoods. In "protected" areas, landlords simply did not rent to blacks, nor were blacks sold homes. More recently, indirect means have been devised in order to prevent blacks from moving into white neighborhoods. These include the use of zoning laws, deed restrictions, and building codes—all of which it has been argued, were at least partially intended to exclude "undesirable" households from an area.[3]

Explicit exclusionary discrimination is purported to place virtually all of the burden of prejudice upon black households, who supposedly face higher home prices because of the subsequent restricted supply. On the other hand, with less direct means of excluding blacks, some of the burden of racial prejudice is assumed to fall upon white households. In this case, buying the protection of a "racially zoned" neighborhood is apt to impose some costs upon whites, including the consumption of more housing than would otherwise be desired. For example, these indirect means of exclusion often involve effective floors on the levels of housing quality available in an area (no rental property, large minimum lot size requirements, etc.). As a consequence, some whites will be forced to "overconsume" housing in order to receive the benefits of the exclusive neighborhood.

Because of recent legal changes brought about by fair housing policies and civil rights legislation, explicit exclusionary practices are becoming less evident. Nonetheless, white prejudices can still impact housing markets as whites attempt to buy housing in locations distinguished by the characteristics (race) of neighbors as well as of neighborhood. In fact, even in the absence of direct or indirect exclusionary discrimination to maintain a neighborhood's racial character, white prejudices will still have profound effects upon housing market outcomes.

A. Muth–Bailey Models of Prejudice

There are numerous models of urban housing markets that describe the impact of white racial prejudices. Most stem from the initial contribution of Martin Bailey (1959, 1966), later extended by Richard Muth (1975). Their basic conceptual framework (hereafter referred to as the Muth–Bailey model) involves the assumptions that whites prefer not to live with nor near blacks and that initially the two races are geographically separated. Whites will reside at or near the black–white neighborhood border only if housing in the area is sufficiently discounted to compensate white households for the disutility of living there. The result is that home prices

---

[3] Prior to the civil rights legislation of the 1960s, exclusionary discrimination was relatively open and to a considerable degree, simply accepted. Even during the 1970s, exclusionary discrimination continued to exist, only in more subtle forms. Recently, the Department of Housing and Urban Development funded experiments referred to as "housing audits" that revealed a wide variety of ways that blacks may be excluded from an apartment complex or neighborhood while minimizing the probability of detection and hence legal recourse. (See Wienk, Reid, Simonson, and Eggers, 1979.)

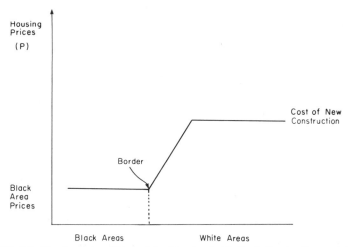

FIGURE 8.1. Housing price differentials: The simple Muth–Bailey border model.

in white areas near the border will be depressed relative to prices in interior white neighborhoods. If black prices at the border exceed white border prices, blacks, who are "free to move," will begin to occupy these white areas, thus expanding the black area and ultimately shifting the border. This process continues until prices on both sides of the border are equal. In equilibrium, housing prices in black areas will, therefore, be lower than prices in white interior areas as shown in Figure 8.1.

If, as is generally assumed, white households live at the urban fringe such that white housing prices are tied to the costs of new construction, house prices in black areas will be depressed below new construction costs. Individual blacks, though free to move into white areas, will have no incentive to do so because of the white prejudice premiums they would have to pay to live there. Consequently, blacks remain sequestered in the ghetto, consuming older housing (but at a discount price).[4] Because the structure of equilibrium prices generates a disincentive for blacks to move into white areas, the market equilibrium that emerges is stable. This assures whites that the status quo of each neighborhood they consider will be maintained (in the absence of some unanticipated exogenous change in the market). Because the Muth–Bailey model concludes that perfect seg-

[4] It should be noted that in the real world of durable housing capital, both land and housing capital earn urban economic rents. Therefore, prices can fall substantially in black areas, even below so-called replacement costs. Failure to recognize this aspect of the housing market has led Courant and Yinger (1977) to erroneously conclude that, if land rents fall below the price of agricultural land at the fringe, the interior urban area will revert to a greenbelt or "graybelt." However, only if *all* rents (to land and structure) fall to below agriculture farm prices could such a phenomenon occur.

regation will be sustained and because white preferences regarding race are defined in terms of distance from the border of the black neighborhood, this and similar models are usually referred to as *border models*. However, as is discussed in paragraphs to follow, models of prejudice in general may not yield the restrictive border model results.

B. Extended Versions of Prejudice Models

The basic Muth–Bailey construct has been easily incorporated into more standard urban price gradient models by Rose-Ackerman (1975), Courant and Yinger (1977), and White (1977). In these modified Muth–Bailey models, blacks and whites participate in the standard bid price competition for locations. Following Muth (1969), it is a typically assumed conclusion that lower income households have steeper bid-price functions and hence tend to live closer to the CBD. Because blacks, in general, have less income than whites, blacks live close to the CBD and whites live near the urban fringe. Thus, as in the more simple model, a black–white border will exist that separates the two populations, with price equalization at the border still holding. Past the border, prices actually rise with distance from the CBD as the premiums whites pay for areas further from the border outweight discounts due to decreased accessibility from the CBD.[5] At some distance, however, these accessibility discounts become greater than the prejudice premiums associated with even further geographic distance from blacks, and the price function again resumes its normal downward slope.

As before, the resulting set of prices across locations generates strong incentives for blacks to remain in the low-priced ghetto. This guarantees the stability of the equilibrium outcome. Thus, whites can be assured that their neighborhood will remain segregated. Relative to blacks, whites will pay for their prejudicial preferences. However, these modified Muth–Bailey models make it more clear that whites actually end up paying no more than if there were no prejudice. Instead, in the presence of prejudice blacks pay less as urban economic rents are depressed. Thus, the results from this modified model, shown in Figure 8.2, are basically the same as for the simpler version.

One interesting difference between this model and the simple Muth–

---

[5] More realistically, whites may pay premiums to be further from the black ghetto simply because with distance from the ghetto comes a declining probability that one's neighborhood will experience a dramatic racial transition. However, in all border models it is simply assumed that whites suffer disutility from being close to the border. As will be shown later, if the desire to be distant from the border is related to the probability of racial transition, other factors that can keep that probability low, even for neighborhoods close to the ghetto, will also likely produce prejudice premiums.

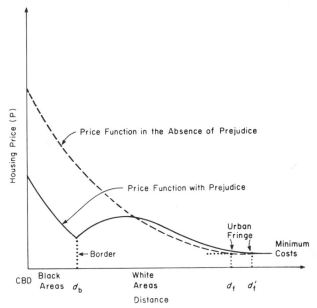

FIGURE 8.2. Housing price differentials: The border model in the context of urban price gradients.

Bailey construct is that households are also segregated by income class as well as by race. Following Muth (1969) and others, higher income households are assumed to locate further from the CBD.[6] Thus, at the black–white border the highest income blacks will be adjacent to the lowest income whites. Consequently, there exists a slight possibility that the structure of housing prices across distances from the CBD may not deter high-income blacks from moving into white neighborhoods.

This point is brought out by Courant and Yinger (1977). However, they fail to stress that whites and blacks will live together only if the slope of each household's bid-price function is the same *and* if the total bids at that location are identical. If prejudice premiums are high enough, house prices in the ghetto can be depressed even below the lowest priced white housing at the urban fringe. Hence, even if the bid-price functions of high-income blacks were essentially flat, they still might not "hop" (as referred to by Courant and Yinger) over the white middle class and attempt to integrate themselves with high-income whites.

[6] The assumption that low-income households have steeper bid-price functions and therefore live closer to the CBD stems from Muth (1969). This assumption is not being defended here. Indeed, given recent evidence, it is probably incorrect. In either case, as long as differences in income exist along with a "natural" geographic distribution of households by income, some degree of segregation will exist, as pointed out by Smith (1980b).

Whether or not higher income blacks will actually "hop" across the racial border and reside in the more distant neighborhoods depends upon a variety of factors including (a) the magnitude of prejudice premiums paid by whites to avoid the border; (b) the relative size of the black and white population; (c) the distance from the border where the price function again begins to fall; and (d) the slope of the bid-price function of high-income blacks.

Diagramatically, only if the average slope of the market price function between locations d_b and d_f' is less than the slope of the bid-price function of the highest income blacks will they find it in their interests to move to "the suburbs." This would lead to an unstable situation given the Muth–Bailey formulation of prejudice. However, as demonstrated in Smith (1980b), the condition required in order for "hopping" to exist is unlikely to occur. Indeed, under a wide variety of assumptions $P(d_b)$ will be lower than $P(d_f')$. In addition, Smith argues that "hopping" is in part an artificial by-product of the restrictive assumptions regarding white prejudice tastes (disutility is defined only in terms of distance to the ghetto), which leads to either the absolute segregation of the border models or apparent disequilibrium chaos.

Another useful modification is an amenity model of prejudice where white prejudice is redefined in terms of the percentage of blacks that live in their immediate neighborhood rather than in terms of distance from all black neighborhoods (i.e., the border). Assuming there exists an inverse relationship between income and distances to the CBD and assuming that the distribution of black incomes is skewed toward lower income levels than are whites, then *in the absence of prejudice,* some geographic concentration is still to be expected, as illustrated in Figure 8.3. In Figure 8.3(a) the population density function for each group is described in terms of distance (instead of income), which in turn yields racial composition curves. Thus, even in the absence of prejudice a degree of defacto racial segregation will exist, due simply to income differentials.[7]

As long as the percentage of blacks declines with distance, then the introduction of prejudice as just defined will simply lower the slope of white bid-price functions, P_d^w.[8] Thus, for black and white households of similar income, black bid-price functions at each location d_i will be steeper, $-P_d^b(d_i) > -P_d^w(d_i)$. As a consequence, whites will migrate outward, and blacks will migrate inward, as depicted in Figure 8.4, until at each lo-

---

[7] For a discussion of the empirical literature that addresses this issue of the proportion of segregation due to economic differences between races, see Smith (1979).

[8] Price functions with respect to distance $P(d)$, for whites and blacks are distinguished by the superscripts w and b, respectively. Slopes of the bid function are designated by P_d with the appropriate superscript.

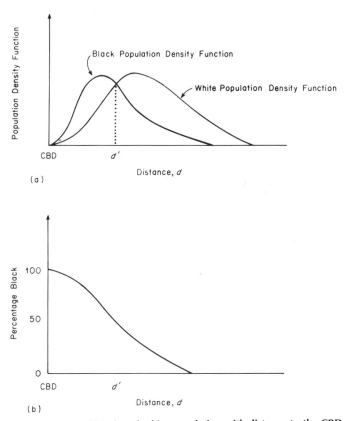

FIGURE 8.3. Distribution of black and white population with distance to the CBD.

cation black and white bids, as well as the slopes of the bid-price functions, are equal: $P^W(d) = P^b(d)$ and $P_d^w = P_d^b$. However, in a world of prejudice, this can only occur if at each location black incomes exceed white incomes, $I^b(d) > I^w(d)$.[9]

Although quantitatively these results differ somewhat from the simple Muth–Bailey model, qualitatively they are the same. The sharp decline in housing prices will not exist as before, but prejudice in the housing market does lower prices in black and integrated areas below nonprejudice levels, resulting in an overall depression of urban economic rents. White preferences are at least partially actualized in that white households end up liv-

[9] Equilibrium requires that at each location $P_d^b = P_d^w$. Following the standard Muth proposition that the slope of the bid-price function P_d declines with income, if P_d^w falls because of the disamenity associated with living with a higher proportion of blacks, then $P_d^b(I^b) = P_d^w(I^w)$ requires that at each distance d_i, $I^w < I^b$.

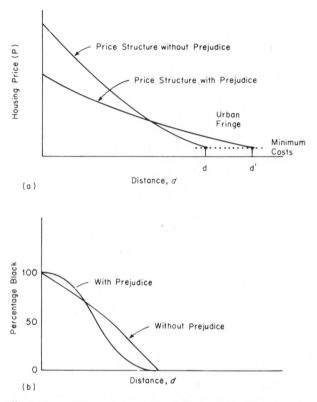

FIGURE 8.4. Effects of prejudice on urban price gradients and racial composition.

ing in neighborhoods with a lower percentage of black neighbors, as white prejudice prices keep many blacks from "fully integrating" all neighborhoods.[10] The major difference, of course, is that some integration will occur. Furthermore, there exists no distinct black–white neighborhood border.

[10] Typically, in prejudice models the black population ends up being more centralized. However, this need not occur. An alternative outcome could be the concentration of blacks in one quadrant of a city, described in the urban monocentric model as a wedge emanating from the CBD. However, this outcome is not easily described in the context of static equilibrium models. For a nonconcentric "pattern of segregation" to emerge as a stable equilibrium outcome, a dynamic urban model could possibly be developed so that land prices at the urban fringe differ for black and white expansion (new development) areas. Clearly, early writers have simply accepted as the initial starting point the historical centralization of blacks, particularly in northern cities. Given this initial geographic concentration of blacks, prejudice models then demonstrate why such patterns are easily maintained.

C. Racial Prejudice and Housing Consumption

A particularly interesting proposition generated from the model above is that for the racial integration to be stable, black incomes in such areas must exceed white incomes. As a result, discounts on home prices in racially integrated areas may not be the only mechanism that brings about a spatial distribution of households by race. Stable integration as defined here would require that, within integrated areas, there must exist heterogenous housing with blacks living in higher quality dwelling units. This condition is easily satisfied within the context of the standard monocentric urban model with a maleable stock of housing capital such that housing is instantaneously produced to satisfy the demands of households currently at each location. However, since the stock of housing in most neighborhoods is, in fact, reasonably homogeneous and since the geographic distribution of houses by quality type is relatively fixed over long periods of time, it is likely that households seeking to "buy" neighborhoods with neighbors of their liking will be forced to alter their consumption of housing in order to achieve the level of neighbor-oriented neighborhood amenities they desire.[11]

If at each location the basic quality of housing in the area is relatively homogeneous and inelastic in supply, then to meet the conditions for stable integration ($I^b > I^w$), either blacks living there will have to underconsume housing relative to their economic status or whites will have to overconsume housing. This, of course, places an additional cost upon either or both household types.[12] As a result, black households will now find the integrated neighborhoods relatively less attractive than the ghetto, and white households may find the *net effective discount* in the integrated area insufficient to keep them there. Thus, in a world of relatively fixed stock of housing capital, urban areas will likely be even more segregated because of prejudice than the simple amenity model of prejudice would predict.

Once it is recognized that neighborhoods are distinguished by both standard spatial amenities and the quality of the stock of housing available there, it becomes evident that another means exists whereby whites can "purchase" segregated neighborhoods. Given that the income distribution of black households is skewed lower relative to whites, areas with

[11] For example, a household with a particularly strong preference to live in the same area as households of substantially higher incomes is apt to find that they must "overconsume" housing to achieve that objective.

[12] Such a cost is essentially the same concept as that developed by Smith (1978), where neighborhood premiums are defined in terms of the loss in consumer surplus to land associated with high land prices in high amenity areas.

higher quality homes would be expected to have a smaller percentage of blacks, even in the absence of other distortions such as that created by white prejudiced prices. Whites, therefore, may acquire a greater assurance of living in a predominantly white neighborhood by buying more housing (i.e., housing services or quality). In other words, just as individual white households have incentive to live further from the CBD to achieve spatial separation from blacks, so do they have an incentive to overconsume housing to achieve the same objective. This phenomenon will be even more pronounced if white prejudice against blacks is related to the economic status of potential black neighbors. In essence, whites may find an area attractive because the quality of the homes there assures them that the area will not undergo significant racial transition since relatively few blacks can afford housing in the area. Furthermore, those blacks with higher incomes that might move into such areas are apt to be viewed as "less objectionable."

Such behavior will be especially important in urban areas that are rapidly growing and for which the black population is expanding. This expansion means that many previously all-white neighborhoods will experience black immigration. Neighborhoods that contain housing whose quality level is consistent with the economic status of a sizeable segment of the black population will be viewed as "less secure," and prices there will be discounted. On the other hand, in areas where housing quality exceeds the economic capabilities of the majority of black households, white prejudice prices will be observed because of the premiums whites are willing to pay for the *assurance* of having white neighbors. In the former case, the discounts in home prices due to *expectations* of racial transition in the future will only speed the process of racial change. In the latter case, the fact that the area is *expected* to remain segregated will generate racially oriented neighborhood premiums that will, in themselves, help assure the maintenance of the status quo.

D. Ghetto Expansion and Owner Occupancy

Because of typically lower levels of wealth among blacks and because of the importance wealth plays in the acquisition of owner-occupied housing,[13] areas that have a large proportion of rental units are likely to be discounted by whites since these areas will be perceived as having a greater probability of experiencing racial change.[14] Again, because of

[13] See Smith and Campbell (1980) and Smith and Mieszkowski (1980) for evidence of the important role wealth plays in the acquisition of owner-occupied housing.

[14] This seems to be the implicit assumption behind "racial zoning" that prohibits multi-family housing within a neighborhood community.

these discounts, these areas will become even more attractive to blacks, some of whom will rent and others of whom will buy discounted owner-occupied housing. Furthermore, in a dynamic context, areas *expected* to undergo racial transition may still have higher "white rents" but have already low prejudice-oriented capital prices. Such a high rent to value ratio is conducive to the conversion of owner-occupied housing into rental units. Thus, black expansion is more likely to push toward discounted areas with a large proportion of rental units, and the expansion of black neighborhoods in itself will lead to the conversion of owner units to rental units. As a result of the dynamics of racial transition and of the behavior of whites to avoid areas of potential transition, the proportion of blacks relative to whites who are observed residing in rental units is expected to be high, even after controlling for incomes and wealth.

Whites, on the other hand, recognize that they can purchase more secure white neighborhoods by residing in areas that not only have high-quality housing but also consist mostly of owner-occupied units. Although the owner-occupied nature of the area might be maintained by restrictive zoning and other mechanisms, it can also be preserved simply by the presence of high property values (from prejudice prices) and by the overconsumption of housing in general. That is, neighborhoods with a high percentage of owner occupancy and high-quality homes will be viewed as more secure from minority intrusion that will result in additional premiums being paid for the area, premiums that will in themselves create still stronger disincentives for blacks to move in.

E. Summary

Models of prejudice predict the existence of positive neighborhood premiums paid by white households to live in predominantly white areas that are geographically separated from black neighborhoods. The result is that housing prices will be observed to be lower in all black areas and will rise (ceteris paribus) in locations (*a*) with increasing distance from those black areas; (*b*) with a declining percentage of black households living there; and–or (*c*) with diminishing expectations of future racial change. In the latter case, expectations of racial change are expected to be correlated with (*a*) nearness to the black ghetto; (*b*) the percentage of rental units in the area; (*c*) the average quality of the stock of housing (the level of housing services per dwelling); and (*d*) and the general level of neighborhood amenities.

In one sense, whites pay for their prejudice, in that the housing prices they must pay are higher than those for blacks. But whites, in general, actually pay no more for housing than they would if there were no prejudice. The major effect is that blacks pay less for housing. Thus, one result of prejudice is an interesting wealth transfer from land and–or property owners to black households as inner city urban economic rents are depressed. In fact, these economic rents attributable to both land and capital can fall to the point where housing prices in the ghetto are below replacement costs at the urban fringe.

The price differentials that emerge create a housing market environment such that it is in the interests of black households (who are "free" to move) to remain in the ghetto. This, coupled with distorted white consumption patterns, will result in a high degree of racial segregation, much more than would otherwise be expected.[15] In the typical case, blacks will be more centralized about the CDB, and whites will be more decentralized in the suburbs.

Segregation, however, need not always be absolute. At any point in time, integrated areas may exist either as transition areas in temporary disequilibrium or as stable integrated neighborhoods. However, for integrated areas to be stable, blacks in the area must have higher incomes than their white neighbors. Thus, unless a significant degree of variance in home quality exists in integrated neighborhoods, a part of the "price" paid to live there will entail the costs of underconsumption of housing by blacks or overconsumption of housing by whites.

Differentials in consumption levels by blacks and whites, however, are a broader phenomenon, observed in more than just integrated areas. Whites in all-white segregated areas are also expected to consume more housing and to have a higher propensity to own than blacks in general. This "overconsumption" of housing provides whites with an additional means to achieve their objective of living in all-white areas, secure from racial transition. Blacks, on the other hand, are more likely to rent and to consume less housing because of the dynamics of racial transition of neighborhoods. Expansion of black neighborhoods will occur in more predominately rental areas with dwellings of moderate quality where prejudice prices are too low to present an effective barrier to black immigration. Consequently, because there exist several reasons why consumption differentials are generated between blacks and whites in the housing market, traditional references to these differentials are inappropriate. Indeed, such phrases as "blacks consume less housing," and "blacks have lower propensities to own" are misrepresentations of the effect of prejudice on housing market participants. Clearly the purported underconsumption of housing by blacks just as easily reflects the overconsumption of housing by whites.

---

[15] See Smith (1979) for an empirical definition of segregation consistent with prejudice in urban housing markets.

Finally, the impact of racial prejudices on owner-occupied and rental housing markets will differ to some extent. Large differentials in price (rents) are less likely. Because of the greater mobility of white renters, *potential* transition areas will not warrant a discount; only *actual* transition areas will. However, since blacks are more likely to be renters, areas with a significant number of rental units will be perceived as less "secure." Therefore, expectations of potential racial transition will keep white capital price premiums either low or nonexistent in these areas, which in and of itself will further promote black immigration.[16]

If models of prejudice are applicable to today's urban housing market, a wide variety of phenomena should be observed if prejudice remains pervasive. These include housing price differentials correlated with the racial composition of the area or with distance to black areas; differentials in housing consumption and ownership patterns between blacks and whites; and a degree of segregation that exceeds what might be reasonably expected in the absence of prejudice. Although integrated neighborhoods may be observed, in most cases they should be observed to be unstable, that is, moving toward complete racial transition. To the extent that an integrated neighborhood achieves any degree of stability, differentials in the income of black and white households should be observed there. The expansion of black neighborhoods into previously white areas should occur in moderate income neighborhoods, especially those with a high percentage of rental units. Conversion of owner-occupied dwellings to rental units is expected to accompany or just precede racial transition.

All these phenomena are consistent with the basic premises and conclusions of models of prejudice, but any one does not entail sufficient evidence to ascertain these models' credibility. In fact, many are also consistent with the existence of direct exclusionary practices.[17] On the other hand, the observance of all of these expected phenomena would provide substantial evidence to support prejudice models, especially if they include Muth–Bailey-type price differentials. Models of prejudice clearly hypothesize that housing in black areas will sell at a discount. Models of exclusion suggest that housing prices in the black ghetto will be unusually high because of the restricted nature of the supply of housing. Indeed, a

---

[16] Rental areas will be viewed as more open to blacks because (*a*) there exists no wealth requirements; (*b*) black incomes are generally sufficient today for most rental units; (*c*) rental areas are, in general, not "overconsumption areas" where whites can feel "protected;" and (*d*) the self-fulfilling prophetic nature of expectations that themselves will help keep prejudice prices to a minimum, thus breaking down a primary barrier to in-migration.

[17] For example, consumption and ownership differentials are hypothesized by models of exclusion, where it is assumed that blacks are not only restricted to the ghetto but that the restriction itself limits the supply of housing to blacks to the more inferior stock of housing (often rental) in the urban area. On the other hand, were this the case, the limited supply should surely result in higher prices in black neighborhoods.

greater concensus regarding the relationship between housing prices and race will considerably help resolve the debate regarding the applicability of prejudice models to today's housing markets.

III. EVIDENCE FROM THE HOUSTON HOUSING MARKET

A series of studies have been concluded that focus on the impact of race on housing markets in Houston, Texas.[18] Taken together, these studies provide a considerable amount of empirical evidence by which many of the hypotheses stated previously may be examined. Included in these studies are analyses of (a) housing price differentials associated with race; (b) differentials in consumption patterns between races; (c) the pattern and nature of segregation in Houston; (d) the movement of minority groups within the metropolitan area; and (e) the process of racial transition within selected neighborhoods.

The data used in these studies were obtained from several sources. Five thousand observations on housing characteristics and home prices came from data complied by the Society of Real Estate Appraisers, (SREA). Of these, 635 observations included detailed information regarding the owner–occupant of each home. These data were obtained through a special survey funded by the Department of Housing and Urban Development, (HUD). Also used were block and census tract data from the 1960 and 1970 censuses as well as a complete school census data from the Houston Independent School District, (HISD).

Analyses performed in these studies included the estimation of (a) hedonic price equations for neighborhoods designated by race; (b) housing consumption functions; and (c) logistic functions of tenure choice. In addition, using revised segregation indices, changes in the spatial distribution (and concentration) of blacks and Hispanics during the past two decades were explained. In this chapter, only brief explanations of the empirical techniques are provided. The primary emphasis is placed on the presentation of the empirical results and their implications. Readers interested in details of the methodology are directed to the full reports.

A. Housing Price Differentials

SREA housing data for 1977, which provided market prices along with structural characteristics, were matched with additional information on

---

[18] See Smith (1977, 1979, 1980a, 1980c, 1981) and Smith and Mieszkowski (1980).

distance to major work centers and key neighborhood attributes. The latter included information on crime, pollution, and measures of school quality as well as census data. The 3736 observations were grouped into five geographic areas designated as (*a*) White; (*b*) Integrated; (*c*) Border–Nontransition; (*d*) Border–Transition; and (*e*) Black. These categories correspond to that used by Berry (1976) in his analysis of price differentials in Chicago.[19] In addition, 2112 observations for 1970 were grouped into the same subareas in order to estimate differences in rates of home value appreciation over an 8-year span of time.

For each area, a *separate* hedonic house price equation was estimated. In all cases the econometric fit was quite respectable ($R^2 > .80$), and most of the estimated coefficients of the 12 independent variables used had the correct sign and were statistically significant.[20] Using a modified version of a technique popularized by Blinder (1973), differences in average house values between the five areas were separated into that part that could be attributed to differences in the *price* of housing as opposed to that that was merely due to differences in the average housing bundle available. From the former, neighborhood hedonic price indices were calculated from which comparisons could be made.[21] Relative to white areas, the *average price* of housing was 21% lower in black areas, 16% lower in integrated areas, 10% lower in border areas perceived to be threatened by racial transition, and 7% lower in border areas that are thought to be relatively secure from black immigration in the immediate future.[22] Although these price differences could in part be attributed to differences in neighborhood characteristics, the net affect of adjusting these indices for the

[19] This designation was chosen because Chicago as well as Houston SREA data were used to analyze housing price differentials. This permitted comparisons between the Chicago results and Berry's findings and between the Chicago and Houston results. Although only the Houston results are discussed here, the empirical findings for Chicago were virtually identical. See Smith and Mieszkowski (1980) for complete details.

[20] The independent variables included (*a*) square feet of living area; (*b*) lot size; (*c*) number of baths; (*d*) number of rooms; (*e*) age of structure; (*f*) dummy variables for the presence of brick exterior, basement, fireplace, garage, and central air-conditioning; and (*g*) qualitative indices for condition and modernization (remodeling).

[21] As quality controlled price indices, these basically measure differences in the average price of housing in each of five neighborhoods.

[22] These results are reasonably consistent with those of Berry (1976) and Schnare (1976), but they do conflict with the empirical findings reported by Kain and Quigley (1970), King and Mieszkowski (1973), and Yinger (1978). Nonetheless, all of these studies make the same mistake of estimating a single hedonic equation for the overall urban area that controls for race by use of dummy variables or of a single continuous race variable. This specification severely constrains the estimated price function by requiring the shadow prices of all housing attributes to be the same in each neighborhood. Furthermore, as demonstrated in Smith and Mieszkowski (1980), if the housing price function does differ (in terms of both the slope coefficients and the intercept term) in white and black areas, then single equation estimation can generate erroneous signs on those traditional race variables.

expected impact of differentials in neighborhood amenities was considered small.[23]

Following the same basic technique, price indices for 1970 were estimated by area and used to calculate the rate of house price inflation from 1970 to 1977. The results show a divergence in neighborhood appreciation rates. During the 1970–1977 period, white upper-middle-income neighborhoods that had been secure from minority intrusion experienced an average annual rate of appreciation of approximately 22%. On the other hand, prices rose an an annual rate of 14% in white border areas, 10% in white border areas threatened by transition, 12% in integrated areas, and 11% in black areas.

Together, these results present a pattern that is fully consistent and supportive of the models of prejudice outlined previously. Prejudice prices do appear to exist for white areas. Furthermore, racial discounts are not just correlated with distance to the all black ghetto. They also appear to be related to the percentage of blacks within a neighborhood and to expectations that the percentage will increase in the near future. Furthermore, the magnitude of prejudice prices is seen to be increasing as the gap between prices in black and white areas widens.[24] The presence of prejudice in the Houston housing market not only can be observed from such general patterns as described in Table 8.1, but also is evident from the observation of particular neighborhoods. One good example is a large

[23] Whether or not differences in the characteristics of each neighborhood account for any of the price differentials reported depends greatly on the weights (i.e., implicit prices) used to evaluate neighborhood characteristics. Because the variances in the neighborhood variables within the separate racially designated areas were small, shadow prices could only be obtained from a metropolitan-wide regression. However, the extremely high correlation between many of these variables and race made the results somewhat untrustworthy. This is especially true with regards to the quality of neighborhood schools and neighborhood crime rates. Only two neighborhood variables were reasonably uncorrelated with respect to race: accessibility and pollution. Estimated coefficients from the overall sample suggest that black area prices would, in the absence of prejudice, be expected to be 7% higher because of better accessibility and 5% lower because of high levels of pollution and thus do not explain the actual 21% discount observed. However, there does exist a major difference in school quality between black and white areas, as measured by student performances. Indeed, in Houston it is perceived that school quality is significantly inferior in predominantly minority Houston Independent School District. The empirical results on the surface indicate that inferior school quality could account for a 10% black–white differential in home prices or half of the 21% discount observed. However, the school variable used (as well as general perception of school quality in Houston) is highly correlated with the racial composition of the area. Furthermore, other evidence strongly suggests that it is this correlation between race and school quality that has generated, to a great extent, white prejudices regarding black and integrated neighborhoods.

[24] To some extent the fact that nonthreatened border areas experienced a lower rate of appreciation than white areas may reflect a change in status for some of these areas from white interior areas in 1970. The same is true for threatened areas that were nonthreatened border in 1970.

TABLE 8.1
Differentials in Price and Rates of Appreciation by Neighborhood

Price differentials (compared with secure white areas)	Percentage
Border areas (not threatened by transition)	− 7
Border areas (threatened by transition)	−10
Integrated areas	−16
Black areas	−21
Annual rates of change in house price (1970–1977)	
White areas (upper-middle income)	22
Border areas (not threatened by transition)	14
Border areas (threatened by transition)	10
Integrated areas	12
Black areas	11

all-white area in southwest Houston. The neighborhood is split by high school boundaries, where one school is currently about 60% minority (black and Hispanic) and the other is predominantly white. Other than the racial composition of the schools, there is virtually no other difference in the neighborhood and housing characteristics of these two areas. Nonetheless, home prices (as measured by hedonic price indices) within the minority school boundaries were found to be discounted 15%. In this particular case, the general high quality of homes and the subsequent high home values have prevented the discounted area from experiencing any significant racial transition. Instead, as might be expected, the area is undergoing another type of demographic change, where white households with school-age children are being replaced by households with no children.

B. Differentials in the Consumption of Housing

Using the subsample of 635 observations for which information was also available on the characteristics of the households living in each house, OLS regressions were applied to analyze the level of housing expenditures and the consumption of specific housing characteristics for both blacks and whites. In some ways the approach taken is comparable to that of Quigley (1974), Straszheim (1974), and Kain and Quigley (1975). However, much more attention is given to such issues as correctly specifying the budget constraint to include a measure or permanent income and wealth and distinguishing households not only by their own race but also by the racial composition of the neighborhood in which they live.

TABLE 8.2
Owner-Occupied Housing Market
Comparisons of Black–White Expenditure
and Consumption Levels

Attribute	Black consumption
Expenditures	10–30% less
Lot size	4% less[a]
Living area	1% more[a]
Quality index	22% less
Home age	30% older

[a] Not significantly different from zero.

As shown in Table 8.2, blacks are found to spend 10–30% less on housing, ceteris paribus, a result fully consistent with models of prejudice. Indeed, within the context of prejudice model hypotheses, this finding is more accurately stated that whites spend about 10–30% more. However, it is somewhat difficult to interpret differences in expenditures per se. That is, these findings could, in part, simply reflect the fact that blacks pay approximately 20% less for comparable housing services. Furthermore, the results of these expenditure analyses were sensitive to alternative definitions of permanent income. Apparently there exists a different relationship between current income and permanent income for blacks and whites. In fact, as suggested by Smith and Mieszkowski (1980), transitory income seems typically a larger proportion of total black incomes. Thus, how permanent income is empirically defined for analytical purposes tends to significantly effect consumption (expenditure) estimates for blacks.

On the other hand, analyses of the consumption levels of key housing attributes as reported in Table 8.2 were much less ambiguous. Relative to whites, blacks were found to consume less housing "quality," defined both in terms of the age of housing and of a single hedonic weighted variable of several attributes normally associated with housing quality. In particular, it was found that blacks, ceteris paribus, purchased homes that were 30% older with about 22% less quality.[25] Again, it must be remembered that if the prejudice models are correct, this so-called underconsumption of housing by blacks is a misnomer and really reflects overconsumption by whites. That is, whites are consuming more than the

[25] This result also tends to verify that indeed, blacks do pay less for housing since the 30% older age and 22% less quality can account for only about 7% less expenditures and hence total house value. If the *expenditure* differential of 30% is correct, this then implies that for equivalent housing, average *prices* for blacks must be 23% lower.

expected level of housing quality and buying newer dwellings to avoid racial integration.[26]

As expected, comparisons of blacks and whites living in integrated areas produced similar estimates of consumption differentials as found between blacks and whites in general. However, in this case, the phenomenon is more likely due to the fact that black incomes are expected to exceed white incomes in integrated areas, even though the stock of housing there is relatively homogeneous.[27] On the other hand, when comparisons were made of black and white households living in the same predominately white areas (perceived as secure from racial transition), no differences were observed either with respect to housing expenditures or the consumption of housing attributes.

Statistically, the average income of blacks in white areas were not significantly higher than those of their white neighbors. However, these black households typically had incomes in excess of $35,000, double the average income of black households in the entire sample. This pattern is more consistent with models of prejudice (particularly amenity models), where white preferences are defined in terms of the socioeconomic status of their neighbors as opposed to only race. In this case, it appears that the percentage of black households earning $35,000 is perceived to be too small to constitute a threat to the stability of the segregated neighborhood or that high-income blacks are considered less undesirable by whites.

C. Home Ownership

The analysis of ownership rates involved somewhat different issues. The approach taken involved the application of logit analysis to approximately 1000 observations of owners and renters. The estimation procedure was quite similar to that used by Li (1977). Although the usual list of explanatory variables found in the literature (such as income, age, and

[26] One must be cautioned, however, that these results may be somewhat city-specific. Indeed, as has been argued here, black consumption levels are to a great extent determined by the type of housing stock present in areas where black neighborhood expansion has occurred. Much of this expansion in Houston has occurred in low density areas with single family detached housing (though often rental). Thus, it is not surprising that black home buyers in Houston do not consume less living space or land.

[27] It should be noted that all observations were for households who had just purchased a home. Hence, as would be expected in the case of unstable integrated neighborhoods, there exists few new white buyers. Consequently, the comparisons of income differences between blacks and whites in the same area had to be made with use of census tract data or the micro-household data survey applied to a geographic area associated with a much broader definition of "integrated." The former approach (using census data) is seriously hampered by the decennial nature of the census. The latter approach (with the micro data), on the other hand, was not totally satisfactory since it really entailed comparing blacks and whites from different neighborhoods.

number of children) were used, special attention was given to the inclusion of wealth and previous tenure (owner versus renter) as important determinants of current ownership. Also, a considerable effort was made to guarantee a reasonable degree of sample representativeness, which is shown by Smith and Mieszkowski (1980) and later, by Smith and Campbell (1981), to be of critical importance in logit analysis.

The logistic function was estimated using an adjusted representative sample. With permanent income, wealth, and previous tenure included along with the traditional demographic variables, results were obtained indicating that blacks, ceteris paribus, have a 10% lower probability of owning. Excluding wealth, ownership rates for blacks were estimated to be 20% lower, a result that is quite consistent with the findings of other research. (See Kain and Quigley, 1972, 1975; Roistacher and Goodman, 1976; Straszheim, 1974; and Struyk, 1975.) Thus, although wealth differentials explain a good part of the overall difference in black–white ownership rates, they do not explain all of it.

The major departure from the literature is not the empirical results per se but their interpretation. In light of outcomes predicted by models of prejudice, these results are in part considered a reflection of abnormally high white ownership rates since whites find living in exclusively owner-occupied areas one additional means to minimize the expected number of blacks that might become their neighbors.

However, it is also possible that this phenomenon (lower ownership rates) is due to the process of integration itself. As predicted by prejudice models, racial transition areas in Houston have, indeed, rapidly converted to rental areas just before and during the transition period. Furthermore, over the past decade it has been those areas near the border with a high percentage of rental units that have undergone racial transition. In addition, the lack of zoning in Houston, which has allowed a significant amount of new, multifamily complexes to be built in middle-class white interior neighborhoods, has helped open the way for some integration in many areas that were all-white in 1970. Owner-occupied units in these areas still warrant high, prejudiced prices since the proportion of multifamily units there does not present a significant threat to the status quo. Thus, many previously all-white census tracts are now partially integrated, but with the minorities living almost exclusively in apartments. Such a phenomenon further reinforces the tendency for blacks to rent.

Two interesting examples are useful in illustrating the relationship between tenure rates and the process of racial change. In 1960, the South Park area of Houston, as described by the census, was nearly 100% middle-class white. The stock of housing was almost exclusively single-family detached housing, approximately 90% owner-occupied. During the mid1960s, black immigration had begun to occur. In 1970 the area, as reported by the census, was technically integrated. By 1970 approximately one third of the owner-occupied units had been converted to rental units as *real* capital values fell. Despite the fact that the initial transition primarily involved only middle-income black households, black incomes there were somewhat less than whites. This would immediately suggest that the observed integration was unstable, and indeed, it was. By 1980, South Park had become predominately minority (about 95%), with about 50% of all housing rental. Thus, the process of racial transition became complete (resegregation), and it brought with it, as expected, a significant shift in owner-occupancy rates.[28]

The second example involves most of the western portions of Houston, which were almost exclusively white in 1970. Because of the housing crunch during the mid 1970s, the pattern of new residential construction changed dramatically. For the first time in Houston history, the construction of multifamily units emerged as equal in importance to the construction of new, single-family dwellings. During this time most of the remaining vacant land in this area was developed for multifamily purposes. Again, because of the lack of zoning, many of these white middle-class and upper-middle-class neighborhoods now have 15–30% multifamily units. In areas where the percentage of rental units is considered "tolerable" (10–20%), no white flight has yet to occur, even though many of these rental units house over 50% minorities. As a result, it has been estimated by Smith (1979) that western portions of Houston now have about 8% black and 10% Hispanic.[29] Nonetheless, expectations are that these areas will remain relatively stable with respect to their racial composition now that no more vacant land exists in these neighborhoods. Because of the general high quality of the owner-occupied homes there and the high neighborhood premiums that are being paid for good accessibility, most single-family units (with market values in the $75–150,000 range) are considered out of the reach of most black families. Thus, the possibility of further black immigration is assumed to be minimal.[30]

Other areas in the south and southwest of Houston that were all-white

[28] It should be noted that a part of this phenomenon may be due to the "redlining" of transition areas. Redlining need not, however, reflect discrimination per se but instead may reflect the general proposition that a significant decline in housing capital values accompanies racial transition. As discussed in Smith, Callaway, and Crackett (1978), such a perception can lead to self-fulfilling prophecies where, in anticipation of depressed prices, lenders withhold mortgage funds, which in turn assures price declines.

[29] Census tracts in western sections of the city, which contained virtually no blacks in 1970, were estimated to have 3–17% black in 1979.

[30] Although these areas have an average of nearly 8% black population, much less than 1% of all owner-occupied housing is owned by blacks. In this particular case, some degree of neighborhood integration is achieved where white incomes are substantially higher than black incomes. However, such would not be the case in the long run if the area were not considered secure from further transition.

in 1970 are experiencing complete racial transition. These areas, too, experienced a significant expansion of new multifamily rental units, but here in many cases the percentage of rental units exceeded 50%. Also, the average quality of homes in these areas was much lower, with house values between $35,000 and $60,000. As a consequence, expectations of transition were higher, and prejudice prices were minimal. Now such areas have as much as 50% minority population, and the prospects for integration being stable in these areas are unlikely. Indeed, some areas in which the process of transition began earlier in the decade are already 85% minority. The only exceptions are the few areas where there exists low–moderate-income housing that is sufficiently heterogeneous and discounted that some whites will remain. In these areas black incomes exceed white, as predicted by models of prejudice.[31]

IV. CONCLUSION

These empirical results and the general observations are consistent with the notion that a neighborhood's social environment is related to general characteristics of the residents in the area and that this environment impacts housing prices in much the same way as do other neighborhood amenities. Although race was emphasized, the same principles apply to such characteristics as income, wealth, and social position. These neighbor-oriented amenities, however, do differ from such standard locational characteristics in that they are endogenous to the market clearing process. Consequently, locational premiums emerge only where a household can be assured that the equilibrium outcome will be consistent with its preferences.

As long as households wish to reside with neighbors of similar characteristics, the expanded version of the prejudice model is applicable. Where households have strong preferences for similar-type neighbors, they will offer higher prices for housing in neighborhoods where the residents there match these tastes. In equilibrium, as households attempt to "buy" through the housing market the type of neighbors they desire, socioeconomic segregation will occur because these preferences will be at least partially satisfied.[32]

[31] One of the primary sources of such low-cost housing in integrated areas is trailer courts, many of which are predominantly white. Such trailer courts interspersed within the more traditional residential areas provide the necessary housing stock heterogeneity required for stable integration.

[32] Note that where households have strong preferences to live in areas with residents different than themselves, the stable equilibrium predicted by prejudice models may break down. Furthermore, even if a stable equilibrium does emerge, it will usually result in lower levels of consumption of neighbor-oriented amenities than in a world without such preferences.

With regards to the race and housing literature, the evidence presented here cannot be considered sufficient proof of the validity of the prejudice model, but the fact that all aspects of the Houston housing market cited are consistent with the expanded prejudice models is certainly persuasive. Furthermore, though both models of exclusionary discrimination and models of prejudice predict the existence of the type of segregation patterns observed and the consumption differentials between blacks and whites that exist, the pattern of housing prices that exists across neighborhoods distinguished by race is really only consistent with prejudice models.

The empirical findings presented here and elsewhere have definite policy relevance to the extent that they tend to confirm the prejudice model. For example, if prejudice models are an accurate description of the housing market, open housing policies alone will not achieve the type of social objective for which they were purportedly created. Equal access to housing that guarantees individuals of all races the *opportunity* to acquire housing wherever they choose may do little to bring about integration. The elimination of direct exclusionary discrimination will not eliminate the market forces generated by white prejudice that continue to effectively keep whites and blacks segregated.

From a pure welfare economics perspective, such an outcome, in the absence of any social (or collective) considerations, is not even Pareto efficient. The externality associated with race leads to social inefficiencies since households, in attempting to segregate themselves on the basis of race, will behave such that housing consumption, tenure, and location decisions will be distorted. Whites will, ceteris paribus, live too far from the CBD, buy too much housing, and have ownership rates that are too high. Ironically, in a world of perfect exclusion, where blacks are not allowed to live in the same areas as whites, most of these inefficiencies disappear.[33] This suggests that in cases where society has no interest, the formation of exclusive neighborhoods or clubs is efficient in that no particular market distortion need emerge to maintain the status quo. Thus, an area might legitimately be set aside for households with no children, household of a particular ethnic or religious background, or households with homogeneous demands for public goods. The problem, of course, is that in such a world of Tiebout-type neighborhoods, social policy that attempts to directly or indirectly redistribute real income at the local level will be frustrated.

---

[33] This is true as long as both submarkets faced similar supplies of housing. That is, if there existed a north–south boundary through the CBD with a wall separating the two areas, then price differentials, location distortions, and consumption differentials should disappear.

REFERENCES

Bailey, M. "A Note on the Economics of Residential Zoning and Urban Renewal." *Land Econ.* 35 (1959): 288–292.

Bailey, M. "The Effects of Race and Other Demographic Factors on the Value of Single Family Homes." *Land Econ.* 42 (1966): 215–220.

Berry, B. "Ghetto Expansion and Single-Family Housing Prices: Chicago, 1968–1972." *J. Urban Econ.* 3 (1976): 397–423.

Blinder, A. "Wage Discrimination: Reduced Form and Structural Estimates." *J. of Hum. Res.* 8 (1973): 436–455.

Courant, P., and Yinger, J. "On Models of Racial Prejudice and Urban Residential Structure." *J. Urban Econ.* 4 (1977): 272–291.

Kain, J., and Quigley, J. "Measuring the Value of Urban Amenities." *J. of Amer. Stat. Association,* 65 (1970): 532–548.

Kain, J., and Quigley, J. "Housing Market Discrimination, Homeownership, and Savings Behavior." *Am. Econ. Rev.,* 62 (1972): 263–277

Kain, J., and Quigley, J. *Housing Markets and Racial Discrimination.* New York: National Bureau of Economic Research, 1975.

King, A. T., and Mieszkowski, P. "Racial Discrimination, Segregation, and the Price of Housing." *J. Polit. Econ.* 81 (1973): 590–606.

Li, M. "A Logit Model of Home Ownership." *Econometrica* 45 (1977): 1081–1099.

Muth, R. *Cities and Housing.* Chicago, Ill.: U. of Chicago Press, 1969.

Muth, R. "Residential Segregation and Discrimination." In *Patterns of Racial Discrimination: Housing,* edited by G. von Furstenburg *et al.* Lexington, Mass.: D. C. Heath, 1974.

Muth, R. *Urban Economic Problems.* New York: Harper, 1975.

Quigley, J. "Racial Discrimination and the Housing Consumption of Black Households." In *Patterns of Racial Discrimination: Housing,* edited by G. von Furstenberg *et al.* Lexington, Mass.: D. C. Heath, 1974.

Roistacher, E., and Good, J. "Race and Home Ownership: Is Discrimination Disappearing?" *Econ. Inq.* 14 (1976): 59–70.

Rose-Ackerman, S. "Racism and Urban Structure." *J. Urban Econ.* 2 (1975): 85–103.

Schnare, A. "Racial and Ethnic Price Differentials in an Urban Housing Market." *Urban Stud.* 13 (1976): 107–120.

Smith, B. A. "Separating Discriminatory Segregation from DeFacto Segregation." Report prepared for the U.S. Department of Housing and Urban Development, Contract No. HUD-1760-77, 1977.

Smith, B. A. "Measuring the Value of Urban Amenities." *J. Urban Econ.* 5 (1978): 370–387.

Smith, B. A. "Defacto versus Discriminatory Segregation." Unpublished manuscript, University of Houston, 1979.

Smith, B. A. "Racial Discrimination: Some New Empirical Evidence." In *Housing Policy for the 1980's,* edited by D. Marshall and R. Montgomery. Lexington, Mass.: D. C. Health, 1980(a).

Smith, B. A. "Blacks in Urban Housing Markets: A Reevaluation." Unpublished manuscript, University of Houston, 1980(b).

Smith, B. A. "An Analysis of Changes in the Geographic Distribution of Black and Hispanic Populations in Houston Since 1970." Report prepared for the Houston Independent School district, 1980(c).

Smith, B. A. "A Study of Racial Discrimination in Housing." In *Research in Urban Economics,* edited by J. V. Henderson. Vol. 1. Greenwich, Conn.: JAI Press, 1981.

Smith, B. A., and Campbell, J. "Housing Demand: The Joint Tenure and Expenditure Decision." Unpublished manuscript, University of Houston, 1980.

Smith, B. A., and Campbell, J. "Pure Sample Bias in Estimating the Demand for Housing." Unpublished manuscript, University of Houston, 1981.

Smith, B. A., and Mieszkowski, P. "A Study of Racial Discrimination in Housing." Report prepared for the U.S. Department of Housing and Urban Development, Contract No. H-2557-RG, 1980.

Smith, B. A., Callaway, G., and Crackett, J. "Lending Patterns in the Houston Metropolitan Area." Report prepared for the Fair Housing Division, City of Houston, Contract No. 18749, 1978.

Straszheim, M. "Racial Discrimination in the Urban Housing Market and Its Effect on Black Housing Consumption." In *Patterns of Racial Discrimination: Housing,* edited by G. von Furstenberg, *et al.* Lexington, Mass.: D. C. Heath, 1974.

Struyk, R. "Determinants of the Rate of Home Ownership of Blacks Relative to White Households." *J. of Urban Econ.,* 2 (1975): 271–286.

White, M. "Urban Models of Race Discrimination." *J. Reg. Sci. Urban Econ.* 7 (1977): 217–232.

Wienk, R., Reid, C., Simonson, J., and Eggers, F. *Measuring Racial Discrimination in American Housing Markets: The Housing Market Practices Survey.* Washington, D.C.: U.S. Department of Housing and Urban Development, 1979.

Yinger, J. "The Black–White Price Differential in Housing: Some Further Evidence." *Land Econ.* 54 (1978): 185–206.

Yinger, J., Galster, G. Smith, B., and Eggers, F. *The Status of Research into Racial Discrimination and Segregation in American Housing Markets.* Washington, D.C.: U.S. Department of Housing and Urban Development, 1979.

IV

REGIONAL AMENITY MARKETS

9

Urban Structure, Wage Rates, and Regional Amenities

DONALD R. HAURIN

I. INTRODUCTION

This chapter draws together two literatures that discuss the methods by which households are compensated for differences in amenity levels across urban areas. One type of research (see Cropper and Arriga-Salinas, 1980; Hoch, 1972, 1975; Izraeli, 1977; Meyer and Leone, 1975; Tolley, 1974) examines whether the compensation for urban disamenities is through adjustments in the nominal wage rate or through changes in the prices of local goods, thus the city's price deflator. The issue, in general, is the identification and separation of these two effects. Also of interest is an analysis of the relationship of the city's industrial structure to the manner of compensation for the amenity differential. Finally, the question arises as to whether "perverse" relations between changes in wages or housing prices and changes in amenity levels will ever be observed in the standard urban model. The model presented in the chapter is capable of analyzing both wage and price compensation for urban disamenities. It is simplified so that the type of compensation can be discussed; however, it is rich enough to include intraurban spatial relations and to identify urban aggregates such as the size of the resident population.

Another set of literature has concentrated on relating disamenities to the internal (spatial) structure of an urbanized area (see Cobb, 1977; Fish, 1975; Freeman, 1971, 1974a, 1974b, 1975; Harrison and Rubinfeld, 1978; Maler, 1977; Papageorgiou, 1973; Polinsky and Rubinfeld, 1975; Polinsky and Shavell, 1975; Small, 1975; Wieand, 1973). Using land value studies,

195

THE ECONOMICS OF
URBAN AMENITIES

this type of modeling has led to the empirical measurement of the loss due to disamenities. However, the interactions of changes in the spatial structure and urban aggregates (population, wages, spatial size) are usually not fully developed.[1]

The solution to these problems requires a structure that accounts for both spatial interactions within a city and external relations with other cities and allows for the identification of changes in urban aggregates. The model presented in this chapter is fairly standard, extended to include disamenities, and it satisfies the above criteria in a straightforward manner.[2] It is simplified in that a spatial central business district (CBD) is not included.[3] However it does consider a variety of alternative structures of the production sector. Questions concerning compensation through wages and the price of local goods (housing) are the primary focus of this analysis.

The remainder of this section will discuss in general terms the form of the model. Since the results of a general formulation would be ambiguous in this case, certain functional forms are assumed in the next section. These assumptions allow for the complete specification of the interrelationships of amenity levels, wages, the price of housing, population, and the spatial size of the urban area. The chapter concludes with examples of the various effects that disamenities may have.

Households are assumed to receive utility from the consumption of a composite good (which is produced in the area and may be exported), locally produced housing, the level of amenities, and leisure. Travel within the city is costly since it reduces leisure time, resulting in the generation of a price of land (housing) gradient equalizing utility levels at all residential locations. Demand functions for the composite good and housing are derived as well as a population density function.

The production sector is characterized by a set of competitive firms with external economies or diseconomies of scale present at the industry level. Firms pay their inputs the value of their marginal products, and a relation between wages and the aggregate industry labor force is then derived from the unit cost function. Pollution, the illustrative disamenity examined here, takes on a simplified form in the urban area. Since spatial variations in pollution levels (due to dissipation, variation in location of

---

[1] The paper by Polinsky and Rubinfeld (1975) contains an excellent discussion about the form of the spatial model usually employed. It also indicates the empirical conclusions that can justifiably be drawn from the model and related regression analysis and the complexities introduced when changes in population and wage rates are allowed.

[2] This model is best described by J. V. Henderson (1977). Since his presentation includes most of the derivations, they will not be repeated here. He includes a discussion of pollution (Chapter 5), but it is directed towards an analysis of the optimal pollution tax.

[3] See Henderson (1977, pp. 32–35) for the details of a spatial CBD.

source, wind patterns) are not critical to the aggregate relations in the urban area, only a uniform level will be considered.[4] The pollution is generated from two sources: The first is external to the urban area and it affects households only, not the production technology of the firms. The other source is the resident industry, where emissions are assumed to be a function of output. This assumption adds another relation between the city aggregates and another layer of complexity.[5]

The other good produced locally is housing, which also must be consumed locally. Tolley (1974) suggested that an urban wage multiplier mechanism is present where, if local wages rise, the price of local goods increases, requiring further compensation of households, leading to further impacts. This mechanism is modeled by including local labor as an input into housing, resulting in the price of housing being directly related to local wage rates. This formulation is not meant to model exactly the production technology in housing but to express the essential effects of Tolley's hypothesis.

The resulting system of relations can then be differentiated with respect to a change in amenity levels. The solution expresses changes in both the urban aggregate statistics and internal spatial relations as a function of the parameters of the system.

II. A MODEL OF AN URBAN AREA WITH POLLUTION

A. The Industrial Sector

Each firm produces a good x which is consumed locally and can be exported. It employs inputs of labor ℓ and business capital k_b subject to the following linear homogeneous technology:

$$x = G(L_x)\ell^{\alpha_1}k_b^{\alpha_2} \qquad \alpha_1 + \alpha_2 = 1. \tag{9.1}$$

Included in the production function is a shifter $G(L_x)$ that each firm views as given since the industry's use of labor L_x is assumed to be substantially

---

[4] Variations in pollution levels are critical to additional changes in the price of housing beyond those noted in this study. This effect of pollution will not be captured in the model; however, it has been explored in other works (Papageorgiou, 1973). Any effects of spatial variations in pollution on city size are assumed to be negligible.

[5] An extension to this article would allow firms to abate emissions through the use of additional inputs if there was an incentive to do so (such as an emissions tax.) An endogenous optimal emissions tax could be specified (see Henderson, 1977, pp. 103–106) and the reactions of the city aggregates derived.

larger than any one firm's use of labor. External economies of scale are present if $G'(L_x) > 0$, diseconomies of scale if $G(0) > 0$, $G'(L_x) < 0$.

With this technology, Euler's theorem implies that each firm's revenues are exhausted by payments to factors. Since land is not included as an input to production of the industrial good (not critical to this model), a point CBD is assumed.

From the value of marginal product equations, each firm's demands for inputs can be derived. Substituting back into Eq. (9.1) yields a relation between the yearly wage rate w and the industry's use of labor:

$$w = C_0 G(L_x)^{1/\alpha_1}, \tag{9.2}$$

where

$$C_0 = (\alpha_1{}^{\alpha_1} \alpha_2{}^{\alpha_2} p_x p_k{}^{-\alpha_2})^{1/\alpha_1}.$$

It is assumed that both the price of capital (p_k) and the price of the output (p_x) are fixed in a national market. From (9.2), it is seen that the variation in wage rates with the size of the labor force depends on the form of scale economies.

Total production in the industry is

$$X = G(L_x) L_x{}^{\alpha_1} K_b{}^{\alpha_2}, \tag{9.3}$$

where the uppercase symbols represent industry aggregates. If pollution (P) is modeled as being emitted by firms then it is assumed that:

$$P = P(X) \quad \text{and} \quad P'(X) > 0. \tag{9.4}$$

In a more complex structure, each firm could abate emissions using additional labor. A firm only has an incentive to do so if it is taxed directly on its own emissions. It is assumed that a single firm's emissions form a small part of total pollution, thus individual acts of abatement would have only negligible effects on the wage rate.

B. The Residential Sector

Households are assumed to prefer a clean environment, designated by the amenity level:

$$a = a(P) \tag{9.5}$$

where

$$a'(P) < 0, \qquad a(0) = a^*.$$

At this point a dispersion pattern for emissions could be introduced, however for simplicity, the amenity level is assumed spatially invariant. Furthermore, households cannot escape pollution by moving across some boundary, rather pollution is modeled as an urban phenomenon. All households in the urbanized area are subject to pollution.

The household utility function is represented as:

$$U(r) = U(x, h, a, e) = C_1 x(r)^{\gamma_1} h(r)^{\gamma_2} a^{\gamma_3} e(r)^{\gamma_4} \tag{9.6}$$

where $\gamma_1 + \gamma_2 = 1$. Also, $U(r)$ is the level of utility at distance r from a centralized workplace, h is the consumption of housing (yearly), x represents the consumption of other goods, and e is leisure time.[6] The budget constraint faced by the household is

$$y = p_x x + p_h(r)h, \tag{9.7}$$

where $p_h(r)$ is the spatially variable price of housing and y is yearly income. Also,

$$e(r) = T - tr, \tag{9.8}$$

where T is total leisure time available and tr is commuting time that is directly related to distance from the CBD.[7]

Households maximize utility subject to their constraints. The result is the demand equations for x and h and a locational equilibrium equation. The latter two are presented in Eqs. (9.9) and (9.10):

$$h(r) = \gamma_2 y p_h(r)^{-1} \tag{9.9}$$

and

$$p_h'(r) = -t\gamma_4 p_h(r)/\gamma_2(T - tr), \tag{9.10}$$

where

$$p_h'(r) = \partial p_h(r)/\partial r.$$

The indirect utility function is

$$V(r) = C_2 y p_h(r)^{-\gamma_2} a^{\gamma_3}(T - tr)^{\gamma_4}, \tag{9.11}$$

where

$$C_2 = \gamma_1^{\gamma_1}\gamma_2^{\gamma_2} p_x^{-\gamma_1}.$$

The specification of a production technology for housing is required to find the aggregate relationships in the city. The simple form chosen is presented in Eq. (9.12):

$$h(r) = \phi k(r)^{\beta_1} n(r)^{\beta_2} \ell_h(r)^{\beta_3}, \tag{9.12}$$

---

[6] Another imported composite good could be added to the model; however, trade balances and trading relations of the city are not critical to the development of the primary results of this study. Thus, for simplicity, x is viewed as a composite good that happens to be the same as that produced by the industrial sector.

[7] Total leisure time is a constant if total work time is assumed to be fixed. A more general formulation would allow for both mechanical and time costs in travel; however, such a change would make the model intractable if implimented in the usual manner by subtracting transport costs from the (income) budget constraint.

where $k(r)$ is housing capital, $n(r)$ is land used in housing, $\ell_h(r)$ is labor used in housing, and $\beta_1 + \beta_2 + \beta_3 = 1$. The competitive producers maximize profits thus determining their demands for factors. Specifically, the quantity of land per household is

$$n(r) = \beta_2 p_h(r) h(r) p_N(r)^{-1}, \tag{9.13}$$

where $p_N(r)$ is the price of land. Labor is introduced in Eq. (9.12) to capture Tolley's wage multiplier effect. It is assumed that the wage rate of these workers is equal to w, the same as the industrial sector.[8] Substituting Eq. (9.13) and similar equations for $\ell_h(r)$ and $k(r)$ results in:

$$p_h(r) = C_3 p_N(r)^{\beta_2} w^{\beta_3}, \tag{9.14}$$

where $C_3 = (\phi \beta_1{}^{\beta_1} \beta_2{}^{\beta_2} \beta_3{}^{\beta_3} p_k{}^{-\beta_1})^{-1}$. Inspecting Eq. (9.14), the wage multiplier effect is evident as well as the relation between the price of land and the price of housing. As the wage rate increases, ceteris paribus, the price of the local good, housing, increases.

The price of housing can be derived in two ways. Using Eq. (9.11) and assuming an open city where the level of utility is fixed at V, the price of housing is determined to be

$$p_h(r) = C_4 y^{1/\gamma_2} a^{\gamma_3/\gamma_2} (T - tr)^{\gamma_4/\gamma_2}, \tag{9.15}$$

where $C_4 = (V^{-1} C_2)^{1/\gamma_2}$. This price of housing function is typical of monocentric urban models where p_h declines with increasing distance from the CBD. An alternative technique is to integrate Eq. (9.10) and solve for the constant of integration by observing that, at the endogenous edge ($\bar{r}$) of the city, the price of housing is determined by the exogenous price of agricultural land ($\bar{p}$) and wages. The result is[9]

$$p_h(r) = \bar{p}_h(T - t\bar{r})^{-C_5}(T - tr)^{C_5}, \tag{9.16}$$

where $C_5 = \gamma_4/\gamma_2$ and $\bar{p}_h = p_h(\bar{r}) = C_3 \bar{p}^{\beta_2} w^{\beta_3}$. [The latter result is derived from Eq. (9.14).]

The spatial variation in the price of land is found by substituting Eq. (9.14) into Eqs. (9.15) or (9.16):

$$p_N(r) = \bar{p}(T - t\bar{r})^{-C_5/\beta_2}(T - tr)^{C_5/\beta_2}. \tag{9.17}$$

---

[8] These laborers are not local workers in Muth's sense (see Muth, 1969, p. 42), where a wage gradient results.

[9] It has now been assumed that yearly income y equals the yearly wage w. This implies that laborers are renters, landlords are absent from the city, and no urban land rentals are returned to households through a mechanism such as a federal land bank.

Equating (9.15) and (9.16) yields

$$a^{\gamma_3/\gamma_2}(T - t\bar{r})^{C_5}w^{1/\gamma_2-\beta_3} = C_3\frac{\bar{p}^{\beta_2}}{C_4}. \qquad (9.18)$$

The above equation relates the level of amenities in the city to the endogenous wage rate and spatial city size. It is part of the system of equations used to determine reactions to changes in air quality.

The aggregate relations of the urban area are now derived. First, the total population L in the city can be determined by integrating the population density relation across space.[10] In Eq. (9.13), the quantity of land per household $n(r)$ is described, thus its inverse yields the required density relationship. Substituting Eq. (9.9) for housing expenditures and Eq. (9.17) for the price of land and integrating from CBD to the city edge $\bar{r}$ yields

$$L = C_7 w^{-1}s_1(\bar{r}), \qquad (9.19)$$

where $s_1(\bar{r}) = T^{C_6+2}(T - t\bar{r})^{-C_6} - (T - t\bar{r})[T + t\bar{r}(1 + C_6)]$,

$$C_6 = \frac{C_5}{\beta_2},$$

$$C_7 = 2\pi\bar{p}/\beta_2\gamma_2 t^2(C_6 + 1)(C_6 + 2).$$

The total population is composed of industrial workers and local workers in housing L_h. To determine L_h, the quantity of local workers at location r can be integrated across space. Thus:

$$L_h(r) = \int_0^{\bar{r}} \ell_h(r)h(r)dr,$$

where $\ell_h(r)h(r)$ is the number of local workers at each location. The VMP equation for labor, which is derived from Eq. (9.12) is

$$\ell_h(r) = \beta_3 p_h(r)h(r)w^{-1},$$

Since housing expenditures per household are a constant fraction of income, $p_h(r)h(r) = \beta_2 w$, then $\ell_h = \beta_3\gamma_2$ for each house. Assuming the number of houses and population are identical, then there are L houses, or:

$$L_h = \beta_3\gamma_2 L. \qquad (9.20)$$

Equation (9.20) describes the relation between the total population in the city and the number employed in local production. The number employed

---

[10] Note that the total population is assumed equal to the total labor force.

in the export industry can be found since we know

$$L = L_x + L_h. \tag{9.21}$$

If it is assumed that the city's industry produces no pollution (it is all externally generated), then the unknowns are L, L_x, L_h, w, and $\bar{r}$, and they can be determined using Eqs. (9.2), (9.18), (9.19), (9.20), and (9.21). If pollution is internally generated, then P and the amenity level are endogenous and Eqs. (9.4) and (9.5) must be considered. Once the urban aggregate relations are found, the prices of housing and land, and housing expenditures, can be determined from Eqs. (9.16), (9.17), and (9.9).

III. SMALL EXTERNAL CHANGES IN THE LEVEL OF POLLUTION

To indicate the results derived from this type of model, the smaller system of five equations and unknowns is differentiated and usually expressed in the form of percentage changes. In Part A of the appendix the differentiated versions of Eqs. (9.2), (9.18), (9.19), (9.20), and (9.21) are presented. Substituting Eq. (9.20') into (9.21') and the result into (9.2') yields the relationship between changes in wage rates and the total population:

$$\frac{dL}{L} = \left(\frac{\alpha_1}{\epsilon}\right) \frac{dw}{w}, \tag{9.22}$$

where ϵ indicates the type of scale economies. Specifically, if ϵ is positive (negative), then economies (diseconomies) of scale are present. The three unknowns dL, dw, and $d\bar{r}$ can now be solved for if there is a change in the amenity level da. Specifically:

$$\frac{dw}{w} = \left[\frac{-\theta_1 s_2}{(\theta_3 s_2 + \theta_2(1 + \theta_0))} \right] \frac{da}{a}, \tag{9.23}$$

$$d\bar{r} = - \left[\frac{\theta_1(1 + \theta_0)}{(\theta_3 s_2 + \theta_2(1 + \theta_0))} \right] \frac{da}{a}, \tag{9.24}$$

$$\frac{dL}{L} = - \left[\frac{\theta_0 \theta_1 s_2}{(\theta_3 s_2 + \theta_2(1 + \theta_0))} \right] \frac{da}{a}, \tag{9.25}$$

where[11]: $\theta_1, \theta_3, s_2 > 0$; $\theta_2 < 0$; $\theta_0 \gtreqless 0$.

[11] The values of the parameters are

$$\theta_0 = \frac{\alpha_1}{\epsilon}, \quad \theta_1 = \frac{\gamma_3}{\gamma_2}, \quad \theta_2 = - \frac{tC_5}{(T - t\bar{r})}, \quad \text{and} \quad \theta_3 = \frac{1}{\gamma_2 - \beta_3}.$$

First, consider the simple case where the industry is operating in a region of (locally) constant returns to scale, therefore $\epsilon = 0$ and $dw/w = 0$. In this case:

$$d\bar{r} = -\left(\frac{\theta_1}{\theta_2}\right)\frac{da}{a}$$

and

$$\frac{dL}{L} = -\left(\frac{\theta_1 s_2}{\theta_2}\right)\frac{da}{a}.$$

Thus, if there was an external decrease in amenities (the city becoming less attractive), the total population and spatial city size would decline. Wages are fixed by assumption. At any location r, the price of housing decreases as revealed from the inspection of Eq. (9.16):

$$\left.\frac{dp_h(r)}{p_h(r)}\right|_r = tC_5(T - t\bar{r})^{-1}d\bar{r} + \frac{\beta_3 dw}{w}. \tag{9.26}$$

This case probably corresponds to the model many researchers have in mind when they hypothesize that compensation for disamenity differentials among regions occurs through differences in the price of housing between areas.

If $\theta_0 = -1$, that is, diseconomies of scale are present, then if there is an external decrease in amenities:

$$\frac{dw}{w} > 0, \qquad \frac{dL}{L} = -\frac{dw}{w} < 0, \qquad d\bar{r} = 0.$$

Inspecting Eq. (9.26) reveals that the price of housing increases due to the rising wage rate. Therefore, in this particular structure compensation for the lower level of amenities occurs through an increase in the wage rate. Offsetting this change in income is a smaller percentage increase in the price of housing if $\beta_3 > 0$. The parameter β_3 represents the urban wage multiplier effect; if this is zero, then the price of housing will not vary. Thus, it is the increase in wages that raises the price of local housing even though the amenity level declines. Observation of changes in the price of housing alone would yield a very misleading interpretation of the value of the change in amenity level.

If $\theta_0 > 0$, economies of scale are present and L, w, $p_h(r)$ and $\bar{r}$ will all change in the same direction if the amenity level changes. However, by examining any of the equations relating da/a to changes in w, $\bar{r}$, or L, one finds a generally ambiguous relation. If θ_0 is large (small positive economies of scale), then wages, city size, and city population all decrease if the amenity level falls. Furthermore, the price of housing at an inhabited location will also decrease. In this case, even though the direction of the change in the price of housing is an "anticipated," the change in the wage rate is not compensatory.

In a situation where there are strong economies of scale ($\theta_0 \to 0$), it is likely that wages, city size, population, and the price of housing will increase in response to a decline in amenities. This result is unusual in that the population flow is not as expected. (See Part B of the appendix for proof.) The reason for this result is that a small increase in population results in a large compensating increase in wages and a smaller (costly) increase in the price of housing. If laborers emigrated from the urban area; as L decreased, wages would fall rapidly and the original utility level could not be reattained.[12]

Finally, if there are strong diseconomies of scale, wages, spatial city size, and the price of housing will increase while population size declines. These results are summarized in Table 9.1.

To summarize, four of the five special cases noted above contain "perverse" changes in either income or the price of housing in response to an external change in amenities. In all cases, the combination of changes compensates workers since their utility level remains constant by assumption. However, observation of either the change in housing prices or in wages alone is not sufficient to totally account for the value of the

[12] The stability of the derived solution is a problem in this case.

TABLE 9.1
Economies and Diseconomies of Scale

$\dfrac{da}{a} < 0$	Diseconomies of scale			Economies of scale	
Value of ϵ	Large negative	-1	0	Small positive	Large positive
$\dfrac{dw}{w}$	$+$	$+$	0	$-$	$+$
$\dfrac{dL}{L}$	$-$	$-$	$-$	$-$	$+$
$d\bar{r}$	$+$	0	$-$	$-$	$+$
$\dfrac{dp_h(r)}{p_h(r)}$	$+$	$+$	$-$	$-$	$+$

change in the amenity level. Furthermore, the exact type of change in the prices of local goods or wages depends on the industrial structure of the city.

IV. A SOLUTION IF THE AMENITY LEVEL
IS ENDOGENOUS

If the industrial sector is the source of pollution, as represented by Eq. (9.4), then the change in the amenity level is:

$$da/a = \epsilon_{a,P} \, \epsilon_{P,X} \, dX/X \qquad (9.27)$$

as industrial output varies. In Eq. (9.27), ϵ_{ij} is the elasticity of i with respect to j. Also, from the VMP equation for labor's input to X:

$$dX/X = (dw/w) + (dL_x/L_x). \qquad (9.28)$$

If a stable urban area is described by the equations that determine the levels of L, L_x, X, a, w, and $\bar{r}$, then the effects of changes in various parameter values, production technology, or external changes in pollution levels can be determined. Changes in internally generated emissions are derived in Eq. (9.27), however in (9.23)–(9.25), reactions to either internal or external pollution are accounted for. For example, when $\epsilon = 0$, it was found that the population of the city declined if the level of externally generated pollution increased. Since $dL_x/L_x = dL/L$, the decline in production workers implies a decrease in output, thus less internally generated pollution. The level of amenities tends to return to its original level, moderating the effects of the change in externally generated pollution.[13]

V. SUMMARY

This chapter presents a model of a monocentric urban area where households are sensitive to the level of amenities. The model assumes

---

[13] A final step in this line of analysis would be to construct a numerical example that solves for the levels of L, w, a, $\bar{r}$, and $p_h(r)$. The responses to changes in parameter values or external pollution could then be measured, the results depending on the structure of the city. However, I do not know of any general insights that would be gained, thus this additional step will not be undertaken.

that households are mobile at a prespecified utility level and determines the city's wage rate, population, and spatial size.

Reactions of these variables to changes in externally generated pollution are found. The emphasis is on determining the compensatory nature of variations in wages and the price of housing. Two polar cases are noted:

1. The compensation for amenity changes is only through a wage change.
2. Compensation is through a change in housing prices.

In general, the manner of compensation depends on the form of scale economies in the industrial sector. Thus no generalization as to the manner of compensation can be made among different types of cities. It is noted that, in certain cases, if the amenity level decreases, a counterintuitive movement of either wages or the price of housing may occur. Since any economies of diseconomies of scale are probably small at the observed levels of city size in the U.S., the model predicts that an increase in disamenities will result in a decline in population. However, the movement of the wage rate and housing prices is still dependent on the structure of the industrial sector. Extensions of the theoretical model are noted, including the possibility of constructing a more comprehensive numerical analysis and an analysis of reactions to an emissions tax.

An example of a recent empirical application of this methodology is the work by Cropper and Arriga-Salinas (1980). They explicitly point out one advantage of the interurban approach, compared to the intraurban approach, to measuring the value of disamenities such as pollution. In intraurban studies, differences in property values reflect differences in the levels of pollution in the urban area. The question of how to value the uniform level of pollution remains unanswered. Specifically, in the Cropper–Arriga-Salinas model, they point out that intraurban models do not evaluate the costs of pollution at the workplace (CBD); the costs are only evaluated based on the residential location.

Their model differs from the one presented here in that it assumes that the spatial size of an urban area is fixed. This assumption simplifies the empirical analysis, but it prohibits a long run interpretation. Also, there is a consistency problem with their free mobility assumption for labor, which implies that the nature of the equilibrium is long run. They estimate (using two-stage least squares) an equation for the real wage rate, a function of population and the pollution level. The assumption of a fixed spatial city size is critical in simplifying the econometric problem to a more manageable form. The equivalent equation in this study is Eq. (9.19) where $\bar{r}$ is a function of the amenity level. In Cropper–Arriga-Salinas, the nominal wage is deflated by a price index, creating the measure of real wages. The price index is based on the prices of local and exported goods, but a local wage multiplier effect is not included. They also do not include the full variety of possible industrial structures mentioned in this study. Their analysis is instructive in that it presents a technique for deriving estimating equations and measures of the willingness to pay for clean air based on interurban wage and price differentials.

APPENDIX

Part A

From (9.20):

$$\frac{dL_h}{L_h} = \frac{dL}{L} \tag{9.20'}$$

From (9.21):

$$\frac{dL}{L} = \left(\frac{L_x}{L}\right)\left(\frac{dL_x}{L_x}\right) + \left(\frac{L_h}{L}\right)\left(\frac{dL_h}{L_h}\right) \tag{9.21'}$$

From (9.18):

$$0 = \left(\frac{\gamma_3}{\gamma_2}\right)\frac{da}{a} - \left[\frac{C_5 t}{(T - t\bar{r})}\right] d\bar{r} + \left(\frac{1}{\gamma_2} - \beta_3\right)\frac{dw}{w} \tag{9.18'}$$

From (9.2):

$$\frac{dw}{w} = \left(\frac{\epsilon}{\alpha_1}\right)\frac{dL_x}{L_x}, \tag{9.2'}$$

where $\epsilon = \left(\frac{dG}{dL_x}\right)\left(\frac{L_x}{G}\right)$ represents the type of scale economies.

From (9.19):

$$\frac{dL}{L} = -\frac{dw}{w} + s_2(\bar{r})d\bar{r}, \tag{9.19'}$$

where $s_2(\bar{r}) = \frac{tC_6}{s_1(\bar{r})} [T^{C_6+2}(T - t\bar{r})^{-C_6-1} - T + 2t\bar{r}(1 + C_6^{-1})] > 0.$

Also, $(T - t\bar{r})s_2(\bar{r})/tC_6 > 1$. This can be shown by substituting the value for $s_2(\bar{r})$ into the inequality, which results in:

$$\frac{[T^{C_6+2}(T - t\bar{r})^{-C_6} - T(T - t\bar{r})] + 2t\bar{r}(T - t\bar{r})(1 + C_6^{-1})}{[T^{C_6+2}(T - t\bar{r})^{-C_6} - T(T - t\bar{r})] - t\bar{r}(T - t\bar{r})(1 + C_6)} > 1.$$

This is true because the first terms in the parentheses in both numerator and denominator are identical and positive.

Part B

Consider a city with strong economies of scale, ϵ is positive and large, thus θ_0 has a small positive value. Rewriting Eq. (9.23):

$$\frac{dw}{w} = \left[\frac{-\theta_1}{(\theta_3 + \theta_2 s_2^{-1}(1 + \theta_0))} \right] \frac{da}{a}.$$

Now

$$\frac{\theta_2}{s_2} = \frac{-tC_5}{(T - t\bar{r})s_2}.$$

It was shown in Part A that: $(T - t\bar{r})s_2 > tC_6 > tC_5$ since $C_6 = C_5/\beta_2$. Therefore: $tC_5/(T - t\bar{r})s_2 < 1$ and $0 > \theta_2/s_2 > -1$. The denominator in the expression for dw/w equals the sum of $\theta_3 = \dfrac{1}{\gamma_2} - \beta_3$ (which is likely to be greater than 1) and a negative fraction (since θ_0 is small). Thus, the denominator is likely to be positive, $\theta_1 > 0$, and therefore, if $da/a > 0$, then $dw/w > 0$. With economies of scale, if $dw/w > 0$, then $dL/L > 0$, thus population size increases by a small amount (since ϵ is large).

REFERENCES

Cobb, S. A. "Site Rent, Air Quality, and the Demand for Amenities." *J. Environ. Econ. Manag.* 4 (Sept. 1977): 214–218.
Cropper, M. L., and Arriga-Salinas, A. S. "Inter-city Wage Differentials and the Value of Air Quality." *J. Urban Econ.* 8 (Sept. 1980): 236–254.
Fish, O. "Externalities and the Urban Rent and Population Density Function: The Case of Air Pollution." *J. Environ. Econ. Manag.* 2 (Sept. 1975): 18–33.
Freeman, A. M. "Air Pollution and Property Values, A Methodological Comment." *Rev. Econ. Stat.* 53 (November 1971): 415–416.
Freeman, A. M. "On Estimating Air Pollution Control Benefits from Land Value Studies." *J. Environ. Econ. Manag.* 1 (May 1974)(a): 74–82.
Freeman, A. M. "Air pollution and property values: A further comment." *Rev. Econ. Stat.* 56 (November 1974)(b): 554–556.
Freeman, A. M. "Spatial Equilibrium, the Theory of Rents, and the Measurement of Benefits from Public Programs: A Comment." *Quart. J. Econ.* (August 1975) 89: 470–473.
Harrison, D., and Rubinfeld, D. "Hedonic Housing Prices and the Demand for Clean Air." *J. Environ. Econ. Manag.* 5 (March 1978): 81–102.
Henderson, J. V. *Economic Theory and the Cities.* New York: Academic Press, 1977.
Hoch, I. "Income and City Size." *Urban Stud.* 9 (Oct. 1972): 299–328.

Hoch, I. "Variations in the Quality of Urban Life among Cities and Regions." In *Public Economics and the Quality of Life*, edited by L. Wingo and R. Evans. Baltimore, Md.: Lexington Books, 1975.

Izraeli, O. "Differentials in Nominal Wages and Prices between Cities." *Urban Stud.* 14 (Oct. 1977): 275–290.

Maler, K. "A Note on the Use of Property Values in Estimating Marginal Willingness to Pay for Environmental Quality." *J. Environ. Econ. Manag.* 4 (Dec. 1977): 355–369.

Meyer, J. R., and Leone, R. A. "The Urban Disamenity Revisited." In *Public Economics and the Quality of Life*, edited by L. Wingo and R. Evans. Lexington Books, Baltimore, Md.: 1975.

Muth, R. F. *Cities and Housing*. Chicago, Ill.: U. of Chicago Press, 1969.

Papageorgiou, G. J. "The Impact of the Environment upon the Spatial Distribution of Population and Land Values." *Econ. Geog.* 49 (July 1973): 251–256.

Polinsky, A. M., and Rubinfeld, D. L. "Property Values and the Benefits of Environmental Improvements: Theory and Measurement." In *Public Economics and the Quality of Life*, edited by L. Wingo and R. Evans. Lexington Books, Baltimore, Md.: 1975.

Polinsky, A. M., and Shavell, S. "The Air Pollution and Property Value Debate." *Rev. Econ. Stat.* 57: (February 1975): 100–104.

Small, K. A. "Air Pollution and Property Values, Further Comment." *Rev. Econ. Stat.* 57 (February 1975): 105–107.

Tolley, G. S. "The Welfare Economics of City Bigness." *J. Urban Econ.* 1 (1974): 324–345.

Wieand, K. F. "Air Pollution and Property Values: A Study of the St. Louis Area." *J. Regional Sci.* 13 (April 1973): 91–95.

10

Amenities and Migration over the Life-Cycle

PHILIP E. GRAVES   JOANNA REGULSKA

I. INTRODUCTION

That amenities are important determinants in the decision of where and when to migrate can hardly be denied (see for example, Liu, 1975). Several studies have emphasized climate with one, Graves (1979), characterizing this variable in considerable detail (temperature and its variance, humidity, and wind velocity being considered) in an analysis that was disaggregated by age and race.

That climate, or indeed any more general set of amenities, should exert a continued influence on migration is not clear at the theoretical level: Sorting among locations should lead to an equilibrium array of household locations, the particular configuration depending on the distribution of preferences. The theoretical construct giving rise to ongoing migration is only briefly outlined here. The emphasis in this Chapter is on empirical results. (See Graves and Linneman, 1979, or Linneman and Graves, 1979, for greater detail.)

The notion is that each location supplies a location-specific bundle of amenities with income and rents compensating for variation in the over-all attractiveness of the amenity bundle at a site. Hence locations in San Francisco or Los Angeles (presumed to be relatively more desirable locations) will be available only for higher rents and, in a world of firm immobility, only if lower wages are accepted for work at this location; Detroit would be expected to have lower rents and higher wages. The way in which migration enters, from an economist's perspective, is that (*a*) either

THE ECONOMICS OF
URBAN AMENITIES

relative locational prices change (e.g., advancements in air-conditioning making the Southwest relatively more attractive), or (*b*) real productivity rises in all locations and some locations offer inferior, in the economic sense, amenity bundles while others offer superior bundles. Movement will take place, with rising incomes and constant spatial technology,[1] until wage–rent compensation is again established in equilibrium. The equilibrium is, of course, immediately disturbed by further rises in income on average, and the process continues.

There is, to be sure, more to migration than this equilibrium view. Job search, viewed as arbitraging real utility levels across space, accounts for a sizable migratory flow.[2] These migration flows may, however, have little systematic component, with movement occurring from low to high utility areas where the utility differentials have randomly emerged. Migration is the disequilibrium reaction in such circumstances.

A strand of literature, the gravity models often used by sociologists, is also cast in a fundamentally equilibrium view of the world (see Niedercorn and Bechdolt, 1969, or Vanderkamp, 1977, for economic interpretations of the gravity models). However, the physics analogy is useful in the context of such models only in explaining gross flows among areas.

The drawback in each of the preceding migration approaches is that the crucial policy (and political) question remains unanswered: Which areas will experience growth as a result of net in-migration, and which will decline? The importance of this question provides the rationale for net migration regression analyses since these analyses relate directly to regional growth and decline. Promising studies using individual data (e.g., Graves and Linneman, 1979; Linneman and Graves, 1979; Polachek and Horvath, 1977) have made substantial strides in better formulating the microeconomic decision to move. However, the probability of movement, combined with similar probit or logit statements regarding *where* the resulting flows will be going, has yet to be conducted.

The purpose of the present effort is to improve significantly on the empirical results in Graves (1979) by reducing the problem of omitted variables. Specifically, the strong age-adjusted climate results may be

---

[1] This ignores innovations, such as air-conditioning, which alter the relative spatial prices of obtaining a given amenity bundle. As a further illustration, domed athletic centers as at Houston or New Orleans effectively alter the cost of receiving a "comfortable baseball experience." Similarly, fresh fruit and other delicacies in the winter are—with the advent of refrigerator cars, trucks, and planes—no longer an amenity not available to those in cold northern climes. These relative price effects are difficult to gauge and may have little systematic effect vis-a-vis the persistence of rising incomes over time.

[2] The locational search may well be undertaken on grounds other than equilization of the present value of skill-adjusted wage differentials (traditional job search). This disequilibrium approach applies as well to "rent search" or "amenity search" since the spatial utility differential can appear in any of the land, labor, or (implicitly) amenity markets.

biased by omitted variables that are correlated with climate. For example, if a city is located on an ocean, its climate is likely to be moderated, hence the climate variable will in part be reflecting the effect of the ocean access amenity. Similarly, low humidity may be correlated with the presence of mountains or, to take a case where the climate effect might be enhanced by variable inclusion, smog may be greater in the warmer western cities. Even in cases where the relationship between climate and an omitted variable is a priori unclear (as for example, climate and crime), random correlations might damage the results when a more inclusive treatment would not.

Population size measured in two ways is also included as a proxy for the net effects of scale economies or diseconomies as those relate to size. Culture or variety of goods, generally, and scale economies in provision of public goods, such as utilities of various sorts, come to mind as attractive amenities of urban life. On the negative side of the ledger, congestion, urban blight, and general aesthetic displeasure associated with substitution of man-made for natural amenities comes to mind. Regional dummies are included to control for other unexamined effects that vary by region.

In Section II the data are described, with findings presented in Section III. Section IV summarizes the chapter. The conclusions in brief are that for whites:

1. Population size is inferior, people moving from large cities.
2. People are still moving *away* from the South, ceteris paribus.
3. Mountain effects are insignificant, and the effects of river, lake, or ocean are mixed, depending on age cohort.

Racial differences and effects on explanatory power are also discussed. Perhaps the most important result, in light of the inclusion of a great many additional control variables, is the continued importance of the climate variables—t-values become much larger, and the quantitative size of effect is little changed.

II. DATA

The variables employed in this study are essentially the economic (income, employment) and climate (1931–1960 averages of temperature variance, humidity, and wind speed) variables of Graves (1979) to which have been added population and population density, crime (property and violent), total suspended particulates (an air-pollution measure), regional dummies, and four subjectively defined variables denoting access to ocean, river, lake, or mountain. A description of all variables as well as their summary statistics is given in Table 10.1.

TABLE 10.1
Variable Definitions and Summary Statistics

Variable	Mean	SD	Description
WHITE TOTAL	2.9258	12.8529	WXX and BXX represent net
W15	3.4304	16.2392	immigration of the respective
W20	9.3057	34.5429	race and age group (e.g., B20
W25	12.7731	27.8832	represents nonwhite in-migra-
W30	6.8895	23.8565	tion of those ages 20–24).
W35	2.6646	17.2423	
W40	2.4207	13.7372	
W45	1.8095	12.1179	
W50	1.7330	10.5128	
W55	1.3534	10.1077	
W60	1.4509	13.8280	
W65	1.4393	19.4116	
W70	1.9430	16.8587	
W75	4.0457	11.3043	
BLACK TOTAL	10.3994	24.8741	
B15	17.8318	38.3767	
B20	36.3147	96.1715	
B25	28.3023	60.3881	
B30	9.0474	32.2133	
B35	5.3851	21.0342	
B40	4.0177	15.5868	
B45	4.4061	13.1624	
B50	5.2485	15.6651	
B55	5.4146	14.6892	
B60	6.0475	19.0881	
B65	8.5799	27.1771	
B70	7.6872	44.6931	
B75	10.6524	32.2283	
DEGDAY	4422.1168	2154.0526	Heating degree days (measure of cold)
ANTMVR	60.9934	10.4981	Annual temperature variance (average July maximum minus average January minimum), 1931–1960 mean values
ANNHUM	59.5036	8.9119	Annual humidity (average of summer and winter values at 1:00 and 7:00 P.M.), 1931–1960 mean values
ANNWIND	9.1701	1.6287	Annual wind (average of January and July readings, in mph), 1931–1960 mean values
COODGDY	1475.7241	955.7620	Cooling degree days (measure of warmth)

TABLE 10.1 (*continued*)

Variable	Mean	SD	Description
UNEMP	5.0270	1.4264	Unemployment rate in 1960
MEINC	5783.0584	782.0599	Median income in 1960
EAST (E)	.1397	.3480	Region dummies, equal to 1 if
NORTH CENTRAL (NC)	.2647	.4428	the city is in that region; zero
SOUTH (S)	.4412	.4984	otherwise
POP	614028.2336	980268.1897	Population size
POPURBAN	81.7676	11.5404	Percentage of SMSA population that is "urban"
TSP	171.4720	69.8321	Total suspended particulate ("smoke pollution")
OCEAN	.1985	.4004	Created dummy variables,
RIVER	.3529	.4797	equal to 1 if the indicated
LAKE	.9412	.2362	amenity is within 25 miles of
MOUNTAIN	.5693	.4970	the SMSA
CRIMVIOL	380.6594	195.4080	Violent crime
CRIMPRO	2734.9523	903.4814	Property crime

The dependent variables are net migration rates for 1960–1970 by race and 5-year age cohorts, the latter enabling life-cycle patterns to be discerned. Whenever possible, beginning-of-period data (ca. 1960) were used to avoid downward bias in variable effects as discussed in Greenwood and Sweetland (1972) and Greenwood (1975). For some variables, such as pollution and crime, adequate data were not available at the beginning-of-period and values circa 1970 were used. The poor performance of crime and pollution may partially stem from this difficulty.

The subjectively defined dummy variables (ocean, river, lake, and mountains) were defined as unity if the amenity in question was within a 25-mile distance from the SMSA. Alternative specifications as well as detailed quantification (stream flow, vertical drop, and so on) were not pursued. Again, the generally poor performance of these variables, discussed later, may to a limited degree result from their definition.

III. REGRESSION RESULTS

In Tables 10.2 and 10.3 age-disaggregated results are presented for white and nonwhite migration respectively. The explanatory power in-

TABLE 10.2
White Net Migration by Age[a]

	Dependent variable											
	W20–24	W25–29	W30–34	W35–39	W40–44	W45–49	W50–54	W55–59	W60–64	W65–69	W70–74	W75–up
Constant	236.7242	17.9110	29.5868	90.7654	78.2711	64.0268	69.2095	86.0306	127.4601	189.4610	157.0767	84.2977
	(5.70)	(.07)	(.21)	(3.82)	(4.67)	(3.92)	(6.46)	(11.87)	(15.92)	(20.70)	(20.86)	(15.55)
POP[b]	−.0020	−.0042	−.0042	−.0032	−.0024	−.0018	−.0018	−.0017	−.0021	−.0018	−.0022	−.0027
	(.22)	(2.05)	(2.30)	(2.63)	(2.46)	(1.75)	(2.35)	(2.70)	(2.32)	(1.08)	(2.25)	(8.74)
POPURBAN	.2258	.1677	−.0544	−.0457	−.0350	−0.0550	−.0346	−.0230	−.0036	.0041	.0153	.0052
	(.43)	(.48)	(.06)	(.08)	(.08)	(.24)	(.13)	(.07)	(.001)	(.001)	(.02)	(.005)
MEINC	−.0139	.0119	.0135	.0030	.0019	.0024	.0010	−.0000	−.0029	−.0063	−.0050	.0009
	(4.21)	(6.29)	(9.13)	(.87)	(.60)	(1.17)	(.31)	(.000)	(1.74)	(4.76)	(4.38)	(.36)
UNEMP	−8.3938	−6.4463	−2.2584	−2.4591	−2.1617	−1.9694	−1.8029	−1.6406	−1.8544	−2.1010	−1.7937	−.8462
	(11.50)	(13.81)	(1.90)	(4.43)	(5.62)	(5.86)	(6.92)	(6.81)	(5.32)	(4.01)	(4.29)	(2.47)
CRIMPRO	.0084	.0061	.0016	.0019	.0034	.0033	.0028	.0019	.0010	.0015	.0022	.0017
	(1.99)	(2.09)	(.16)	(.44)	(2.36)	(2.87)	(2.92)	(1.54)	(.28)	(.37)	(1.10)	(1.76)
CRIMVIOL	−.0079	.0076	.0045	.0011	−.0042	−.0057	−.0061	−.0076	−.0084	−.0129	−.0148	−.0084
	(.09)	(.16)	(.06)	(.007)	(.18)	(.42)	(.68)	(1.23)	(.93)	(1.29)	(2.49)	(2.07)
TSP	−.0538	.0023	−.0100	−.0138	−.0128	−.0126	−.0114	−.0109	−.0150	−.0178	−.0143	−.0132
	(1.17)	(.005)	(.09)	(.35)	(.49)	(.59)	(.68)	(.75)	(.86)	(.71)	(.68)	(1.48)
DEGDAY	.0062	.0053	.0066	.0065	.0063	.0058	.0057	.0062	.0090	.0131	.0180	.0058
	(1.12)	(1.69)	(2.94)	(5.53)	(8.53)	(9.18)	(12.67)	(17.72)	(22.69)	(28.32)	(28.17)	(21.18)
COODGDY	.0002	.0108	.0136	.0105	.0100	.0096	.0094	.0105	.0157	.0227	.0194	.0112
	(.000)	(3.38)	(6.10)	(7.10)	(10.56)	(12.22)	(16.54)	(24.55)	(33.51)	(40.99)	(43.91)	(38.06)

ANTMVR	$-.8523$	$-.7002$	$-.9425$	$-.8484$	$-.8610$	$-.8211$	$-.8216$	$-.9539$	-1.3404	-1.9738	-1.6360	$-.9529$
	(1.04)	(1.43)	(2.92)	(4.62)	(7.82)	(8.93)	(12.59)	(20.18)	(24.35)	(31.07)	(31.31)	(27.48)
ANNWIND	-2.2930	-3.5526	-4.3698	-3.5859	-3.1840	-2.8653	-2.4092	-2.2846	-2.6273	-3.5573	-2.7724	-1.1900
	(.80)	(3.90)	(6.65)	(8.76)	(11.35)	(11.54)	(11.49)	(12.29)	(9.93)	(10.71)	(9.54)	(4.55)
ANNHUM	$-.9831$	$-.3148$	$-.4714$	$-.5785$	$-.5462$	$-.4912$	$-.5087$	$-.6337$	$-.8557$	-1.2938	-1.1101	$-.8096$
	(1.67)	(.35)	(.88)	(2.59)	(3.80)	(3.85)	(5.83)	(10.75)	(11.98)	(16.11)	(17.40)	(23.95)
E	-9.6439	-10.6119	4.7040	3.8476	4.3920	4.4781	2.8141	2.0222	-2.9818	-4.5282	-5.7396	-5.8072
	(.32)	(.79)	(.17)	(.22)	(.49)	(.64)	(.35)	(.22)	(.29)	(.39)	(.92)	(2.45)
NC	-2.0325	-8.7251	-1.5529	-2.1780	$.9538$	2.7647	2.5372	3.3963	$.1940$	1.2534	$-.1260$	$.1128$
	(.01)	(.45)	(.02)	(.06)	(.02)	(.20)	(.24)	(.61)	(.001)	(.03)	(.004)	(.001)
S	$.5326$	-1.9240	-1.6818	-4.4283	$-.8118$	1.2152	$.3367$	$-.9748$	-6.2126	-7.9972	-6.5326	$.2216$
	(.001)	(.03)	(.02)	(.30)	(.02)	(.05)	(.005)	(.05)	(1.27)	(1.24)	(1.21)	(.004)
OCEAN	-8.1142	-4.2331	1.1722	$-.6018$	-1.2250	-1.0399	-1.0210	$.1169$	1.5355	3.2518	2.3076	-3.1437
	(.55)	(.30)	(.03)	(.01)	(.09)	(.08)	(.11)	(.002)	(.19)	(.49)	(.36)	(1.74)
RIVER	10.9113	12.2303	6.2408	5.0442	3.3523	2.5796	1.5235	$.7602$	-1.6095	-3.5230	-2.8737	$-.5955$
	(2.53)	(6.48)	(1.90)	(2.43)	(1.96)	(1.31)	(.64)	(.19)	(.52)	(1.47)	(1.44)	(.16)
LAKE	-26.1338	-18.8027	-15.1112	-17.4169	-8.3325	-3.2266	-3.1614	-1.4514	1.9671	7.0824	4.4055	-2.7656
	(3.04)	(3.20)	(2.33)	(6.05)	(2.28)	(.43)	(.58)	(.14)	(.16)	(1.24)	(.71)	(.72)
MOUNTAIN	-5.0231	1.2535	2.8541	2.0994	1.2335	1.3053	$.9824$	$.2704$	$-.3810$	$-.8831$	$-.5305$	$-.3589$
	(.43)	(.05)	(.32)	(.34)	(.19)	(.27)	(.21)	(.02)	(.02)	(.07)	(.04)	(.05)
R^2	.537	.681	.592	.603	.625	.613	.641	.681	.729	.772	.797	.828

[a] t-values in parentheses; 137 observations.
[b] Population is in thousands of people.

217

TABLE 10.3
Nonwhite Net Migration by Age[a]

	Dependent variable											
	B20–24	B25–29	B30–34	B35–39	B40–44	B45–49	B50–54	B55–59	B60–64	B65–69	B70–74	B75–up
Constant	602.7508 (5.80)	133.3264 (.94)	−74.0451 (.96)	−46.4683 (.71)	−39.7656 (.84)	−7.0637 (.04)	11.4387 (.07)	61.4738 (2.24)	17.6362 (.94)	67.7003 (.72)	−99.7814 (.51)	86.5313 (.83)
POP[b]	−.0583 (.30)	.0213 (.13)	.0061 (.04)	−.0100 (.19)	−.0099 (.29)	−.0096 (.38)	−.0140 (.59)	.0020 (.01)	−.0028 (.01)	−.0071 (.04)	.0460 (.60)	.0011 (.001)
POPURBAN	.6712 (.58)	−.0879 (.03)	.1316 (.002)	.1355 (.49)	.0888 (.34)	.0594 (.21)	.1598 (1.06)	−.0828 (.33)	.0872 (.18)	.0585 (.04)	−.1005 (.04)	−.2897 (.74)
MEINC	−.0350 (4.10)	.1550 (2.66)	.1525 (8.55)	.0077 (4.11)	.0068 (5.17)	.0059 (5.43)	.0006 (.04)	.0035 (1.51)	.0008 (.045)	−.0038 (.47)	−.0020 (.04)	.0076 (.74)
UNEMP	−18.6071 (8.58)	−10.3199 (8.77)	−3.2697 (2.92)	−1.1936 (.73)	.3119 (.08)	.5083 (.30)	−.2884 (.07)	−.9252 (.78)	−.7390 (.25)	1.4009 (.48)	1.5908 (.20)	−1.1832 (.24)
CRIMPRO	.8672 (.32)	.0142 (2.83)	.0001 (.000)	−.0007 (.04)	.0001 (.13)	.0002 (.006)	−.0028 (1.04)	.0036 (2.05)	.0028 (.65)	.0046 (.89)	.0062 (.51)	.0097 (2.72)
CRIMVIOL	−.0290 (.18)	−.0511 (1.83)	.0001 (.001)	.0077 (.26)	.0007 (.003)	.0034 (.11)	.0049 (.16)	−.0294 (6.77)	−.0222 (1.96)	−.0359 (2.68)	−.0448 (1.35)	−.0572 (4.75)
TSP	−.0740 (.34)	−.0212 (.09)	.0295 (.59)	−.0153 (.30)	−.0066 (.09)	.0120 (.42)	.0419 (3.51)	.0040 (.04)	.0394 (1.80)	−.0263 (.42)	−.0835 (1.37)	−.0522 (1.16)
DEGDAY	.0530 (12.51)	.0261 (10.06)	.1129 (.06)	−.0007 (.04)	.0004 (.03)	.0004 (.03)	.0034 (1.69)	.0022 (.80)	.0038 (1.22)	.0035 (.54)	.0096 (1.30)	.0089 (2.44)
COODGDY	.0305 (2.03)	.0255 (4.73)	.0059 (.83)	.0014 (.09)	.0014 (.14)	.0027 (.76)	.0046 (1.49)	.0011 (.10)	.0060 (1.46)	.0012 (.03)	.0169 (1.30)	.0053 (.43)

	(1)	(2)	(3)	(4)	(5)	(6)	(7)	(8)	(9)	(10)	(11)	(12)
ANTMVR	-4.5077 (4.39)	-3.1734 (7.23)	-.3787 (.34)	.1316 (.08)	-.1608 (.19)	-.2362 (.57)	-.3632 (.92)	-.2878 (.34)	-.5742 (2.64)	-.5631 (.68)	.7320 (.37)	-1.6290 (3.96)
ANNWND	1.4498 (.05)	1.2721 (.12)	1.4283 (.52)	.4774 (.10)	.1268 (.01)	-.2028 (.04)	.0667 (.003)	-.9278 (.38)	-1.2007 (1.24)	-.0577 (.001)	.6248 (.03)	.2218 (.008)
ANNHUM	-3.4133 (3.08)	-1.7333 (2.63)	.4192 (.51)	.3521 (.67)	.1885 (.31)	-.0491 (.03)	-.1368 (.16)	-.1250 (.077)	-.4037 (1.59)	-.0326 (.003)	.6335 (.34)	-.5318 (.51)
E	-50.7967 (1.35)	16.4209 (.47)	12.4099 (.89)	-3.9197 (.17)	-1.8415 (.06)	-.7811 (.01)	-3.1328 (.17)	2.4607 (.06)	3.8288 (.28)	-26.2062 (3.55)	-20.9792 (.74)	2.3480 (.02)
NC	-59.9299 (1.58)	-1.1576 (.002)	-11.7043 (.62)	-21.7293 (4.30)	-11.3767 (1.91)	-7.3046 (1.11)	-11.1566 (1.78)	2.5006 (.05)	3.9807 (.26)	-27.3563 (3.26)	-13.8765 (.27)	10.0366 (.31)
S	-57.8184 (1.74)	-18.2784 (.58)	-28.7043 (4.74)	-27.7664 (8.31)	-12.7635 (2.84)	-12.9273 (4.10)	-17.2074 (5.01)	-7.6737 (.58)	-5.2207 (.53)	-28.9777 (4.32)	2.5094 (.01)	7.7337 (.22)
OCEAN	-6.0389 (.05)	.4517 (.009)	-6.4807 (.59)	-7.0454 (1.30)	-7.9878 (2.70)	-5.7453 (1.97)	-2.8548 (.33)	-1.3307 (.04)	-.1641 (.001)	-4.6257 (.27)	3.4357 (.05)	-7.9921 (.56)
RIVER	21.3656 (1.48)	15.8632 (2.72)	6.6228 (1.57)	2.1234 (.30)	.3741 (.01)	.1271 (.002)	3.9804 (1.67)	2.3278 (.33)	1.0632 (.14)	-2.1051 (.14)	-9.0874 (.86)	-4.5466 (.46)
LAKE	-103.5120 (7.25)	-28.4577 (1.82)	-13.8671 (1.43)	-8.7507 (1.07)	-2.2667 (.12)	-1.7389 (.10)	-4.6365 (.47)	-6.6473 (.56)	-3.0563 (.23)	3.6080 (.09)	-14.6350 (.46)	-7.9259 (.29)
MOUNTAIN	3.8624 (.04)	10.4118 (.93)	2.5340 (.18)	-1.8309 (.18)	.7155 (.04)	-.8269 (.09)	.4045 (.14)	-.1962 (.002)	-4.3106 (1.78)	-2.7053 (.19)	4.3487 (.16)	-.5087 (.005)
R^2	.630	.738	.715	.625	.558	.558	.548	.435	.550	.485	.354	.472

[a] t-values in parentheses; 137 observations.
[b] Population is in units of 10,000 people.

219

creases, as compared to Graves' (1979) findings, by an average of 24% for whites (from .37 to .46 on average)—a substantial increase in light of the large number of variables already in the equation.

In terms of overall results, Graves's (1979) earlier analysis, which indicated that climate variables are more important for whites than for nonwhites, continues to be supported. This suggests that the income elasticity of demand for climate amenities is nonconstant (increasing with income) since nonwhites have much smaller incomes than whites on average. Alternative explanations are that incomes grew in absolute terms more for whites than nonwhites over the 1960–1970 period or that historically determined initial locations varied systematically by race, the true interpretation perhaps involving a combination of these explanations. As in the earlier study, movement toward cold and warm locations, but away from high annual temperature variance as well as from humidity and wind, was observed.

A theoretical implication of the model is largely confirmed in comparing the present results with earlier findings: The size and significance of the income and unemployment variable coefficients are increased by inclusion of more amenities. Any given variation in these economic variables will represent a larger expected real utility differential the more amenities are held constant in the regression. Hence a given nominal income or unemployment differential should lead to more migration in the present analysis, an expectation borne out by the data (particularly for whites).

Considering the new variables, population size is seen to exert a negative effect on in-migration of all age groups of both racial groups (population size, then, is an inferior good), with the population density variable being insignificant for both races.

Crime is largely insignificant, although in-migration of older migrants of both races appears to be inhibited by crimes of violence. The only significant coefficients on property crime (for older white migrants) are of the "wrong" sign. Pollution (TSP) consistently inhibits white in-migration, with a mixed sign pattern for nonwhites, although the effects are insignificant. As suggested by Graves (1976), such movements as occur due to crime or pollution can be conducted readily *within* cities, hence anomalous and insignificant findings across cities are perhaps not surprising.

Relative to the (omitted) West, net in-migration to other regions is largely negative although typically insignificantly so. A consistent pattern of movement by both races *away* from the South is seen when other amenities are held constant—a result different from that obtained when amenities are uncontrolled.

The subjectively defined variables (ocean, river, lake, and mountain) are largely insignificant, holding climate and other amenities constant.

There appears, among certain age groups, to be some movement toward rivers and away from lakes, but there is no significant or consistent pattern of movement toward or away from mountains. These findings suggest that other amenities, particularly climate, are predominant, the presumed effect of mountains being due perhaps to low humidity or some other variable that is usually uncontrolled. This is not too surprising. Although oceans or mountains might appear desirable for their recreational or aesthetic properties, the percentage of time actually spent enjoying them is small relative to the time spent enjoying the desirable climates frequently associated with them.

IV. SUMMARY

The analysis presented here continues to support the importance of climate in observed migration patterns. The new variables fail to add a great deal to the explanation, exceptions being population size for all groups and region for certain groups. As expected on theoretical grounds, income and unemployment differentials exert stronger effects the more amenities are controlled since they are then to a greater extent reflecting expected real utility differentials.

REFERENCES

Graves, P. E. "A Reexamination of Migration, Economic Opportunity, and the Quality of Life." *J. Reg. Sci.* 16 (March 1976): 107–112.

Graves, P. E. "A Life-Cycle Empirical Analysis of Migration and Climate, by Race." *J. Urban Econ.* 6 (April 1979): 135–147.

Graves, P. E., and Linneman, P. D. "Household Migration: Theoretical and Empirical Results." *J. Urban Econ.* 6 (July 1979): 383–404.

Greenwood, M. J. "Research on Internal Migration in the United States: A Survey." *J. Econ. Lit.* 13 (June 1975): 397–433.

Greenwood, M. J., and Sweetland, D. "The Determinants of Migration between Standard Metropolitan Statistical Areas." *Demography* 9 (November, 1972): 665–681.

Linneman, P. D., and Graves, P. E. "Amenities, Job Search, and the Migration Decision: A Multinomial Logit Analysis." University of Colorado #141 (October 1979).

Liu, B. "Differential Net Migration Rates and the Quality of Life." *Rev. Econ. Stat.* 52 (August 1975): 329–337.

Niedercorn, J. H., and Bechdolt, B. V. "An Economic Derivation of the 'Gravity Law' of Spatial Interaction." *J. Reg. Sci.* 9 (August, 1969): 272–282.

Polachek, S., and Horvath, F. "A Life Cycle Approach to Migration." In *Research in Labor Economics,* edited by R. Ehrenberg. Greenwich, Conn.: JAI Press, 1977.

Vanderkamp, J. "The Gravity Model and Migration Behaviour: An Economic Interpretation." *J. Econ. Stud.* 4 (November, 1977): 89–102.

Subject Index